W9-CDP-432

Oedipus

MYTH AND DRAMA

EDITED BY

Martin Kallich, NORTHERN ILLINOIS UNIVERSITY

Andrew MacLeish, UNIVERSITY OF MINNESOTA

Gertrude Schoenbohm, NORTHERN ILLINOIS UNIVERSITY

The Odyssey Press, New York

COPYRIGHT © 1968 BY WESTERN PUBLISHING COMPANY, INC.
Published by The Odyssey Press, a Division of Western Publishing Company, Inc.
All Rights Reserved
PRINTED IN THE UNITED STATES
Library of Congress Catalog Card Number 67-18744
A 0 9 8 7 6 5 4 3 2

ACKNOWLEDGMENTS

The editors are grateful to the following authors, publishers, and periodicals for permission to use the material listed below:

AMERICAN BOOK COMPANY: from H. A. Grueber, *Myths of Greece and Rome* (New York: American Book Company, 1893), pp. 392–393. Copyright 1893 and 1921 by American Book Company.

CAMBRIDGE UNIVERSITY PRESS: from R. C. Jebb, *Sophocles, The Plays and Fragments* (Cambridge: Cambridge University Press, 1893) Part I, pp. 7–199.

THE CLARENDON PRESS: from C. Maurice Bowra, *Sophoclean Tragedy* (Oxford: The Clarendon Press, 1944), pp. 174–211. By permission of The Clarendon Press, Oxford. John Dennis, *The Impartial Critick: Or, Some Observations Upon A Late Book, Entitled, A Short View of Tragedy, Written by Mr. Rymer* (1963), edited by Joel E. Spingarn in *Critical Essays of the Seventeenth Century* (Oxford: The Clarendon Press, 1908), 3 volumes. III, 151–166. By permission of The Clarendon Press, Oxford. "Preface to Troilus and Cressida" (1679), edited by W. P. Ker in *Essays of John Dryden* (Oxford: The Clarendon Press, 1926) 2 volumes. I, 208–221. By permission of The Clarendon Press, Oxford. Bonamy Dobrée, *Restoration Tragedy, 1660–1720* (Oxford: The Clarendon Press, 1929), pp. 115–117. By permission of The Clarendon Press, Oxford.

DOVER PUBLICATIONS: passage from S. H. Butcher, *Aristotle's Theory of Poetry and Fine Art* (4th ed., New York: Dover Publications, Inc., 1951), pp. 11–107.

THE GERMAN QUARTERLY: from William H. Rey, "Geist und Blut in Hofmannsthal's *Oedipus und die Sphinx*," *The German Quarterly*, XXI (March, 1958), 84–93. Translated into English by Gertrude Schoenbohm.

THE HOGARTH PRESS: from Sigmund Freud, "Preface to Reik's *Ritual: Psycho-Analytical Studies*" (1919), in *The Standard Edition of The Complete Psychological Works of Sigmund Freud,* edited by James Strachey (London: The Hogarth Press, 1955), XVII, 261–263. Sigmund Freud, "Psycho-analysis" (1923), in *The Standard Edition of the Complete Psychological Works of Sigmund Freud,* edited by James Strachey (London: The Hogarth Press, 1955), XVIII, 247, 252–253. Sigmund Freud, "Dostoevsky and Parricide" (1928), in *The Standard Edition of the Complete Psychological Works of Sigmund Freud,* edited by James Strachey (London: The Hogarth Press, 1961) XXI, 188.

HOUGHTON MIFFLIN COMPANY: from Helen Child Sargent and George L. Kittridge, *English and Scottish Popular Ballads* (Boston: Houghton Mifflin Co., 1932), p. 25.

INTERNATIONAL UNIVERSITIES PRESS: from Theodor Reik; *Dogma and Compulsion* (New York: International Universities Press, 1951), pp. 319–326.

LONGMAN, HURST, REES, ORME, & BROWN: from David Erskine Baker, *Biographia Dramatica: or A Companion to the Playhouse: Containing Historical and Critical Memoirs and Original Anecdotes of British and Irish Dramatic Writers* (London: Longman, Hurst, Rees, Orme, & Brown, 1812), 3 volumes. I, 448–449; III, 93.

THE MACMILLAN COMPANY: from Alfred North Whitehead, *Science and the Modern World* (New York: The Macmillan Company, 1925), pp. 14–16. Copyright 1925 by The Macmillan Company; copyright renewed 1953 by Evelyn Whitehead.

METHUEN AND COMPANY, LTD.: from H. D. F. Kitto, *Greek Tragedy: A Literary Study* (London: Methuen, 1950), pp. 135–141.

PANTHEON BOOKS: from *The Collected Works of Carl Gustav Jung,* edited by Herbert Read, Michael Fordham, and Gerhard Adler. Vol. V, *Symbols of Transformation* (New York: Pantheon Books, 1956), 224–225, 328–331, 181–182. First published in German in 1912.

RANDOM HOUSE, INC.: from Sigmund Freud, *The Interpretation of Dreams* (1900) in *The Basic Writings of Sigmund Freud,* translated and edited by A. A. Brill (New York: Random House, The Modern Library, 1938), pp. 306–311. Copyright 1938 by Random House, Inc. Copyright renewed 1965 by Gioia B. Bernheim and Edmund R. Brill. Reprinted by permission.

WILLIAM H. REY: from William H. Rey, "Geist und Blut in Hofmannsthal's *Oedipus und die Sphinx,*" *The German Quarterly,* XXI (March, 1958), 84–93. Translated into English by Gertrude Schoenbohm.

THE UNIVERSITY OF CHICAGO PRESS: from Gilbert Murray, *The Literature of Ancient Greece* (Chicago: The University of Chicago Press, 1956), pp. 239–242.

UNIVERSITÄTSVERLAG WAGNER: from Eduard Lachmann, "Hofmannsthal's Drama *Oedipus und die Sphinx,*" Enzinger Festschrift, Schlern-Schriften-

Reihe (Innsbruck: Universitätsverlag Wagner, 1953), pp. 148–152. Translated into English by Gertrude Schoenbohm. Printed by permission.

S. Fischer Verlag: from Hugo von Hofmannsthal, *Oedipus und die Sphinx,* Dramen II (Frankfurt am Main: S. Fischer Verlag, 1954). Translated into English by Gertrude Schoenbohm.

A. B. Watt & Son: from Sir James George Frazer, *The Golden Bough: A Study in Magic and Religion* (London: A. B. Watt & Son, 1935), 12 volumes. The selection comes from *The Magic Art and the Evolution of Kings,* II, 113–117. Reprinted by permission of Trinity College, Cambridge, England, the owners of the copyright.

Watts and Company: from Lord Raglan, *The Hero: A Study in Tradition, Myth, and Drama* (London: Watts and Co., 1949), pp. 177–185. First published in 1936.

George West and Henry Clements: from Gerard Langbaine, *An Account of the English Dramatic Poets* (Oxford; George West and Henry Clements, 1691), pp. 167, 320–321.

Contents

EPIGRAPH

Alfred North Whitehead (1861–1947) was one of the great philosophers of all time. He lectured in mathematics at Cambridge University and was, for fourteen years, at the Imperial College of Science. In 1924 he came to Harvard University.

The effect of Greek dramatic literature was many-sided so far as concerns the various ways in which it indirectly affected medieval thought. The pilgrim fathers of the scientific imagination as it exists today are the great tragedians of ancient Athens, Aeschylus, Sophocles, Euripides. Their vision of fate, remorseless [14] and indifferent, urging a tragic incident to its inevitable issue, is the vision possessed by science. Fate in Greek Tragedy becomes the order of nature in modern thought. The absorbing interest in the particular heroic incidents, as an example and a verification of the workings of fate, reappears in our epoch as concentration of interest on the crucial experiments. It was my good fortune to be present at the meeting of the Royal Society in London when the Astronomer Royal for England announced that the photographic plates of the famous eclipse, as measured by his colleagues in Greenwich Observatory, had verified the prediction of Einstein

Reprinted with permission of The Macmillan Company from *Science and the Modern World* by Alfred North Whitehead, pp. 14–16. Copyright 1925 by The Macmillan Company, renewed 1953 by Evelyn Whitehead.

that rays of light are bent as they pass in the neighbourhood of the sun. The whole atmosphere of tense interest was exactly that of the Greek drama: we were the chorus commenting on the decree of destiny as disclosed in the development of a supreme incident. There was dramatic quality in the very staging:—the traditional ceremonial, and in the background the picture of Newton to remind us that the greatest of scientific generalizations was now, after more than two centuries, to receive its first modification: Nor was the personal interest wanting: a great adventure in thought had at length come safe to shore.

Let me here remind you that the essence of dramatic tragedy is not unhappiness. It resides in the solemnity of the remorseless working of things. This inevitableness of destiny can only be illustrated in terms of human life by incidents which in fact involve unhappiness. For it is only by them that the futility of escape can be made evident in the drama. This remorseless inevitableness is what pervades scientific thought. The laws of physics are the decrees of fate.

The conception of the moral order in the Greek plays was certainly not a discovery of the dramatists. It must have passed into the literary [15] tradition from the general serious opinion of the times. But in finding this magnificent expression, it thereby deepened the stream of thought from which it arose. The spectacle of a moral order was impressed upon the imagination of a classical civilisation. . . .

PREFACE

This book is about you, and its time is the present. For you the time of this book begins on a hot August morning at a seaport city on the island of Honshu in southwestern Japan. It is 8:15 A.M. Suddenly a light of unparalleled brilliance breaks over the city as if the sun itself were splitting apart. The city and 80,000 of its people vanish. The day is Thursday, August 6, 1945; the city is Hiroshima; the event is the dropping of the first atomic bomb by an American plane named "Enola Gay."

The dropping of this bomb forced the capitulation of Japan, and World War II came to an end. It left the survivors of Hiroshima sitting on the ash heap of their own past, picking at their sores and asking the same question that the hero of the Old Testament, Job, asked: Why?

Looking back at this event from the perspective of only a few years, we see that it caused a surrender: the surrender of twentieth-century man to the fear which now plagues his daily life. From this fear arises the age-old question: Why?, and we realize that we are not much different from our ancestors of almost three thousand years ago. Now we are compelled to ask such fundamental questions as: What is it in man's nature that compels him to act as he does? What is the nature of the forces that control man's life? Is man's presence on earth really a kind of grim joke? All these are summed up in the single question concerning identity: Who am I?

This book points to the persistence of this questioning in its most popular and effective form: the Oedipus tragedies. The three plays included here represent a time span covering almost the entire development of Western civilization from 430 B.C. to the twentieth century. This implies not only the importance of the Oedipus myth, universal in time and space, but also man's constant preoccupation with it. These plays tell the story of a wise man who was not quite wise enough to know himself. They are ordered, conscious manifestations of man's concern with fate, with chance, and with the forces of the cosmos—all those forces inside and outside of man which condition his relationships with his parents and his fellow men. Such is the content of tragedy, the most earnest artistic expression of man's suffering.

In short, this book has three general aims: to provide a basis for an understanding of perhaps the most important myth of ancient and modern civilizations, of primitive and sophisticated cultures; to stimulate an awareness of significant ways in which this myth is reflected in man's unconscious life; and, last of all, to encourage investigation of changing ideas about the content of tragedy and its form in various ages.

To assist you in achieving these goals the editors have included with the plays related critical, mythological, and psychological materials as well as anthropological materials dealing with the myth. These representative selections from the best writings in the four areas provide a wide scope of suggestion for class discussion and papers of varying length and difficulty.

In this collection of materials, the Oedipus legend in its dramatic form has been emphasized. But the possibility of finding the Oedipus theme in different contexts and different literary forms should also be considered. For such has been the contribution of Freud—his interpretation of the Oedipus complex and its influence upon the unconscious. We, in our time, cannot fully appreciate the significance of myth unless we consider its influence on such diverse works as Shakespeare's *Hamlet,* Matthew Arnold's *Sohrab and Rustum,* Feodor Dostoevsky's *Brothers Karamazov,* D. H. Lawrence's *Sons and Lovers,* Lytton Strachey's *Queen Victoria,* and Eugene O'Neill's *Mourning Becomes Electra.*

M. K.
A. MacL.
G. S.

The Plays

Oedipus the King

Sophocles

Regarded by many as the masterpiece of all Greek tragedy, *Oedipus the King* (c. 430–415 B.C.) is the major work of Sophocles (495–406 B.C.). Written in the early years of the war between Athens and Sparta, the play reflects the unfortunate days when a plague devastated Athens.

Long before the action of the play begins, the young Oedipus had come to Thebes where he found its king, Laius, recently dead and the city ravaged by the Sphinx. He solved the Sphinx' riddle, which troubled every man before him, and she killed herself. In gratitude, Thebes offered the crown to Oedipus, its savior. He accepted, married Jocasta, the widow of the slain King Laius, and reigned in prosperity for many years. As the play opens, the Thebans ask him to save the city once again from a dreadful plague which has fallen upon it.

That *Oedipus* has been read for the past twenty-four hundred years is proof of its universal appeal. As the hero is a symbolic representation of fifth-century Athens, so he is also the center of an important intellectual revolution which resulted in a new conception of man: the idea that man was fully capable of understanding and, eventually,

From R. C. Jebb, *Sophocles, The Plays and Fragments* (Cambridge: Cambridge University Press, 1893), Part I, 7–199. The text has been modernized by the editors. The page numbers in brackets refer to right-hand pages in Jebb's edition; the Greek appears on the left-hand pages.

dominating his environment. The depiction of a powerful political king, a *tyrannos,* encouraged the conception of man as the master of the universe, a self-made ruler who has the ability to "win the prize of an all-prosperous fortune."

The imagery of the play associates its hero with the victorious progress of man. Oedipus is compared to man the conqueror and inventor with all the achievements which have raised him to civilization and made him ruler of the world. He is presented as helmsman, conqueror of the sea and land, ploughman, hunter, and tamer of wild nature. And these images make Oedipus symbolic of the most impressive and revolutionary achievements of the whole human race.

But, by the end of the play, the symbol undergoes a change. The prophecy of the gods has been fulfilled and Oedipus apparently knows himself for what he is: not the measurer of the world but one who is measured by fate.

"The chorus sees in Oedipus . . . an example to mankind. In this self-recognition of Oedipus, man recognizes himself. Man [tries to] measure himself and the result is not that man is the measure of all things. The chorus . . . states what it understands to be the result of the great calculation: "Generations of mankind that must die, I add up the total of your life and find it equal to zero."[1]

But this dreary statement, while it is an understandable reaction to the shock of the play's discovery, is not the last word on Oedipus. Man is not zero, for Oedipus rises again from the ruin of his life as the last section of the play makes clear.

Sophocles continued to write into his very old age. In *Oedipus at Colonus,* written at the very end of his life, the now-mellowed creator of the tortured Oedipus brings him, in his blindness, to Athens, where King Theseus offers him sanctuary. Here Oedipus hears a voice calling from heaven and passes to the realm of the gods confident and unobserved. As C. M. Bowra observes, describing the apotheosis of Oedipus,

". . . Sophocles makes it abundantly clear that Oedipus is

[1] Bernard M. W. Knox, *Oedipus at Thebes* (New Haven: Yale University Press, 1957), p. 157. We are indebted to pages 107–158 of this book for much of what appears in the preceding three paragraphs.

in no sense to blame for what he has done and that his expulsion from Thebes was an act of callous cruelty. His end is the atonement for his sufferings, and perhaps in it Sophocles saw the solution of the question which had troubled him all his life; through suffering, even through injustice done to him, the great man becomes a god."[2]

The structure of *Oedipus* is that of classic tragedy. It consists of a Prologue depicting Oedipus counseling the Theban elders, the Parados or first Choral Ode, four Episodes, each followed by a Choral Ode called a Stasimon, and the Exodus in which the doom of Oedipus is sealed.

CHARACTERS IN THE PLAY

OEDIPUS, King of Thebes

PRIEST OF ZEUS

CREON, brother of Jocasta

CHORUS of Theban Elders

TEIRESIAS, a blind prophet

JOCASTA, Queen of Thebes; wife of Oedipus, widow of Laius, the late King of Thebes

MESSENGER from Corinth

HERDSMAN formerly in the service of Laius

SECOND MESSENGER

MUTE PERSONS, a train of Suppliants (old men, youths, children)

THE CHILDREN, Antigone and Ismene, daughters of Oedipus and Jocasta

[2] *Ancient Greek Literature* (Oxford: Oxford University Press, 1933), p. 105. Robert Graves, *The Greek Myths* (Baltimore: Penguin Books, 1955), II, 9–24 retells the whole story and indicates the sources.

SCENE: *Before the royal palace of Oedipus at Thebes. In front of the large central doors there is an altar; a smaller altar stands also near each of the two side-doors. Suppliants—old men, youths, and young children—are seated on the steps of the altars. They are dressed in white tunics and cloaks,—their hair bound with white fillets. On the altars they have laid down olive-branches wreathed with fillets of wool. The Priest of Zeus, a venerable man, is alone standing, facing the central doors of the palace. These are now thrown open. Followed by two attendants, who place themselves on either side of the doors, Oedipus enters, in the robes of a king. For a moment he gazes silently on the groups at the altars, and then speaks.*

OEDIPUS: My children, latest-born to Cadmus who was of old, why are you set before me thus with wreathed branches of suppliants, while the city reeks with incense, rings with prayers for health and cries of woe? I considered it unfitting, my children, to hear these things at the mouth of others, and have come hither myself, I, Oedipus renowned of all.

Tell me, then, venerable man—since it is your natural part to speak for these—in what mood are you placed here, [11] with what dread or what desire? Be sure that I would gladly give all aid; hard of heart would I be, did I not pity such suppliants as these.

PRIEST OF ZEUS: Nay, Oedipus, ruler of my land, you see of what years we are who beset your altars,—some, nestlings still too tender for far flights,—some, bowed with age, priests, as I of Zeus,—and these, the chosen youth; while the rest of the folk sit with wreathed [13] branches in the market-places, and before the two shrines of Pallas, and where Ismenus gives answer by fire.

For the city, as you yourself see, is now too sorely vexed, and can no more lift her head from beneath the angry waves of death; a blight is on her in the fruitful blossoms of the land, in the herds among the pastures, in the barren pangs of women; and above all the flaming god, the malign plague, has swooped on us, and ravages the town; by whom the house of Cadmus is made waste, but dark Hades rich in groans and tears. [15]

It is not as deeming you ranked with gods that I and these children are suppliants at your hearth, but as deeming you first of men, both in life's common chances, and when mortals have to do with more than man: seeing that you came to the town of Cadmus, and did free us from the tax that we rendered to the hard songstress; and this, though you knew nothing from us that could help you, nor had been schooled; no, by a god's aid, 'tis said and believed did you uplift our life.

And now, Oedipus, king glorious in all eyes, we beseech you, all we suppliants, to find for us some succour, whether by the whisper of a god you know it, or perhaps as in the power of man; for I see that, when men have been proved in deeds past, [17] the issues of their counsels, too, most often have effect.

On, best of mortals, again uplift our State! On, guard your fame,—since now this land calls you saviour for your former zeal; and never be it our memory of your reign that we were first restored and afterward cast down: nay, lift up this State in such a way that it fall no more!

With good omen you gave us that past happiness; now also show yourself the same. For if you are to rule this land, even as you are now its lord, 'tis better to be lord of men than of a waste: since neither walled town nor ship is anything, if it is void and no men dwell within it with you. [19]

OEDIPUS: O my piteous children, known, well known to me are the desires wherewith you have come: well know I that you suffer all; yet, sufferers as you are, there is not one of you whose suffering is as mine. Your pain comes on each one of you for himself alone, and for no other; but my soul mourns at once for the city, and for myself, and for you.

So that you rouse me not, truly, as one sunk in sleep: no, be sure that I have wept full many tears, gone many ways in wanderings of thought. And the sole remedy which, well pondering, I could find, this I have put into act. I have sent the son of Menoeceus, Creon, my own wife's brother, to the Pythian house of Phoebus, to learn by what deed or word I might deliver this town. [21] And already, when the lapse of days is reckoned, it troubles me what he is doing; for he delays strangely, beyond the fitting time. But when he comes, then shall I be no true man if I do not all that the god shows.

PRIEST: Nay, in season have you spoken; at this moment these signal to me that Creon draws near.

OEDIPUS: O king Apollo, may he come to us in the brightness of saving fortune, even as his face is bright!

PRIEST: Indeed, to all appearance, he brings comfort; else would he not be coming crowned thus thickly with berry-laden bay.

OEDIPUS: We shall know soon: he is within hearing distance.—

Enter Creon.

Prince, my kinsman, son of Menoeceus, what news have you brought us from the god?

CREON: Good news: I tell you that even troubles hard to bear,—if by chance all goes well,—will end in perfect peace. [23]

OEDIPUS: But what is the oracle? So far, your words make me neither bold nor yet afraid.

CREON: If you wish to hear while these are present, I am ready to speak; or else to go within.

OEDIPUS: Speak before all: the sorrow which I bear is for these more than for my own life.

CREON: With your permission, I will tell what I heard from the god. Phoebus our lord bids us plainly to drive out a defiling thing, which (he says) has been harboured in this land, and not to harbour it, so that it cannot be healed.

OEDIPUS: By what rite shall we cleanse ourselves? What is the manner of the misfortune?

CREON: By banishing a man, or by bloodshed in payment of bloodshed, since it is that blood which brings the tempest on our city.

OEDIPUS: And who is the man whose fate he thus reveals?

CREON: Laius, king, was lord of our land before you were pilot of this State. [25]

OEDIPUS: I know it well—by hearsay, for I never saw him.

CREON: He was slain; and the god now bids us plainly to wreak vengeance on his murderers—whosoever they be.

OEDIPUS: And where are they upon the earth? Where shall the dim track of this old crime be found?

CREON: In this land,—said the god. What is sought for can be caught; only that which is not watched escapes.

OEDIPUS: And was it in the house, or in the field, or on strange soil that Laius met his bloody end?

CREON: 'Twas on a visit to Delphi, as he said, that he had left our land; and he came home no more, after he had once set forth.

OEDIPUS: And was there none to tell? Was there no comrade of his journey who saw the deed, from whom information might have been gained, and used?

CREON: All perished, save one who fled in fear, and could tell for certain only one thing of all that he saw.

OEDIPUS: And what was that? One thing might show the clue to many, could we get but a small beginning for hope. [27]

CREON: He said that robbers met and fell on them, not with the strength of one man, but with very many hands.

OEDIPUS: How, then, unless there was some dealing in bribes from here, should the robber have dared thus far?

CREON: Such things were surmised; but, Laius once slain, amid our troubles no avenger arose.

OEDIPUS: But, when royalty had fallen thus, what trouble in your path can have hindered a full search?

CREON: The riddling Sphinx had made us let dark things go, and was inviting us to think of what lay at our doors.

OEDIPUS: Well, I will start afresh, and once more make dark things plain. Right worthily has Phoebus, and worthily have you, bestowed this care on the cause of the dead; and so, as is suitable, you shall find me too leagued with you in seeking vengeance for this land, and for the god besides. On behalf of no far-off friend, [29] no, but in my own cause, shall I dispel this taint. For whoever was the slayer of Laius might wish to take vengeance on me also with a hand as fierce. Therefore, in doing right to Laius, I serve myself.

Come, hasten my children, rise from the altar-steps, and lift these suppliant boughs; and let some other summon hither the folk of Cadmus, warned that I mean to leave nothing untried;

for our health (with the god's help) shall be made certain—or our ruin.

PRIEST: My children, let us rise; we came at first to seek what this man promises of himself. And may Phoebus, who sent these oracles, come to us therewith, our saviour and deliverer from the pestilence.

Exeunt Oedipus and Priest. Enter Chorus of Theban Elders.

CHORUS: *(singing) Strophe 1.* O sweetly-speaking message of Zeus, in what spirit have you come from golden Pytho to glorious [31] Thebes? I am on the rack, terror shakes my soul, O Delian healer to whom wild cries rise, in holy fear of you, what thing you will work for me, perchance unknown before, perchance renewed with the revolving years: tell me immortal Voice, born of Golden Hope!

Antistrophe 1. First I call on you, daughter of Zeus, divine Athena, and on your sister, guardian of our land, Artemis, who sits on her throne of fame, above the circle of our Agora, [33] and on Phoebus the far-darter: O shine forth on me, my threefold help against death! If ever aforetime, in arrest of ruin hurrying on the city, you drove a fiery pest beyond our borders, come now also!

Strophe 2. Woe is me, countless are the sorrows that I bear; a plague is on all our host, and thought can find no weapon for defence. The fruits of the glorious earth grow not; by no birth of children do women surmount the pangs in which they shriek; and life on life may you see sped like bird on nimble wing, aye, swifter than resistless fire, to the shore of the western god.

Antistrophe 2. By such deaths, past numbering, the city perishes: unpitied, her children lie on the ground, spreading pestilence, with none to mourn: and meanwhile young wives and grey-haired mothers with them, uplift a wail at the steps of the altars, some here, some there, [35] entreating for their weary woes. The prayer to the Healer rings clear, and blent therewith, the voice of lamentation: for these things, golden daughter of Zeus, send us the bright face of comfort.

Strophe 3. And grant that the fierce god of death, who now with no brazen shields, yet amid cries as of battle, wraps me in the flame of his onset, may turn his back in speedy flight from our land, borne by a fair wind to the great deep of Amphitrite, or to those waters in which none find haven, even to the Thracian wave; for if night leave anything undone, [37] day follows to accomplish this. O you who wieldest the powers of the fire-fraught lightning, O Zeus our father, slay him beneath your thunderbolt!

Antistrophe 3. Lycean King, gladly would I see your shafts also from your bent bow's string of woven gold, go abroad in their might, our champions in the face of the foe; yea, and the flashing fires of Artemis wherewith she glances through the Lycean hills. And I call him whose locks are bound with gold, who is named with the name of this land, ruddy Bacchus to whom Bacchants cry, the comrade of the Maenads, to draw near with the blaze [39] of his blithe torch, our ally against the god unhonoured among gods.

Oedipus enters during the closing strains of the choral song.

OEDIPUS: You pray: and in answer to your prayer,—if you will give a loyal welcome to my words and minister to your own disease,—you may hope to find succour and relief from woes. These words will I speak publicly, as one who has been a stranger to this report, a stranger to the deed; for I should not be far on the track, if I were tracing it alone, without a clue. But as it is,—since it was only after the time of the deed that I was numbered a Theban among Thebans,—to you, the Cadmeans all, I do thus proclaim.

Whoever of you knows by whom Laius son of Labdacus was slain, [41] I bid him to declare all to me. And if he is afraid, I tell him to remove the danger of the charge from his path by denouncing himself; for he shall suffer nothing else unlovely, but only leave the land, unhurt. Or if any one knows an alien, from another land, as the assassin, let him not keep silence; for I will pay his reward, and my thanks shall rest with him besides.

But if you keep silence—if any one, through fear, shall seek to screen friend or self from my behest—hear you what I then shall do. I charge you that no one of this land, of which I hold the power and the throne, give shelter or speak word unto that murderer, whoever he be,—make him partner of his prayer or sacrifice, or serve him with the lustral rite; [43] but that all ban him their homes, knowing that *this* is our defiling thing, as the oracle of the Pythian god has newly shown me. I then am in this way the ally of the god and of the slain. And I pray solemnly that the slayer, whoever he be, whether his hidden guilt is lonely or has partners, evilly, as he is evil, may wear out his unblest life. And for myself I pray that if, with my knowledge, he should become an inmate of my house, I may suffer the same things which even now I called down upon others. And on you I lay it to make all these words good, for my sake, and for the sake of the god, and for our land's, thus blasted with barrenness by angry heaven.

For even if the matter had not been urged on us by a god, it was not fitting that you should leave the guilt thus unpurged, when one so noble, and he your king, had perished; rather were you bound to search it out. And now, since 'tis I who hold the powers which once he held, [45] who possess his bed and the wife who bare children to him; and since, had his hope of issue not been frustrated, children born of one mother would have made ties between him and me—but, as it was, fate swooped upon his head; by reason of these things will I uphold this cause, just as though it were the cause of my own father, and will leave nothing untried in seeking to find him whose hand shed that blood, for the honour of the son of Labdacus and of Polydorus and elder Cadmus and Agenor who was of old.

And for those who obey me not, I pray that the gods send them neither harvest of the earth nor fruit of the womb, but that they be wasted by their lot that now is, or by one yet more dire. [47] But for all you, the loyal folk of Cadmus to whom these things seem good, may Justice, our ally, and all the gods be with you graciously for ever.

LEADER OF THE CHORUS: As you have put me on my oath, on my oath, O King, I will speak. I am not the slayer, nor can I point to him who slew. As for the question, it was for Phoebus, who sent it, to tell us this thing—who can have wrought the deed.

OEDIPUS: Justly said; but no man on the earth can force the gods to what they will not.

LEADER: I would gladly say what seems to me next best after this.

OEDIPUS: If there is yet a third course, do not hesitate to show it.

LEADER: I know that our lord Teiresias is the seer most like to our lord Phoebus; from whom, O King, a searcher of these things might learn them most clearly.

OEDIPUS: Not even this have I left out of my cares. On the hint of Creon, I have twice sent a man to bring him; and this long while I marvel why he is not here. [49]

LEADER: Indeed (his skill apart) the rumours are but faint and old.

OEDIPUS: What rumours are they? I look to every story.

LEADER: Certain wayfarers were said to have killed him.

OEDIPUS: I, too, have heard it, but none sees him who saw it.

LEADER: Nay, if he knows what fear is, he will not stay when he hears your curses, so dire as they are.

OEDIPUS: When a man shrinks not from a deed, neither is he scared by a word.

LEADER: Well, here is one to put him to the test. For here they bring at last the godlike prophet, in whom alone of men the truth lives.

Enter Teiresias, led by a boy.

OEDIPUS: Teiresias, whose soul grasps all things, the lore that may be told and the unspeakable, the secrets of heaven and the low things of earth,—you feel, though you cannot see, [51] what a plague haunts our State,—from which, great prophet, we find in you our protector and only saviour. Now, Phoebus—if indeed you know it not from the messengers—sent answer to our question that the only riddance from this pest which could come was if we should learn aright the slayers of Laius, and slay them, or send them into exile from our land. Do you, then, grudge neither voice of birds nor any other way or seer-lore that you have, but rescue yourself and the State, rescue me, rescue all that is defiled by the dead. For we are in your hand; and man's noblest task is to help others by his best means and powers.

TEIRESIAS: Alas, how dreadful to have wisdom where it profits not the wise! Aye, I knew this well, [53] but let it slip out of mind; else would I never have come here.

OEDIPUS: What now? How sad you have come in!

TEIRESIAS: Let me go home; most easily will you bear your own burden to the end, and I mine, if you will consent.

OEDIPUS: Your words are strange, nor kindly to this State which nurtured you, when you withhold this response.

TEIRESIAS: No, I see that you, on your part, do not open your lips in season: therefore I speak not, that I also may not have your misfortune.

OEDIPUS: For the love of the gods, turn not away, if you have knowledge: all we suppliants implore you on our knees.

TEIRESIAS: Aye, for you are all without knowledge; but never will I reveal my griefs—that I may not tell yours.

OEDIPUS: What do you say? You know the secret, and will not tell it, but are minded to betray us and to destroy the State?

TEIRESIAS: I will pain neither myself nor you. Why vainly ask these things? You will not learn them from me. [55]

OEDIPUS: What, basest of the base,—for you would anger a very stone,—will you never speak out? Can nothing touch you? Will you never make an end?

TEIRESIAS: You blame my mood, but do not see that to which you are wedded: no, you find fault with me.

OEDIPUS: And who would not be angry to hear the words with which you now slight this city?

TEIRESIAS: The future will come of itself, though I shroud it in silence.

OEDIPUS: Then, seeing that it must come, you on your part should tell me of it.

TEIRESIAS: I will speak no further; rage, then, if you will, with the fiercest wrath your heart knows.

OEDIPUS: Aye, indeed, I will not spare—so angry I am—to speak all my thought. Know that you seem to me even to have helped in plotting the deed, and to have done it, short of [57] slaying with your hands. If you had eyesight, I would have said that the doing, also, of this thing was yours alone.

TEIRESIAS: Indeed?—I charge you that you abide by the decree of your own mouth, and from this day speak neither to these nor to me: *you are* the accursed defiler of this land.

OEDIPUS: So brazen with your blustering taunt? And how do you trust to escape your due?

TEIRESIAS: I have escaped: in my truth is my strength.

OEDIPUS: Who taught you this? It was not, at least, your art.

TEIRESIAS: You: for you spurred me into speech against my will.

OEDIPUS: What speech? Speak again that I may learn it better.

TEIRESIAS: Did you not grasp my sense before? Or are you tempting me to talk?

OEDIPUS: No, I did not grasp it so that I can call it known:—speak again. [59]

TEIRESIAS: I say that you are the slayer of the man whose slayer you seek.

OEDIPUS: Now you shall rue that you have twice said words so dire.

TEIRESIAS: Would you have me say more, that you may be more angry?

OEDIPUS: Say what you will; it will be said in vain.

TEIRESIAS: I say that you have been living in unguessed shame with your nearest kin, and see not to what woe you have come.

OEDIPUS: Do you indeed think that you shall always speak thus without smarting?

TEIRESIAS: Yes, if there is any strength in truth.

OEDIPUS: Indeed, there is,—for all except you; for you that strength is not, since you are maimed in ear, and in mind, and in eye.

TEIRESIAS: Aye, and you are a poor wretch to utter taunts which every man here will soon hurl at you.

OEDIPUS: Night, endless night has you in her keeping, so that you can never hurt me, or any man who sees the sun.

TEIRESIAS: No, your doom is not to fall by *me:* Apollo is enough, whose care it is to work that out.

OEDIPUS: Are these Creon's plots, or yours?

TEIRESIAS: No, Creon is no plague to you; you are your own.

OEDIPUS: O wealth, and empire, and skill surpassing skill in life's keen rivalries, [61] how great is the envy that cleaves to you, if for the sake, yea, of this power which the city has put into my hands, a gift unsought, Creon the trusty, Creon my old friend, has crept on me by stealth, yearning to thrust me out of it, and has suborned such a scheming juggler as this, a tricky quack, who has eyes only for his gains, but in his art is blind!

Come, now, tell me, where have you proved yourself a seer? Why, when the Watcher was here who wove dark song, did you say nothing that could free this folk? Yet the riddle, at least, was not for the first comer to read; there was need of a seer's skill; and no such skill were you found to have either, by help of birds, or as known from any god: no, I came, I, Oedipus, the ignorant, and made her mute, when I had seized the answer by my wit, untaught of birds. [63] And it is I whom you are trying to oust, thinking to stand close to Creon's throne. I think that you and the plotter of these things will regret your zeal to purge the land. Indeed, if you did not seem to be an old man you would have learned at your cost how bold you are.

LEADER: To our thinking, both this man's words and yours, Oedipus, have been said in anger. Not for such words is our need, but to seek how we shall best discharge the mandates of the god.

TEIRESIAS: King though you are, the right of reply, at least, must be judged the same for both; of that I too am lord. Not to you do I live servant, but to Loxias; and so I shall not stand enrolled under Creon for my patron. And I tell you—since you have taunted me even with blindness—that you have sight, yet see not in what misery you are, nor where you dwell, nor with whom. Do you know of what stock you are? And you have been an unwitting foe to your own kin, in the shades, and on the earth above; [65] and the double lash of your mother's and your father's curse shall one day drive you from this land in dreadful haste, with darkness then on the eyes that now see true.

And what place shall not be harbour to your shriek, what of all Cithaeron shall not ring with it soon, when you have learned the meaning of the nuptials in which, within that house, you found a fatal haven, after a voyage so fair? And a throng of other ills you do not guess, which shall make you level with your true self and with your own brood.

Therefore heap your scorns on Creon and on my message: for no one among men shall ever be crushed more miserably than you.

OEDIPUS: Are these taunts to be indeed borne from *him?*—Hence, ruin take you! Go, this instant! Back!—away!—go away from these doors!

TEIRESIAS: I would never have come, not I, if you had not called me.

OEDIPUS: I knew not that you were about to speak folly, or it would have been long before I called you to my house. [67]

TEIRESIAS: Such am I,—as you think, a fool; but for the parents who conceived you, sane.

OEDIPUS: What parents? Stay . . . and who is my father?

TEIRESIAS: This day shall show your birth and shall bring your ruin.

OEDIPUS: What riddles, what dark words you always speak.

TEIRESIAS: Nay, are you not most skilled in unraveling dark speech?

OEDIPUS: Make that my reproach in which you will find me great.

TEIRESIAS: Yes, 'twas just that fortune that undid you.

OEDIPUS: But, if I delivered this town, I care not.

TEIRESIAS: Then I will go: so do you, boy, take me hence.

OEDIPUS: Aye, let him take you: while here, you are a hindrance, a trouble: when you have vanished, you will vex me no more.

TEIRESIAS: I will go when I have done my errand, fearless of your frown: for you can never destroy me. And I tell you—the man of whom you have for a long time [69] been in search, uttering threats, and proclaiming a search into the murder of Laius—that man is here,—in appearance an alien sojourner, but soon, he shall be found a native Theban, and shall not be glad of his fortune. A blind man, he who now has sight, a beggar, who now is rich, he shall make his way to a strange land, feeling the ground before him with his staff. And he shall be found at once brother and father of the children with whom he consorts; son and husband of the woman who bore him; heir to his father's bed, shedder of his father's blood.

So go in and think on that; and if you find that I have been at fault, say thenceforth that I have no understanding in prophecy.

Teiresias is led out by the boy. Oedipus enters the palace.

CHORUS: *(singing) Strophe 1.* Who is he of whom the divine voice from the Delphian rock has [71] spoken, as having wrought with red hands horrors that no tongue can tell?

It is time that he ply in flight a foot stronger than the feet of storm-swift steeds: for the son of Zeus is springing on him, all armed with fiery lightnings, and with him come the dread, unerring Fates.

Antistrophe 1. Yea, newly given from snowy Parnassus, the message has flashed forth to make all search for the unknown man. Into the wild wood's covert, among caves and rocks he is roaming, fierce as a bull, [73] wretched and forlorn on his joyless path, still seeking to put from him the doom spoken at Earth's central shrine: but that doom ever lives, ever flits around him.

Strophe 2. Dreadly, indeed, dreadly does the wise augur move me, who approve not, nor am able to deny. How to speak, I know not; I am fluttered with forebodings; neither in the present have I clear vision, nor of the future. Never in past days, nor in these, have I heard how the house of Labdacus or the son of Polybus had, either against the other, any quarrel I could bring as proof in assailing the public fame of Oedipus, and seeking to avenge the line of Labdacus for the undiscovered murder. [75]

Antistrophe 2. Nay, Zeus indeed and Apollo are keen of thought, and know the things of earth; but that mortal seer wins knowledge above mine, of this there can be no sure tests; though man may surpass man in lore. Yet, until I see the word made good, never will I assent when men blame Oedipus. Before all eyes, the winged maiden came against him of old, and he was seen to be wise; he bore the test, in welcome service to our State; never, therefore, by the verdict of my heart shall he be adjudged guilty of crime.

Enter Creon.

CREON: Fellow-citizens, having learned that Oedipus the king lays dire charges against me, I come here, indignant. If, in the present troubles, he thinks that he has suffered from *me,* [77] by word or deed, anything that tends to harm, in truth I crave not my full term of years, when I must bear such blame as this. The wrong of this rumour touches me not in one point alone, but has the largest scope, if I am to be called a traitor in the city, a traitor too by you and by my friends.

LEADER OF THE CHORUS: But this taunt came under stress, perchance, of anger, rather than from the purpose of the heart.

CREON: And the saying was uttered, that *my* counsels won the seer to utter his falsehoods?

LEADER: Such things were said—I know not with what meaning.

CREON: And was this charge laid against me with steady eyes and steady mind?

LEADER: I know not; I see not what my masters do: but here comes our lord forth from the house.

Enter Oedipus.

OEDIPUS: Sirrah, how did you come here? Are you so bold that you have come to my house, [79] who are the proved assassin of its master,—the palpable robber of my crown? Come, tell me, in the name of the gods, was it cowardice or folly that you saw in me, that you plotted to do this thing? Did you think that I would not note this deed of yours creeping on me by stealth, or, aware, would not ward it off? Now is not your foolish attempt,—to seek, without followers or friends, a throne,—a prize which followers and wealth must win?

CREON: Mark me now,—in answer to your words, hear a fair reply, and then judge for yourself on the basis of knowledge.

OEDIPUS: You are apt in speech, but I have a poor understanding for your lessons, since I have found you my malignant foe.

CREON: Now first hear how I will explain this very thing—[81]

OEDIPUS: But one thing do not explain—that you are not false.

CREON: If you think that stubbornness without sense is a good gift, you are not wise.

OEDIPUS: If you think that you can wrong a kinsman and escape the penalty, you are not sane.

CREON: Justly said, I grant thee: but tell me what is the wrong that you say you have suffered from me.

OEDIPUS: Did you advise, or did you not, that I should send for that reverend seer?

CREON: And now I am still of the same mind.

OEDIPUS: How long is it, then, since Laius—

CREON: Since Laius . . . ? I do not take your drift . . .

OEDIPUS: —was swept from men's sight by a deadly violence?

CREON: The count of years would run far into the past.

OEDIPUS: Was this seer, then, practicing his craft in those days?

CREON: Yes, skilled as now, and in equal honour.

OEDIPUS: Made he, then, any mention of me at that time?

CREON: Never, certainly, when I was within hearing.

OEDIPUS: But did you not hold a search concerning the murder?

CREON: Due search we held, of course—and learned nothing.

OEDIPUS: And how was it that this sage did not tell his story *then?*

CREON: I know not; where I lack light, 'tis my custom to be silent. [83]

OEDIPUS: Thus much, at least, you know, and could declare with light enough.

CREON: What is that? If I know it, I will not deny.

OEDIPUS: That, if he had not conferred with you, he would never have named *my* slaying of Laius.

CREON: If he says so, you know it best; but I claim to learn from you as much as you now have learned from me.

OEDIPUS: Learn your fill: I shall never be found guilty of the blood.

CREON: Say, then—you have married my sister?

OEDIPUS: The question does not allow denial.

CREON: And you rule the land as she does with like sway?

OEDIPUS: She obtains from me all she desires.

CREON: And do not I rank as a third peer of you two?

OEDIPUS: Aye, 'tis just there that you are seen as a false friend.

CREON: Not so, if you would reason with your own heart as I with mine. And first weigh this,—whether you think that any one would choose to rule amid terrors rather than in unruffled peace,—granting that he is to have the same powers. Now I, for one, have no yearning in my nature to be a king rather than to do kingly deeds, no, nor has any man who knows how to keep a sober mind. For now I win all favors from you without fear; [85] but, were I ruler myself, I should be doing much even against my own pleasure.

How, then, could royalty be sweeter for me to have than painless rule and influence? Not yet am I so misguided as to desire other honours than those which profit. Now, all wish me joy; now every man has a greeting for me; now, those who have requests to you crave speech with me, since therein is all their hope of success. Then why should I resign these things, and take those? No mind will become false, while it is wise. Nay, I am no lover of such policy, and, if another put it into practice, I could never bear to act with him.

And, in proof of this, first, go to Pytho, and ask if I brought you true word of the oracle; [87] then next, if you find that I have planned anything in concert with the soothsayer, take and slay me, by the sentence not of one mouth, but of two—by my own, no less than yours. But make me not guilty in a corner, on unproved surmise. It is not right to adjudge bad men good at random, or good men bad. I count it a like thing for a man to cast off a true friend as to cast away the life in his own bosom, which most he loves. But, you will learn these things with sureness in time, for time alone shows a just man; but you could discern a knave even in one day.

LEADER: Well has he spoken, O King, for one who takes care not to fall: the quick in counsel are not sure.

OEDIPUS: When the stealthy plotter is moving on me quickly, I, too, must be quick with my counterplot. If I await him in repose, his ends will have been gained, and mine missed.

CREON: What do you want then? To cast me out of the land?

OEDIPUS: Not so: I desire your death—not your banishment—

that you may show forth what kind of thing envy is.

CREON: You speak as one resolved not to yield or to believe?

OEDIPUS: No; for you do not persuade me that you are worthy of belief.

CREON: No, for I find you not sane.

OEDIPUS: Sane, at least, in my own interest.

CREON: But you should be so in mine also.

OEDIPUS: No, you are false. [89]

CREON: But if you understand nothing?

OEDIPUS: Yet must I rule.

CREON: Not if you rule ill.

OEDIPUS: Hear him, O Thebes!

CREON: Thebes is for me also—not for you alone.

Jocasta enters from the palace.

LEADER: Cease, princes; and in good time for you I see Jocasta coming yonder from the house, with whose help you should settle your present feud.

JOCASTA: Misguided men, why have you raised such foolish strife of tongues? Are you not ashamed, while the land is thus sick, to stir up troubles of your own? Come, go into the house,—and you Creon, to your home,—and forbear to make much of a petty grief.

CREON: Kinswoman, Oedipus your lord claims to do dread things to me, even one or the other of two ills,—to thrust me from the land of my fathers, or to slay me. [91]

OEDIPUS: Yea; for I have caught him, lady, working evil, by ill arts, against my person.

CREON: Now may I see no good, but perish accursed, if I have done you any of what you charge me with!

JOCASTA: O, for the gods' love, believe it, Oedipus—first, for the awful sake of this oath to the gods,—then for my sake and for theirs who stand before you!

The following lines between the Chorus and Oedipus and between the Chorus, Jocasta, and Oedipus are chanted responsively.

CHORUS: *Strophe 1.* Consent, reflect, hearken, O my king, I pray you!

OEDIPUS: What grace, then, would you have me grant you?

CHORUS: Respect him who in other times was not foolish, and who now is strong in his oath.

OEDIPUS: Now do you know what you crave?

CHORUS: Yes.

OEDIPUS: Declare, then, what you mean.

CHORUS: That you should never use an unproved rumour to cast a dishonouring charge on a friend who has bound himself with an oath.

OEDIPUS: Then be very sure that, when you seek this, for me you are seeking destruction, or exile from this land.

CHORUS: *Strophe 2.* No, by him who stands in the front of all the heavenly host, [93] no, by the Sun! Unblest, unfriended, may I die by the uttermost doom, if I have that thought! But my unhappy soul is worn by the withering of the land, and again by the thought that our old sorrows should be crowned by sorrows springing from you two.

OEDIPUS: Then let him go, though I am surely doomed to death, or to be thrust dishonoured from the land. Your lips, not his, move my compassion by their plaint; but he, wherever he be, shall be hated.

CREON: You appear as sullen in yielding as vehement in the excesses of your wrath; but such natures are justly most difficult for themselves to bear.

OEDIPUS: You will not leave me in peace, and be gone?

CREON: I will go my way; I have found you undiscerning, but in the eyes of these I am just.

Exit Creon.

CHORUS: *Antistrophe 1.* Lady, why do you delay to take yonder man into the house? [95]

JOCASTA: I will do so, when I have learned what has happened.

CHORUS: Blind suspicion, bred of talk, arose; and, on the other part, injustice wounds.

JOCASTA: It was on both sides?

CHORUS: Both.

JOCASTA: And what was the story?

CHORUS: It is enough, I think, enough—when our land is already vexed—that the matter should rest where it ceased.

OEDIPUS: Do you see to what you have come, for all your honest purpose, in seeking to relax and blunt my zeal?

CHORUS: *Antistrophe 2.* King, I have said it not once alone—be sure that I should have been shown a madman, bankrupt in sane counsel, if I put you away—you, who gave a true course to my beloved country when distraught by troubles—you, who now also are like to prove our prospering guide. [97]

JOCASTA: In the name of the gods, tell me also, O King, on what account you have conceived this steadfast wrath.

OEDIPUS: That I will do; for I honour you, lady, above yonder men:—the cause is Creon, and the plots that he has laid against me.

JOCASTA: Speak on—if you can tell clearly how the feud began.

OEDIPUS: He says that I stand guilty of the blood of Laius.

JOCASTA: Of his own knowledge? Or on hearsay from another?

OEDIPUS: No, he has made a rascal seer his mouthpiece; as for himself, he keeps his lips wholly pure.

JOCASTA: Then absolve yourself of the things of which you speak; listen to me, and learn for your comfort that there is no mortal who can claim the gift of prophecy. I will give you solid proof of that.

An oracle came to Laius once—I will not say from Phoebus himself, but from his ministers—that the doom should overtake him to die by the hand of his child, [99] who should spring from him and me.

Now Laius,—as, at least, the rumour says,—was murdered one day by foreign robbers at a place where three highways meet. And the child's birth was not three days past, when Laius pinned its ankles together, and had it thrown, by others' hands, on a trackless mountain.

So, in that case, Apollo did not bring it about that the babe should become the slayer of his father, or that Laius should die—the dread thing which he feared—by his child's hand. Thus did the messages of seer-craft map out the future. Do not pay any attention to them. Whatever needful things the god seeks, he himself will easily bring to light.

OEDIPUS: What restlessness of soul, lady, what tumult of the mind has just come upon me since I heard you speak!

JOCASTA: What anxiety has startled you, that you say this?

OEDIPUS: I thought I heard this from you,—that Laius was slain where three highways meet.

JOCASTA: Yes, that was the story; it has not died out yet.

OEDIPUS: And where is the place where this happened?

JOCASTA: The land is called Phocis; and branching roads lead to the same spot from Delphi and from Daulia. [101]

OEDIPUS: And what is the time that has passed since these things took place?

JOCASTA: The news was published to the town shortly before you were first seen in power over this land.

OEDIPUS: O Zeus, what have you decreed to do to me?

JOCASTA: And why, Oedipus, does this thing weigh upon your soul?

OEDIPUS: Ask me not yet; but tell me what was the stature of Laius, and how ripe his manhood.

JOCASTA: He was tall,—the silver just lightly strewn among his hair; and his form was not greatly unlike yours.

OEDIPUS: Unhappy that I am! I think that I have been laying myself even now under a dread curse, and did not know it.

JOCASTA: How say you? I tremble when I look on you, my king.

OEDIPUS: I have dread misgivings that the seer can see. But you will make it clearer if you will tell me one thing more.

JOCASTA: Indeed—though I tremble—I will answer all that you ask, when I hear it. [103]

OEDIPUS: Did he go in small force, or with many armed followers, like a chieftain?

JOCASTA: Five they were in all,—a herald one of them; and there was one carriage, which bore Laius.

OEDIPUS: Alas! 'Tis now clear indeed.—Who was he who gave you these tidings, lady?

JOCASTA: A servant—the sole survivor who came home.

OEDIPUS: Is he by chance at hand in the house now?

JOCASTA: No, truly; so soon as he came thence, and found you reigning instead of Laius, he supplicated me, with hand laid on mine, that I would send him to the fields, to the pastures of the flocks, that he might be far from the sight of this town. And I sent him; he was worthy, for a slave, to win even greater favor than that.

OEDIPUS: Would, then, that he could return to us without delay!

JOCASTA: It is easy: but why do you command this?

OEDIPUS: I fear, lady, that my own lips have been unguarded; and therefore am I eager to behold him. [105]

JOCASTA: Indeed, he shall come. But I too, I think, have a claim to learn what lies heavy on your heart, my king.

OEDIPUS: Yes, and it shall not be kept from you, now that my forebodings have advanced so far. Who, indeed, is more to me than you, to whom I should speak in passing through such a fortune as this?

My father was Polybus of Corinth,—my mother, the Dorian Merope; and I was held the first of all the folk in that town, until something happened to me, worthy, indeed, of wonder, though not worthy of my own anger concerning it. At a banquet, a man full of wine cast it at me in his cups that I was not the true son of my father. And I, vexed, restrained myself for that day as best I might; but on the next I went to my mother and father, and questioned them; and they were angry for the taunt with him who had let that word fly. So on their part I had comfort; yet the thing was ever rankling in my heart; for it still crept abroad with strong rumour. And, unknown to mother or father, I went to Delphi; and Phoebus sent me [107] forth disappointed of that knowledge for which I came, but in his response set forth other things, full of sorrow and terror and woe; even that I was fated to defile my mother's bed; and that I should show to men a brood which they could not endure to behold; and that I should be the slayer of the father who conceived me.

And I, when I had listened to this, turned to flight from the land of Corinth, thenceforth knowing of its region by the stars alone, to some spot where I should never see fulfilment of the infamies foretold in my evil doom. And on my way I came to the regions in which you say that this prince perished. Now, lady, I will tell you the truth. When in my journey I was near to those three roads, there met me a herald, and a man seated in a carriage drawn by colts, as you have described; [109] and he who was in front, and the old man himself, were for thrusting me rudely from the path. Then, in anger, I struck him who pushed me aside—the driver; and the old man, seeing it, watched the moment when I was passing, and, from the carriage, brought his goad with two teeth down directly upon my head. Yet was he paid with interest; by one swift blow from the staff in this hand he was rolled right out of the carriage, on his back; and I slew every man of them.

But if this stranger had any tie of kinship with Laius, who is now more wretched than the man before you? What mortal could prove more hated of heaven? Whom no stranger, no citizen, is allowed to receive in his house; whom it is unlawful that any one accost; [111] whom all must repel from their homes! And this—this curse—was laid on me by no mouth but my own! And I pollute the bed of the slain man with the hands by which he perished. Say, am I vile? O, am I not utterly unclean?—seeing that I must be banished, and in banishment see not my own people, nor set foot in my own land, or else be joined in wedlock to my mother, and slay my father, even Polybus, who begat and reared me.

Then would not he speak aright of Oedipus, who judged these things sent by some cruel power above man? Forbid, forbid, you pure and awful gods, that I should see that day! No, may I be swept from among men, before I behold myself visited with the brand of such a doom!

LEADER OF THE CHORUS: To us, indeed, these things, O King, are fraught with fear; yet have hope, until at last you have gained full knowledge from him who saw the deed.

OEDIPUS: Hope, in truth, rests with me thus far alone; I can await the man summoned from the pastures.

JOCASTA: And when he has appeared—what would you have of him?

OEDIPUS: I will tell you. If his story be found to tally with yours, I, at least, shall stand clear of disaster.

JOCASTA: And what of special note did you hear from me? [113]

OEDIPUS: You were saying that he spoke of Laius as slain by

robbers. If, then, he still speaks, as before, of several, I was not the slayer: a solitary man could not be held the same with that band. But if he names one lonely wayfarer, then beyond doubt this guilt leans to me.

JOCASTA: Be assured that thus, at least, the tale was first told; he cannot revoke that, for the city heard it, not I alone. But even if he should diverge somewhat from his former story, never, King, can he show that the murder of Laius, at least, is truly square to prophecy; of whom Loxias plainly said that he must die by the hand of my child. Nevertheless that poor innocent never slew him, but perished first itself. So henceforth, for what touches divination, I would not look to my right hand or my left. [115]

OEDIPUS: You judge well. But nevertheless send some one to fetch the peasant, and do not neglect this matter.

JOCASTA: I will send without delay. But let us come into the house: I will do nothing except at your good pleasure.

Oedipus and Jocasta go into the palace.

CHORUS: *(singing) Strophe 1.* May destiny still find me winning the praise of reverent purity in all words and deeds sanctioned by those laws of range sublime, called into life throughout the high clear heaven, whose father is Olympus [117] alone; their parent was no race of mortal men, no, nor shall oblivion every lay them to sleep; the god is mighty in them, and he grows not old.

Antistrophe 1. Insolence[1] breeds the tyrant; Insolence, once vainly surfeited on wealth that is not suitable nor good for it,

[1] The Greek word for this is *hybris,* often translated as *arrogance* or *pride.* Part of Professor Jebb's annotation of the Second Stasimon is given here: "The second episode has been marked by the overbearing harshness of Oedipus towards Creon; by the rise of a dreadful suspicion that Oedipus is . . . bloodguilty for Laius; and by the avowed contempt of Jocasta, not, indeed, for Apollo himself, but for the . . . [mantic art, prophetic skill] of his ministers. These traits furnish the two interwoven themes of the second stasimon: (1) the prayer for *purity* in word as in deed; (2) the deprecation of that *pride* which goes before a fall;—whether it be the insolence of the *tyrannos,* or such intellectual arrogance as Jocasta's speech bewrays. The tone of warning reproof towards Oedipus, while only allusive, is yet in contrast with the firm though anxious sympathy of the former ode, and serves to attune the feeling of the spectators for the approach of the catastrophe." [116]

when it has scaled the topmost ramparts, is hurled to a dire doom, wherein no service of the feet can serve. But I pray that the god never quell such rivalry as benefits the State; the god will I ever hold for our protector. [119]

Strophe 2. But if any man walks haughtily in deed or word, with no fear of Justice, no reverence for the images of gods, may an evil doom seize him for his ill-starred pride, if he will not win his vantage fairly, nor keep him from unholy deeds, but must lay profaning hands on sanctities.

Where such things are, what mortal shall boast any more that he can ward the arrows of the gods from his life? [121] In fact, if such deeds are in honour, why should we join in the sacred dance?

Antistrophe 2. No more will I go reverently to earth's central and inviolate shrine, no more to Abae's temple or Olympia, if these oracles do not prove true, so that all men shall point at them with the finger. Nay, King,–if you are rightly called,–Zeus all-ruling, may it not escape you and your ever-deathless power!

The old prophecies concerning Laius are fading; already men are setting them at nought, and nowhere is Apollo glorified with honours; the worship of the gods is perishing. [123]

Jocasta comes forth, bearing a branch, wreathed with festoons of wool, which, as a suppliant, she is about to lay on the altar of the household god, Lycean Apollo, in front of the palace.

JOCASTA: Princes of the land, the thought has come to me to visit the shrines of the gods, with this wreathed branch in my hands, and these gifts of incense. For Oedipus excites his soul overmuch with all manner of alarms, nor, like a man of sense, judges the new things by the old, but is at the will of the speaker, if he speak terrors.

Since, then, by counsel I can do no good, to you, Lycean Apollo, for you are nearest, I have come, a suppliant with these symbols of prayer, that you may find us some riddance from uncleanness. For now we are all afraid, seeing *him* affrighted, even as they who see fear in the helmsman of their ship.

While Jocasta is offering her prayers to the god, a Messenger, evidently a stranger, enters and addresses the Elders of the Chorus.

MESSENGER: Might I learn from you, strangers, where is the house of the King Oedipus? Or, better still, tell me where he himself is—if you know. [125]

LEADER OF THE CHORUS: This is his dwelling, and he himself, stranger, is within; and this lady is the mother of his children.

MESSENGER: Then may she be ever happy in a happy home, since she is his heaven-blest queen.

JOCASTA: Happiness to you also, stranger! It is the due of your fair greeting.—But say what you have come to seek or to tell.

MESSENGER: Good tidings, lady, for your house and for your husband.

JOCASTA: What are they? And from whom have you come?

MESSENGER: From Corinth: and at the message which I will soon speak you will rejoice—doubtless; yet perhaps grieve.

JOCASTA: And what is it? How does it have a double potentiality?

MESSENGER: The people wish to make him king of the Isthmian land, as it was said there.

JOCASTA: How then? Is the aged Polybus no more in power?

MESSENGER: No, truly: for death holds him in the tomb.

JOCASTA: How say you? Is Polybus dead, old man?

MESSENGER: If I do not speak the truth, I am content to die. [127]

JOCASTA: O handmaid, away with all speed, and tell this to thy master! O you oracles of the gods, where do you stand now! This is the man whom Oedipus long feared and shunned, lest he should slay him; and now this man has died in the course of destiny, not by his hand.

Oedipus enters from the Palace.

OEDIPUS: Jocasta, dearest wife, why have you summoned me forth from these doors?

JOCASTA: Hear this man, and judge, as you listen, to what the awful oracles of the gods have come.

OEDIPUS: And he—who may he be, and what news has he for me?

JOCASTA: He is from Corinth, to tell that your father Polybus lives no longer, but has perished.

OEDIPUS: How, stranger? Let me have it from your own mouth.

MESSENGER: If I must first make these tidings plain, know indeed that he is dead and gone.

OEDIPUS: By treachery, or by visit of disease?

MESSENGER: A light thing in the scale brings the aged to their rest.

OEDIPUS: Ah, he died, it seems, of sickness?

MESSENGER: Yea, and of the long years that he had counted.

OEDIPUS: Alas, alas! Why, indeed, my wife, should one look to the hearth of the Pythian seer, or to the birds that scream above our heads, on whose showing I [129] was doomed to slay my father? But he is dead, and hid already beneath the earth; and here am I, who have not put hand to spear.—Unless, perhaps, he was killed by longing for me: thus, indeed, I should be the cause of his death. But the oracles as they stand, at least, Polybus has swept with him to his rest in Hades: they are worth nothing.

JOCASTA: Nay, did I not predict this to you long ago?

OEDIPUS: You did: but I was misled by my fear.

JOCASTA: Now no more take any of those things to heart.

OEDIPUS: But surely I must needs fear my mother's bed?

JOCASTA: Nay, what should mortal fear, for whom the decrees of Fortune are supreme, and who has clear foresight of nothing? [131] It is best to live at random, as one may. But do not fear concerning wedlock with your mother. Many men before now have so fared in dreams also: but he to whom these things are as nothing bears his life most easily.

OEDIPUS: All these bold words of yours would have been well, were not my mother living; but as it is, since she lives, I must necessarily fear—though you speak reassuringly.

JOCASTA: Nevertheless your father's death is a great sign to cheer us.

OEDIPUS: Great, I know; but my fear is of her who lives.

MESSENGER: And who is the woman about whom you fear?

OEDIPUS: Merope, old man, the consort of Polybus.

MESSENGER: And what is it in her that excites your fear?

OEDIPUS: A heaven-sent oracle of dread import, stranger.

MESSENGER: Lawful, or unlawful, for another to know?

OEDIPUS: Lawful, surely. Loxias once said that I was doomed to espouse my own mother, and to shed with my own hands my father's blood. Therefore my home in Corinth was long kept [133] at a distance by me; with a fortunate outcome, indeed,—yet still it is sweet to see the face of parents.

MESSENGER: Was it indeed for fear of this that you were an exile from that city?

OEDIPUS: And because, old man, I did not wish to be the slayer of my father.

MESSENGER: Then why have I not freed you, King, from this fear, seeing that I came with friendly purpose?

OEDIPUS: Indeed you should have reward due from me.

MESSENGER: Indeed it was chiefly for this that I came—that, on your return home, I might reap some good.

OEDIPUS: No, I will never go near my parents.

MESSENGER: Ah, my son, it is plain enough that you know not what you do.

OEDIPUS: How, old man? For the gods' love, tell me.

MESSENGER: If for these reasons you shrink from going home.

OEDIPUS: Aye, I dread lest Phoebus prove himself true for me.

MESSENGER: You dread to be stained with guilt through your parents?

OEDIPUS: Even so, old man—this it is that always frightens me.

MESSENGER: Do you know, then, that your fears are wholly groundless?

OEDIPUS: How so, if I was born of those parents?

MESSENGER: Because Polybus was nothing to you in blood.

OEDIPUS: What do you say? Was Polybus not my father?

MESSENGER: No more than he who speaks to you, but just so much. [135]

OEDIPUS: And how can my father be equal with him who is as nothing to me?

MESSENGER: Indeed, he did not beget you, any more than I.

OEDIPUS: Why then did he call me his son?

MESSENGER: Know that he had received you as a gift from my hands long ago.

OEDIPUS: And yet he loved me so dearly, who came from another's hand?

MESSENGER: Yes, his former childlessness brought him to it.

OEDIPUS: And you—had you bought me or found me by chance, when you gave me to him?

MESSENGER: Found you in Cithaeron's winding glens.

OEDIPUS: And why were you roaming in those regions?

MESSENGER: I was there in charge of mountain flocks.

OEDIPUS: What, you were a shepherd—a wandering worker?

MESSENGER: But your preserver, my son, in that hour.

OEDIPUS: What was my condition when you took me in your arms?

MESSENGER: The ankles of your feet might bear witness.

OEDIPUS: Ah me, why do you speak of that old trouble?

MESSENGER: I freed you when you had your ankles pinned together.

OEDIPUS: Aye, it was a dread brand of shame that I took from my cradle. [137]

MESSENGER: From that happening you were called by the name which is still yours.

OEDIPUS: O, for the gods' love—was the deed my mother's or father's? Speak!

MESSENGER: I know not; he who gave you to me knows that better than I.

OEDIPUS: What, you got me from another? You did not find me yourself?

MESSENGER: No: another shepherd gave you to me.

OEDIPUS: Who was he? Can you tell me clearly?

MESSENGER: I think he was called one of the household of Laius.

OEDIPUS: The king who ruled this country long ago?

MESSENGER: The same: it was in his service that the man was a shepherd.

OEDIPUS: Is he still alive, that I might see him?

MESSENGER: Indeed, you people of the country should know best.

OEDIPUS: Is there any of you here present that knows the shepherd of whom he speaks—that has seen him in the pastures or the town? Answer! The hour has come when these things should be finally revealed.

LEADER OF THE CHORUS: It seems that he speaks of no other than the peasant whom you are already eager to see; but our lady Jocasta might best tell of that.

OEDIPUS: Lady, do you know of him whom we lately summoned? Is it of him that this man speaks? [139]

JOCASTA: Why ask of whom he spoke? Regard it not . . . waste not a thought on what he said . . . it would be idle.

OEDIPUS: It must not be that, with such clues in my grasp, I should fail to bring my birth to light.

JOCASTA: For the gods' sake, if you have any care for your own life, give up this search! My anguish is enough.

OEDIPUS: Be of good courage; though I be found the son of a slave mother,—aye, a slave for three generations,—you will not be proved base-born.

JOCASTA: Yet hear me, I implore you: do not do it.

OEDIPUS: I must not hear of not discovering the whole truth.

JOCASTA: Yet I wish you well—I advise you for the best.

OEDIPUS: Then these best counsels vex my patience.

JOCASTA: Ill-fated one! May you never come to know who you are!

OEDIPUS: Go, some one, bring me the herdsman hither,—and leave that woman to glory in her princely stock.

JOCASTA: Alas, alas, miserable!—that word alone can I say to you, and no other word henceforth for ever.

She rushes into the palace.

LEADER: Why has the lady gone, Oedipus, in a transport of wild grief? I fear [141] a storm of sorrow will break forth from this silence.

OEDIPUS: Break forth what will! Be my race never so lowly, I must crave to learn it. That woman—for she is proud with more than a woman's pride perhaps thinks shame of my base birth. But I, who hold myself son of Fortune that gives good, will not be dishonoured. She is the mother from whom I spring; and the months, my kinsmen, have marked me sometimes lowly, sometimes great. Such being my lineage, never more can I prove false to it, or spare to search out the secret of my birth. [143]

CHORUS: *(singing) Strophe.* If I am a seer or wise of heart, O

Cithaeron, you shall not fail—by yonder heaven, you shall not!—to know at tomorrow's full moon that Oedipus honours you as native to him, as his nurse, and his mother, and that you are celebrated in our dance and song, because you are well-pleasing to our prince. O Phoebus to whom we cry, may these things find favour in your sight!

Antistrophe. Who was it, my son, that of the race whose years are many that bore you in wedlock with Pan, the mountain-roaming [145] father? Or was it a bride of Loxias that bore you? For dear to him are all the upland pastures. Or perchance it was Cyllene's lord, or the Bacchants' god, dweller on the hill-tops, that received you, a new-born joy, from one of the Nymphs of Helicon, with whom he most has pleasure.

OEDIPUS: Elders, if it is for me to guess, who have never met with him, I think I see the herdsman of whom we have long been in quest; for in his venerable age he tallies with yonder stranger's years, and besides I know those who bring him, I think, as servants [147] of my own. But perhaps you may have the advantage of me in knowledge, if you have seen the herdsman before.

LEADER: Yes, I know him, be sure; he was in the service of Laius—trusty as any man, in his shepherd's place.

The herdsman is brought in.

OEDIPUS: I ask you first, Corinthian stranger, is this he whom you mean?

MESSENGER: The very man whom you see.

OEDIPUS: Ho, you, old man—I would have you look this way, and answer all that I ask you. You were once in the service of Laius?

HERDSMAN: I was—a slave not bought, but reared in his house.

OEDIPUS: Employed in what labour, or what way of life?

HERDSMAN: For the best part of my life I tended flocks.

OEDIPUS: And what were the regions that you mainly frequented?

HERDSMAN: Sometimes it was Cithaeron, sometimes the neighbouring ground.

OEDIPUS: Have you seen this man in those parts—

HERDSMAN: Doing what? . . . What man do you mean? . . .

OEDIPUS: This man here—or have you ever met him before? [149]

HERDSMAN: Not that I could speak at once from memory.

MESSENGER: And no wonder, master. But I will bring clear recollection to his ignorance. I am sure that he well knows of the time when we abode in the region of Cithaeron,—he with two flocks, I, his comrade, with one—three full half-years, from spring to Arcturus; and then for the winter I used to drive my flock to my own fold, and he took his to the fold of Laius. Did any of this happen as I tell, or did it not?

HERDSMAN: You speak the truth—though it is long ago. [151]

MESSENGER: Come, tell me now—do you know of having given me a boy in those days, to be reared as my own foster-son?

HERDSMAN: What now? Why do you ask the question?

MESSENGER: Yonder man, my friend, is he who then was young.

HERDSMAN: Plague take you—be silent once for all!

OEDIPUS: Ha! chide him not, old man—your words need chiding more than his.

HERDSMAN: And wherein, most noble master, do I offend?

OEDIPUS: In not telling of the boy about whom he asks.

HERDSMAN: He speaks without knowledge—he is busy to no purpose.

OEDIPUS: You do not want to speak with a good grace, but you shall or be punished.

HERDSMAN: No, for the gods' love, do not misuse an old man!

OEDIPUS: Ho, some one—pinion him this instant!

HERDSMAN: Alas, why? what more would you learn?

OEDIPUS: Did you give this man the child of whom he speaks?

HERDSMAN: I did,—and I wish that I had perished that day!

OEDIPUS: Well, you will come to that, unless you tell the honest truth.

HERDSMAN: No, I am much more lost, if I speak.

OEDIPUS: The fellow is bent, it seems, on more delays . . .

HERDSMAN: No, no!—I said before that I gave it to him.

OEDIPUS: From where had you got it? In your own house, or from another?

HERDSMAN: It was not my own—I had received it from a man.

OEDIPUS: From whom of the citizens here? from what home?

HERDSMAN: Give up, for the gods' love, master, refrain from asking more!

OEDIPUS: You are lost if I have to question you again.

HERDSMAN: It was a child, then, of the house of Laius. [153]

OEDIPUS: A slave? or one born of his own family?

HERDSMAN: Ah me—I am on the dreaded brink of speech.

OEDIPUS: And I of hearing; yet must I hear.

HERDSMAN: You must know, then, that it was said to be his own child—but your lady within could best say how these things are.

OEDIPUS: How? She gave it to you?

HERDSMAN: Yes, O King.

OEDIPUS: For what end?

HERDSMAN: That I should make away with it.

OEDIPUS: Her own child, the wretch?

HERDSMAN: Yes, from fear of evil prophecies.

OEDIPUS: What were they?

HERDSMAN: The tale ran that he must slay his father.

OEDIPUS: Why, then, did you give him up to this old man?

HERDSMAN: Through pity, master, as thinking that he would bear him away to another land, from which he himself came; but he saved him for the direst woe. For if you are what this man says, know that you were born to misery.

OEDIPUS: O, O! All brought to pass—all true! O light, may I now look my last on you—I who have been found accursed in birth, accursed in wedlock, accursed in the shedding of blood!

He rushes into the palace.

CHORUS: *(singing) Strophe 1.* Alas, you generations of men, how mere a shadow do I count your life! [155] Where, where is the mortal who wins more of happiness than just the seeming, and, after the semblance, a falling away? Yours is a fate that warns me,—yours, yours, unhappy Oedipus—to call no earthly creature blest.

Antistrophe 1. For he, O Zeus, sped his shaft with peerless skill, and won the prize of an all-prosperous fortune; he slew the maiden with crooked talons who sang darkly; he arose for our land as a tower against death. And from that time, Oedipus, you have been called our king, and have been honoured supremely, bearing sway in great Thebes.

Strophe 2. But now whose story is more grievous in men's ears? [157] Who is a more wretched captive to fierce plagues and troubles, with all his life reversed?

Alas, renowned Oedipus! The same bounteous place of rest sufficed you, as child and as father also, that you should make thereon your nuptial couch. O, how can the soil wherein your father sowed, unhappy one, have suffered you in silence so long?

Antistrophe 2. Time the all-seeing has found you out in your despite: he judges the monstrous marriage wherein begetter and begotten have long been one.

Alas, you child of Laius, would, would that I had never seen you! I wail as one who pours a dirge [159] from his lips; truth to tell, it was you that gave me new life, and through you darkness has fallen upon my eyes.

Enter Second Messenger from the palace.

SECOND MESSENGER: You who are ever most honoured in this land, what deeds shall you hear, what deeds behold, what burden of sorrow shall be yours, if, true to your race, you still care for the house of Labdacus! For I believe that neither Ister nor Phasis could wash this house clean, so many are the ills that it shrouds, or will soon bring to light,—ills wrought not unwittingly, but on purpose. And those griefs smart most which are seen to be of our own choice. [161]

LEADER: Indeed those which we knew before fall not short of claiming sore lamentation: besides them, what do you announce?

SECOND MESSENGER: This is the shortest tale to tell and to hear: our royal lady Jocasta is dead.

LEADER: Alas, unfortunate one! From what cause?

SECOND MESSENGER: By her own hand. The worst of all that has happened is spared us, for there was no one there to see. Nevertheless, so far as my own memory serves, you shall learn that unhappy woman's fate.

When, frantic, she had passed within the vestibule, she rushed straight towards her nuptial couch, clutching her hair with the fingers of both hands; once within the chamber, she dashed the doors together at her back; then called on the name of Laius, long since a corpse, mindful of that son, begotten long ago, by whom the father was slaim, leaving the mother to breed accursed offspring with his own.

And she bewailed the wedlock wherein, wretched, she had borne a two-fold brood, [163] husband by husband, children by her child. And how thereafter she perished, is more than I know. For with a shriek Oedipus burst in, and suffered us not to watch her woe unto the end; on him, as he rushed around, our eyes were set. To and fro he went, asking us to give him a sword,–asking where he should find the wife who was no wife, but a mother whose womb had borne alike himself and his children. And, in his frenzy, a power above man was his guide; for it was none of us mortals who were near. And with a dread shriek, as though some one beckoned him on, he sprang at the double doors, and from their sockets forced the bending bolts, and rushed into the room.

There we saw the woman hanging by the neck in a twisted noose of swinging cords. [165] But he, when he saw her, with a dread, deep cry of misery, loosed the halter by which she hung. And when the hapless woman was stretched upon the ground, then was the sequel dread to see. For he tore from her raiment the golden brooches with which she was decked, and lifted them, and struck directly on his own eye-balls, uttering words like these: 'No more shall you behold such horrors as I was suffering and working! Long enough have you looked on those whom you ought never to have seen, failed in knowledge of those whom I yearned to know–henceforth you shall be dark!'

To such dire refrain, not once alone but oft he struck his eyes with lifted hand; and at each blow the bloody eye-balls bedewed his beard, nor sent forth sluggish drops of gore, but all at once a dark shower of bood came down like hail. [167]

From the deeds of two, such ills have broken forth, not on one alone, but with mingled woe for man and wife. The old happiness of their ancestral fortune was once happiness indeed;

but today—lamentation, ruin, death, shame, all earthly ills that can be named—all, all are theirs.

LEADER: And has the sufferer now any relief from pain?

SECOND MESSENGER: He cries for some one to unbar the gates and show to all the Cadmeans his father's slayer, his mother's—the unholy word must not pass my lips,—as purposing to cast himself out of the land, and abide no more, to make the house accursed under his own curse. However, he lacks strength, and one to guide his steps; for the anguish is more than man may bear. And he will show this to you also; for lo, the bars of the gates are withdrawn, and soon you shall behold a sight which even he who abhors it must pity.

The central door of the palace is now opened. Oedipus comes forth, leaning on attendants; the bloody stains are still upon his face. The following lines between Oedipus and the Chorus are chanted responsively.

CHORUS: *Strophe 1.* O dread fate for men to see, [169] O most dreadful of all that have met my eyes! Unhappy one, what madness has come on you? Who is the unearthly foe that, with a bound of more than mortal range, has made your ill-starred life his prey?

Alas, alas, you hapless one! No, I cannot even look on you, though there is much that I would eagerly ask, eagerly learn, much that draws my wistful gaze,—with such a shuddering do you fill me!

OEDIPUS: Woe is me! Alas, alas, wretched that I am! Whither, whither am I borne in my misery? How is my voice swept abroad on the wings of the air? [171] Oh my Fate, how far have you sprung!

CHORUS: To a dread place, dire in men's ears, dire in their sight.

OEDIPUS: O horror of darkness that endfolds me, visitant unspeakable, resistless, sped by a wind too fair!

Ay me! and once again, ay me!

How is my soul pierced by the stab of these goads, and above all by the memory of sorrows!

CHORUS: Yea, amid woes so many a twofold pain may well be yours to mourn and to bear.

OEDIPUS: *Antistrophe 1.* Ah, friend, you still are steadfast in your care of me,—you still have patience to care for the blind man! Ah me! [173] Your presence is not hid from me—no, dark though I am, yet I know your voice very well.

CHORUS: Man of dread deeds, how could you in such a manner quench your vision? What more than human power urged you?

OEDIPUS: *Strophe 2.* Apollo, friends, Apollo was he that brought these my woes to pass, these my miserable, miserable woes: but the hand that struck the eyes was none save mine, wretched that I am! Why was I to see, when sight could show me nothing sweet?

CHORUS: These things were even as you say.

OEDIPUS: Say, friends, what can I more behold, what can I love, what greeting can touch my ear with joy? Haste, lead me from the land, friends, lead me hence, the utterly lost, the thrice accursed, yea, the mortal most abhorred of heaven!

CHORUS: Wretched alike for your fate and for your sense of it, would that I had never so much as known you! [175]

OEDIPUS: *Antistrophe 2.* Perish the man, whoever he was, that freed me in the pastures from the cruel shackle on my feet, and saved me from death, and gave me back to life,—a thankless deed! Had I died then, to my friends and to your own soul I would not have been so sore a grief.

CHORUS: I also would have had it thus.

OEDIPUS: Then I would not have come to shed my father's blood, nor have been called among men the spouse of her from whom I sprang: but now I am forsaken of the gods, son of a defiled mother, successor to his bed who gave me my own wretched being: [177] and if there be yet a woe surpassing woes, it has become the portion of Oedipus.

CHORUS: I know not how I can say that you have counselled well: for you would be better dead than living and blind.

OEDIPUS: Do not advise me further that these things are not best done thus: give me counsel no more. For, if I had sight, I do not know with what eyes I could even have looked on my father, when I came to the place of the dead, or indeed on my miserable mother, since against both I have sinned such sins as strangling could not punish. But do you think that the sight of children, born as mine were born, was lovely for me to look upon? No, no, not lovely to my eyes for ever! No, nor was this town with its towered walls, nor the sacred statues of the gods, since I, thrice wretched that I am,—I, noblest of the sons of Thebes, [179]—have doomed myself to know these no more, by my own command that all should thrust away the impious one,—even him whom gods have shown to be unholy—and of the race of Laius!

After bearing such a stain upon me, was I to look with steady eyes on this folk? No, in truth, no. Were there yet a way to choke the fount of hearing, I would not have hesitated to make a fast prison of this wretched carcass, so that I should have known nor sight nor sound; for it is sweet that our thought should dwell beyond the sphere of griefs.

Alas, Cithaeron, why did you have a shelter for me? When I was given to you, why did you not slay me immediately, that thus I might never have revealed my origin to men? Ah, Polybus,—ah, Corinth, and you that were called the ancient house of my fathers, how fair in appearance was I your nurseling, and what ills were festering beneath! [181] For now I am found evil, and of evil birth. O you three roads, and you secret glen,—you coppice, and narrow way where three paths met—you who drank from my hands that father's blood which was my own,—you remember, perchance, what deeds I wrought for you to see,—and then, when I came here, what fresh deeds I went on to do?

O marriage-rites, you gave me birth, and when you had brought me forth, again you bore children to your child, you created an incestuous kinship of fathers, brothers, sons,—brides, wives, mothers,—yea, all the foulest shame that is wrought among men! But, indeed, it is unfitting to name what it is unfitting to do:—hasten, for the gods' love, hide me somewhere beyond the land, or slay me, or cast me into the sea, where you shall never behold me more! Approach,—consent to lay your hands on a wretched man;—hearken, fear not,—my plague can rest on no other mortal. [183]

Enter Creon.

LEADER: No, here is Creon, at an opportune time for your requests, be they for action or advice; for he alone is left to guard the land in your place.

OEDIPUS: Ah me! how indeed shall I meet him? What claim to belief can be shown on my part? For in the past I have been found wholly false to him.

CREON: I have not come in mockery, Oedipus, nor to reproach you with any bygone fault. *(to the attendants)* But you, if you respect the children of men no more, revere at least the all-nurturing flame of our lord the Sun,—cease showing thus nakedly a pollution such as this,—one which neither earth can welcome, nor the holy rain, nor the light. No, take him into the house as quickly as you can; for it best accords with piety that kinsfolk alone should see and hear a kinsman's woes. [185]

OEDIPUS: For the gods' love—since you have done a gentle violence to my prediction, you who have come in a spirit so noble to me, a man most vile—grant me a favor:—for your good I will speak, not for my own.

CREON: And what favor are you so eager to have from me?

OEDIPUS: Cast me out of this land with all speed, to a place where no mortal shall be found to greet me again.

CREON: This would I have done, be sure, but that I wished first to learn all my duty from the god.

OEDIPUS: No, his command has been set forth in full,—to let me perish, the parricide, the unholy one, that I am.

CREON: Such was the purport; yet, seeing to what a pass we have come, it is better to learn clearly what should be done.

OEDIPUS: Will you, then, seek a response on behalf of such a wretch as I am?

CREON: Yes, for you yourself will now surely put faith in the god.

OEDIPUS: Yes; and on you I lay this charge, to you I will make this entreaty:—give to her who is within such burial as you yourself would; for you will fittingly render the last rites to your own. But for me—never let this city of my father be condemned to have me dwelling in it while I live: no, let me abide on the hills, where yonder is [187] Cithaeron, famed as mine,—which my mother and father, while they lived, set for my appointed tomb,—that thus I may die by the decree of them who sought to slay me. However, of this much am I sure,—that neither sickness nor anything else can destroy me; for I would never have been snatched from death, but in reserve for some strange doom.

No, let *my* fate go whither it will: but concerning my children,—I pray you, Creon, take no thought for the care of my sons; they are men, so that, wherever they may be, they can never lack the means to live. But my two girls, poor unfortunate ones,—who never knew my table laid with food [189] without their father's presence, but ever in all things shared my daily bread,—I pray you, care for *them;* and—if you can—let me touch them with my hands and indulge my grief. Grant it, prince, grant it, you noble heart! Ah, could I but once touch them with my hands, I should think that they were with me, even as when I had sight. . . .

Creon's attendants lead in the children Antigone and Ismene.

Ha? O you gods, can it be my loved ones that I hear sobbing,—can Creon have taken pity on me and sent me my children—my darlings? Am I right?

CREON: Yes: it is of my contriving, for I knew your joy in them of old,—the joy that now is yours.

OEDIPUS: Then blessed be you, and, for reward of this act, may heaven prove to you a kinder guardian than it has to me! My children, where are you? Come here,—here to the hands of him whose mother was your own, [191] the hands whose acts have brought it about that your father's once bright eyes should be such orbs as these,—his, who seeing nothing, knowing nothing, became your father by her from whom he sprang! For you also do I weep—behold you I cannot—when I think of the bitter life in days to come which men will make you live. To what company of the citizens will you go, to what festival, from which you shall not return home in tears, instead of sharing in the holiday? But when you are now come to years ripe for marriage, who shall he be, who shall be the man, my daughters, [193] that will hazard accepting the reproaches which will be injurious alike to my offspring and to yours? For what misery is lacking? Your father slew his father, he had children of her who bore him, and begot you at the sources of his own being! Such are the taunts that will be cast at you; and who will then wed? The man lives not, no, it cannot be, my children, but you must wither in barren maidenhood.

Ah, son of Menoeceus, hear me—since you are the only father left to them, for we, their parents, are lost, both of us,—allow them not to wander poor and unwed, who are your kinswomen, nor abase them to the level of my woes. No, pity them, when you see them at this tender age so utterly forlorn, save for you. Signify your promise, generous man, by the touch of your hand! To you, my children, I would have given much [195] counsel, were your minds mature; but now I would have this to be your prayer—that you live where occasion permits, and that the life which is your portion may be happier than your father's.

CREON: Your grief has had large enough scope: now pass into the house.

OEDIPUS: I must obey, though it is in no way sweet.

CREON: Yes: for it is in season that all things are good.

OEDIPUS: Do you know, then, on what conditions I will go?

CREON: You shall name them; thus I shall know them when I hear.

OEDIPUS: See that you send me to dwell beyond this land.

CREON: You ask me for what the god must give.

OEDIPUS: No, to the gods I have become most hateful.

CREON: You shall have your wish presently.

OEDIPUS: So you consent?

CREON: It is not my habit to speak idly what I do not mean.

OEDIPUS: Then it is time to lead me hence.

CREON: Come, then,—but let your children go. [197]

OEDIPUS: No, do not take these from me!

CREON: Do not desire to be master in all things: for the mastery which you did win has not followed you through life.

CHORUS: (*singing*) Dwellers in our native Thebes, behold, this is Oedipus, who knew the famed riddle, and was a man most mighty; on whose fortunes what citizen did not gaze with envy? Behold into what a stormy sea of dread trouble he has come!

Therefore, while our eyes wait to see the destined final day, we must call no one happy who is of mortal race, until he has crossed life's border, free from pain. [199]

Oedipus

John Dryden and Nathaniel Lee

Oedipus by Dryden and Lee was probably first acted late in 1678 or early in 1679. In his *Vindication of the Duke of Guise* (1683), Dryden explained his share in the writing of the play: "I writ the first and third Acts of *Oedipus,* and drew the scenery of the whole Play."[1] Thus critics have often compared the styles of these collaborating dramatists of the Restoration period (1660–1700). Yet, as Sir Walter Scott has observed, ". . . as the whole was probably corrected by Dryden, the tragedy has the appearance of general consistence and uniformity."[2]

In this *Oedipus,* numerous borrowings from Sophocles' play are evident—the suppliants of Act I. Oedipus and Jocasta of Act III, and Oedipus and Aegeon of Act IV. But this is not the only source. Dryden and Lee also took from the ancient Roman Seneca the idea of raising the ghost of Laius who identifies his murderer to the magician Tiresias. However, in Seneca this episode is narrated by Creon who reports it to Oedipus; in the English version it is dramatized. Likewise, Dryden and Lee took from the nearly contemporary French Pierre Corneille the idea of the romantic subplot of Eurydice and Adrastus, but in Cor-

John Dryden and Nathaniel Lee, *Oedipus,* in *Dryden: The Dramatic Works,* ed. Montague Summers (London: The Nonesuch Press, 1932), IV, 351–427.

[1] *The Works of John Dryden*, ed. by Walter Scott and George Saintsbury (Edinburgh: W. Patterson, 1882), VII, 203.

[2] *Ibid.,* VI, 126.

neille this subject has a happy ending. Moreover, Shakespeare supplied a few significant details: the characterization and the physical appearance of Creon, ugly and humpbacked, are derived from *Richard III,* and the sleepwalking of Oedipus must have been suggested by Lady Macbeth.

Despite these borrowings, the play has a vigor and originality all its own. As the official prompter at Drury Lane, one of the two theaters in London at the time, reports, "This Play was admirably well acted: . . . it took prodigiously, being acted 10 days together."[3] It was performed for over fifty years, with occasional revivals up to the latter half of the eighteenth century.

Scott has written a noteworthy critical introduction to this play. It may be found in his edition of Dryden's works, Volume VI, from which one of the above quotations has been made. The Preface and Prologue were written by Dryden.

PREFACE

Though it be dangerous to raise too great an expectation, especially in works of this Nature, where we are to please an unsatiable Audience, yet 'tis reasonable to prepossess them in favour of an Author; and therefore both the Prologue and Epilogue inform'd you, that Oedipus was the most celebrated piece of all Antiquity. That Sophocles, not only the greatest Wit, but one of the greatest Men in Athens, made it for the Stage at the Publick Cost, and that it had the reputation of being his Master-piece, not only amongst the Seven of his which are still remaining, but of the greater Number which are perish'd. Aristotle has more than once admir'd it in his Book of Poetry, Horace has mention'd it: Lucullus, Julius Caesar, and other noble Romans, have written on the same Subject, tho' their Poems are wholly lost; but Seneca's is still preserv'd. In our own Age, Corneille has attempted it, and it appears by his Preface, with great success. But a judicious Reader will easily observe,

[3] John Downes, *Roscius Anglicanus: or An Historical Review of the Stage from 1660 to 1706* (London: H. Playford, 1708), p. 48. This book is the standard source of information on theatrical affairs during the Restoration period.

how much the Copy is inferiour to the Original. He tells you himself, that he owes a great part of his success to the happy Episode of Theseus and Dirce; which is the same thing, as if we should acknowledge, that we are indebted for our good fortune, to the under-plot of Adrastus, Euridice, and Creon. The truth is, he miserably fail'd in the Character of his Hero: if he desir'd that Oedipus should be pitied, he shou'd have made him a better man. He forgot that Sophocles had taken care to shew him in his first entrance, a just, a merciful, a successful, a Religious Prince; and, in short, a Father of his Country: instead of these he has drawn him suspicious, designing, more anxious of keeping the Theban Crown, than solicitous for the safety of his People: Hector'd by Theseus, contemn'd by Dirce, and scarce maintaining a second part in his own Tragedie. This was an errour in the first concoction; and therefore never to be mended in the second or the third: He introduc'd a greater Heroe than Oedipus himself: for when Theseus was once there, that Companion of Hercules must yield to none: The Poet was oblig'd to furnish him with business, to make him an Equipage suitable to his dignity, and by following him too close, to lose his other King of Branford in the Crowd. Seneca on the other side, as if there were no such thing as Nature to be minded in a Play, is always running after pompous expression, pointed sentences, and Philosophical notions, more proper for the Study than the Stage: The French-man follow'd a wrong scent; and the Roman was absolutely at cold Hunting. All we cou'd gather out of Corneille, was, that an Episode must be, but not his way: and Seneca supply'd us with no new hint, but only a Relation which he makes of his Tiresias raising the Ghost of Lajus: which is [351] here perform'd in view of the Audience, the Rites and Ceremonies so far his, as he agreed with Antiquity, and the Religion of the Greeks: but he himself was beholden to Homer's Tiresias in the Odysses for some of them: and the rest have been collected from Heliodore's Æthiopiques, and Lucan's Erictho. Sophocles indeed is admirable every where: And therefore we have follow'd him as close as possibly we cou'd: But the Athenian Theater (whether more perfect than ours is not now disputed) had a perfection differing from ours. You see there in every Act a single Scene, (or two at most) which manage the business of the Play, and after that succeeds the Chorus, which commonly takes up more time in Singing, than there has been employ'd in speaking. The Principal person appears almost constantly through the Play; but the inferiour parts seldome above once in the whole Tragedie. The conduct of our Stage is much more difficult, where we are oblig'd never to lose any considerable character which we have once presented. Custom likewise has obtain'd, that we must form an under-plot of second Persons, which must be depending on the first, and their by-walks must be like those in a Labyrinth, which all of 'em lead into the great Parterre: or like so many several lodging Chambers, which have their out-lets into the same Gallery. Perhaps after all, if we cou'd think so, the ancient method, as 'tis the easiest, is also the most Natural, and the best. For variety, as 'tis manag'd, is too often subject to breed distraction: and while we wou'd please too many ways, for want of art in the conduct, we please in none. But we have given you more already than was necessary for a Preface, and for ought we know, may gain no more by our instructions, than that Politick Nation is like to do, who have taught their Enemies to fight so long, that at last they are in a condition to invade them.

DRAMATIS PERSONAE

OEDIPUS
ADRASTUS
CREON
TIRESIAS
HAEMON
ALCANDER
DIOCLES
PYRACMON
PHORBAS
DYMAS
AEGEON
GHOST OF LAIUS

Women

JOCASTA
EURYDICE
MANTO

PRIESTS, CITIZENS, ATTENDANTS, etc.

SCENE, *Thebes*

PROLOGUE

When Athens all the Graecian State did guide,
And Greece gave Laws to all the World beside,
Then Sophocles with Socrates did sit,
Supreme in Wisdom one, and one in Wit:
And Wit from Wisdom differ'd not in those,
But as 'twas Sung in Verse, or said in Prose.
Then Oedipus, on Crowded Theaters,
Drew all admiring Eyes and listning Ears;
The pleas'd Spectator shouted every Line,
The noblest, manliest, and the best Design!
And every Critick of each learned Age
By this just Model has reform'd the Stage. [352]
Now, should it fail, (as Heav'n avert our fear!)
Damn it in silence, lest the World should hear.
For were it known this Poem did not please,
You might set up for perfect Salvages:
Your Neighbours would not look on you as men:
But think the Nation all turn'd Picts agen.
'Faith, as you manage matters, 'tis not fit
You should suspect your selves of too much Wit.
Drive not the jest too far, but spare this piece:
And, for this once, be not more Wise than Greece.
See twice! Do not pell-mell to Damning fall,
Like true born Brittains, who ne're think at all:
Pray be advis'd; and though at Mons[1] you won,

[1] A battle fought between the Dutch and the French on August 17, 1678.

On pointed Cannon do not always run.
With some respect to antient Wit proceed;
You take the four first Councils for your Creed.
But, when you lay Tradition wholly by,
And on the private Spirit alone relye,
You turn Fanaticks in your Poetry.
If, notwithstanding all that we can say,
You needs will have your pen'worths of the Play:
And come resolv'd to Damn, because you pay,
  Record it, in memorial of the Fact,
  The first Play bury'd since the Wollen Act.[2] [353]

ACT I. SCENE *Thebes.*

The Curtain rises to a plaintive Tune, representing the present condition of Thebes; Dead Bodies appear at a distance in the Streets; Some faintly go over the Stage, others drop.

Enter Alcander, Diocles, Pyracmon.

ALCANDER: Methinks we stand on Ruines; Nature shakes
About us; and the Universal Frame
So loose, that it but wants another push
To leap from off its Hindges.
DIOCLES: No Sun to chear us; but a bloody Globe
That rowls above; a bald and Beamless Fire;
His Face o're-grown with Scurf: the Sun's sick too;
Shortly he'll be an Earth.
PYRACMON: Therefore the Seasons
Lie all confus'd; and by the Heaven's neglected,
Forget themselves: Blind Winter meets the Summer
In his Mid-way, and, seeing not his Livery,

[2] An act, effective August 1, 1678, which prescribed the wrapping of corpses in woolen material before burial.

Has driv'n him headlong back: And the raw damps,
With flaggy Wings fly heavily about,
Scattering their Pestilential Colds and Rheumes
Through all the lazy Air.
ALCANDER: Hence Murrains follow,
On bleating Flocks, and on the lowing Herds:
At last, the Malady
Grew more domestick, and the faithful Dog
Dy'd at his Masters Feet.
DIOCLES: And next his Master:
For all those Plagues which Earth and Air had brooded,
First on inferiour Creatures try'd their force;
And last they seiz'd on man.
PYRACMON: And then a thousand deaths at once advanc'd,
And every Dart took place; all was so sudden,
That scarce a first man fell; one but began
To wonder, and straight fell a wonder too;
A third, who stoop'd to raise his dying Friend,
Dropt in the pious Act. Heard you that groan? *(Groan within.)*
DIOCLES: A Troop of Ghosts took flight together there:
Now Death's grown riotous, and will play no more
For single Stakes, but Families and Tribes:
How are we sure we breathe not now our last,
And that next minute,
Our Bodies cast into some common Pit,
Shall not be built upon, and overlaid
By half a people?
ALCANDER: There's a Chain of Causes
Link'd to Effects; invincible Necessity
That what e're is, could not but so have been;
That's my security.

To them, enter Creon.

CREON: So had it need, when all our Streets lye cover'd
With dead and dying men,
And Earth exposes Bodies on the Pavements
More than she hides in Graves!

Betwixt the Bride and Bridegroom have I seen
The Nuptial Torch do common offices
Of Marriage and of Death.
DIOCLES: Now, Oedipus,
(If he return from War, our other plague)
Will scarce find half he left, to grace his Triumphs.
PYRACMON: A feeble Pæan will be sung before him.
ALCANDER: He would do well to bring the Wives and Children
Of conquer'd Argians, to renew his Thebes.
CREON: May Funerals meet him at the City Gates
With their detested Omen.
DIOCLES: Of his Children.
CREON: Nay, though she be my Sister, of his Wife.
ALCANDER: O that our Thebes might once again behold
A Monarch Theban born!
DIOCLES: We might have had one.
PYRACMON: Yes, had the people pleas'd.
CREON: Come, y'are my Friends:
The Queen my Sister, after Lajus's death,
Fear'd to lye single; and supply'd his place
With a young Successour.
DIOCLES: He much resembles
Her former Husband too; [356]
ALCANDER: I always thought so.
PYRACMON: When twenty Winters more have grizzl'd his black Locks
He will be very Lajus.
CREON: So he will:
Mean time she stands provided of a Lajus,
More young and vigorous too, by twenty Springs.
These Women are such cunning Purveyors!
Mark where their Appetites have once been pleas'd,
The same resemblance in a younger Lover
Lyes brooding in their Fancies the same Pleasures,
And urges their remembrance to desire.
DIOCLES: Had merit, not her dotage, been consider'd,
Then Creon had been King; but Oedipus,
A stranger!

CREON: That word stranger, I confess
Sounds harshly in my Ears.
DIOCLES: We are your Creatures.
The people prone, as in all general ills,
To sudden change; the King in Wars abroad,
The Queen a Woman weak and unregarded;
Eurydice the Daughter of dead Lajus,
A Princess young and beautious, and unmarried.
Methinks from these disjointed propositions
Something might be produc'd.
CREON: The Gods have done
Their part, by sending this commodious plague,
But oh the Princess! her hard heart is shut,
By Adamantine Locks, against my Love.
ALCANDER: Your claim to her is strong: you are betroth'd.
PYRACMON: True; in her Nonage.
ALCANDER: But that let's remov'd.
DIOCLES: I heard the Prince of Argos, young Adrastus,
When he was hostage here—
CREON: Oh name him not! the bane of all my hopes;
That hot-brain'd, head-long Warriour, has the Charms
Of youth, and somewhat of a lucky rashness,
To please a Woman yet more Fool than he.
That thoughtless Sex is caught by outward form
And empty noise, and loves it self in man.
ALCANDER: But since the War broke out about our Frontiers
He's now a Foe to Thebes!
CREON: But is not so to her; see, she appears;
Once more I'll prove my Fortune: you insinuate [357]
Kind thoughts of me into the multitude;
Lay load upon the Court; gull 'em with freedom;
And you shall see 'em toss their Tails, and gad,
As if the Breeze had stung 'em.
DIOCLES: We'll about it. *(Exeunt Alcander, Diocles, Pyracmon.)*

Enter Eurydice.

CREON: Hail, Royal Maid; thou bright Eurydice!
A lavish Planet reign'd when thou wert born;

And made thee of such kindred mold to Heaven,
Thou seem'st more Heaven's than ours.
  EURYDICE: Cast round your Eyes;
Where late the Streets were so thick sown with men,
Like Cadmus Brood they justled for the passage:
Now look for those erected heads, and see 'em
Like Pebbles paving all our publick ways:
When you have thought on this, then answer me,
If these be hours of Courtship?
  CREON: Yes, they are;
For when the Gods destroy so fast, 'tis time
We should renew the Race.
  EURYDICE: What, in the midst of horrour!
  CREON: Why not then?
There's the more need of comfort.
  EURYDICE: Impious Creon!
  CREON: Unjust Eurydice! can you accuse me
Of love, which is Heaven's precept, and not fear
That Vengeance, which you say pursues our Crimes,
Should reach your Perjuries?
  EURYDICE: Still th' old Argument.
I bad you cast your eyes on other men,
Now cast 'em on your self: think what you are.
  CREON: A Man.
  EURYDICE: A Man!
  CREON: Why doubt you? I'm a man,
  EURYDICE: 'Tis well you tell me so, I should mistake you
For any other part o'th' whole Creation,
Rather than think you man: hence from my sight,
Thou poyson to my eyes.
  CREON: 'Twas you first poison'd mine; and yet methinks,
My face and person shou'd not make you sport.
  EURYDICE: You force me, by your importunities,
To shew you what you are. [358]
  CREON: A Prince, who loves you:
And since your pride provokes me, worth your love,
Ev'n at his highest value.

EURYDICE: Love from thee!
Why love renounc'd thee e're thou saw'st the light:
Nature her self start back when thou wert born;
And cry'd the work's not mine:——
The Midwife stood aghast; and when she saw
Thy Mountain back and thy distorted legs,
Thy face it self,
Half minted with the Royal stamp of man;
And half o'recome with beast, stood doubting long,
Whose right in thee were more:
And knew not, if to burn thee in the flames,
Were not the holier work.
CREON: Am I to blame, if Nature threw my body
In so perverse a mould? yet when she cast
Her envious hand upon my supple joints,
Unable to resist, and rumpled 'em
On heaps in their dark lodging, to revenge
Her bungled work she stampt my mind more fair:
And as from Chaos, huddled and deform'd,
The Gods strook fire, and lighted up the Lamps
That beautify the sky, so he inform'd
This ill-shap'd body with a daring soul:
And making less than man, he made me more.
EURYDICE: No; thou art all one errour; soul and body.
The first young tryal of some unskill'd Pow'r;
Rude in the making Art, and Ape of Jove.
Thy crooked mind within hunch'd out thy back;
And wander'd in thy limbs: to thy own kind
Make love, if thou canst find it in the world:
And seek not from our Sex to raise an off-spring,
Which, mingled with the rest, would tempt the Gods
To cut off humane Kind.
CREON: No; let 'em leave
The Argian Prince for you: that Enemy
Of Thebes has made you false, and break the Vows
You made to me.
EURYDICE: They were my Mothers Vows,

Made when I was at Nurse.
CREON: But hear me, Maid;
This blot of Nature, this deform'd, loath'd Creon, [359]
Is Master of a Sword, to reach the blood
Of your young Minion, spoil the Gods fine work,
And stab you in his heart.
EURYDICE: This when thou doest,
Then may'st thou still be curst with loving me:
And, as thou art, be still unpitied, loath'd;
And let his Ghost——No let his Ghost have rest;
But let the greatest, fiercest, foulest Fury,
Let Creon haunt himself. *(Exit Eurydice.)*
CREON: 'Tis true, I am
What she has told me, an offence to sight:
My body opens inward to my soul,
And lets in day to make my Vices seen
By all discerning eyes, but the blind vulgar.
I must make haste er'e Oedipus return,
To snatch the Crown and her; for I still love;
But love with malice; as an angry Cur
Snarls while he feeds, so will I seize and stanch
The hunger of my love on this proud beauty,
And leave the scraps for Slaves.

Enter Tiresias, leaning on a staff, and led by his Daughter Manto.

What makes this blind prophetick Fool abroad?
Wou'd his Appollo had him, he's too holy
For Earth and me; I'll shun his walk; and seek
My popular friends. *(Exit Creon.)*
TIRESIAS: A little farther; yet a little farther,
Thou wretched Daughter of a dark old man,
Conduct my weary steps: and thou who seest
For me and for thy self, beware thou tread not
With impious steps upon dead corps;——Now stay:
Methinks I draw more open, vital air,
Where are we?
MANTO: Under Covert of a wall:

The most frequented once, and noisy part
Of Thebes, now midnight silence reigns even here;
And grass untrodden springs beneath our feet.

TIRESIAS: If there be nigh this place a Sunny banck,
There let me rest a while: a Sunny banck!
Alas! how can it be, where no Sun shines!
But a dim winking Taper in the Skyes,
That nods, and scarce holds up his drowzy head
To glimmer through the damps.

A Noise within, follow, follow, follow, A Creon, A Creon, A Creon.

Hark! a tumultuous noise, and Creon's name
Thrice eccho'd.

MANTO: Fly, the tempest drives this way.

TIRESIAS: Whither can Age and blindness take their flight?
If I could fly, what cou'd I suffer worse,
Secure of greater Ills!

Noise again, Creon, Creon, Creon.

Enter Creon, Diocles, Alcander, Pyracmon; follow'd by the Crowd.

CREON: I thank ye, Countrymen; but must refuse
The honours you intend me, they're too great;
And I am too unworthy; think agen,
And make a better choice.

1. CITIZEN: Think twice! I ne're thought twice in all my life:
That's double work.

2. CITIZEN: My first word is always my second; and therefore I'll have
No second word: and therefore once again I say, A Creon.

ALL: A Creon, a Creon, a Creon.

CREON: Yet hear me, Fellow Citizens.

DIOCLES: Fellow Citizens! there was a word of kindness.

ALCANDER: When did Oedipus salute you by that familiar name?

1. CITIZEN: Never, never; he was too proud

CREON: Indeed he could not, for he was a stranger:
But under him our Thebes is half destroyed.
Forbid it Heav'n the residue should perish
Under a Theban born.

'Tis true, the Gods might send this plague among you,
Because a stranger rul'd: but what of that,
Can I redress it now?
3. CITIZEN: Yes, you or none.
'Tis certain that the Gods are angry with us
Because he reigns.
CREON: Oedipus may return: you may be ruin'd.
1. CITIZEN: Nay, if that be the matter, we are ruin'd already.
2. CITIZEN: Half of us that are here present, were living men but
Yesterday, and we that are absent do but drop and drop,
And no man knows whether he be dead or living. And
Therefore, while we are sound and well, let us satisfie our
Consciences, and make a new King.
3. CITIZEN: Ha, if we were but worthy to see another Coronation,
And then if we must dye, we'll go merrily together. [361]
ALL: To the question, to the question.
DIOCLES: Are you content, Creon should be your King?
ALL: A Creon, a Creon, a Creon.
TIRESIAS: Hear me, ye Thebans, and thou Creon, hear me.
1. CITIZEN: Who's that would be heard; we'll hear no man:
We can scarce hear one another.
TIRESIAS: I charge you by the Gods to hear me.
2. CITIZEN: Oh, 'tis Apollo's Priest; we must hear him; 'tis the old blind Prophet, that sees all things.
3. CITIZEN: He comes from the Gods too, and they are our betters:
And therefore in good manners we must hear him: Speak, Prophet.
2. CITIZEN: For coming from the Gods that's no great matter,
They can all say that; but he's a great Scholar, he can make
Almanacks, and he were put to't, and therefore I say hear him.
TIRESIAS: When angry Heav'n scatters its plagues among you,
Is it for nought, ye Thebans! are the Gods
Unjust in punishing? are there no Crimes
Which pull this Vengeance down?
1. CITIZEN: Yes, yes, no doubt, there are some Sins stirring
That are the cause of all.

3. CITIZEN: Yes there are Sins; or we should have no Taxes.

2. CITIZEN: For my part, I can speak it with a safe Conscience,
I ne're sinn'd in all my life.

1. CITIZEN: Nor I.

3. CITIZEN: Nor I.

2. CITIZEN: Then we are all justified, the sin lyes not at our doors.

TIRESIAS: All justified alike, and yet all guilty;
Were every man's false dealing brought to light,
His Envy, Malice, Lying, Perjuries,
His Weights and Measures, th'other mans Extortions,
With what Face could you tell offended Heav'n
You had not sinn'd?

2. CITIZEN: Nay, if these be sins, the case is alter'd; for my part I never
Thought any thing but Murder had been a sin.

TIRESIAS: And yet, as if all these were less than nothing,
You add Rebellion to 'em; impious Thebans!
Have you not sworn before the Gods to serve
And to obey this Oedipus, your King,
By publick voice elected; answer me,
If this be true!

2. CITIZEN: This is true; but it's a hard World Neighbours,
If a mans Oath must be his master.

CREON: Speak Diocles; all goes wrong. [362]

DIOCLES: How are you Traytors Countrymen of Thebes?
This holy Sir, who presses you with Oaths,
Forgets your first; were you not sworn before
To Lajus, and his Blood?

ALL: We were, we were.

DIOCLES: While Lajus has a lawful Successor,
Your first Oath still must bind: Eurydice
Is Heir to Lajus, let her marry Creon:
Offended Heav'n will never be appeas'd
While Oedipus pollutes the Throne of Lajus,
A stranger to his Blood.

ALL: We'll no Oedipus, no Oedipus.

1. CITIZEN: He puts the Prophet in a Mouse-hole.

2. CITIZEN: I knew it would be so; the last man ever speaks the best reason.

TIRESIAS: Can benefits thus dye, ungrateful Thebans!
Remember yet, when, after Lajus's death,
The Monster Sphinx laid your rich Country waste,
Your Vineyards spoil'd, your labouring Oxen slew;
Your selves for fear mew'd up within your Walls.
She, taller than your Gates, o're-look'd your Town,
But when she rais'd her Bulk to sail above you,
She drove the Air around her like a Whirlwind,
And shaded all beneath; till stooping down,
She clap'd her leathern wing against your Tow'rs,
And thrust out her long neck, ev'n to your doors.

DIOCLES, ALCANDER, PYRACMON: We'll hear no more.

TIRESIAS: You durst not meet in Temples
T'invoke the Gods for aid, the proudest he
Who leads you now, then cowr'd, like a dar'd Lark:
This Creon shook for fear,
The Blood of Lajus, cruddled in his Veins:
Till Oedipus arriv'd,
Call'd by his own high courage and the Gods,
Himself to you a God: ye offer'd him
Your Queen, and Crown; (but what was then your Crown!)
And Heav'n authoriz'd it by his success:
Speak then, who is your lawful King?

ALL: 'Tis Oedipus.

TIRESIAS: 'Tis Oedipus indeed: your King more lawful
Than yet you dream: for something still there lyes
In Heaven's dark Volume, which I read through mists:
'Tis great, prodigious; 'tis a dreadful birth, [363]
Of wondrous Fate; and now, just now disclosing.
I see, I see! how terrible it dawns.
And my Soul sickens with it:

1. CITIZEN: How the God shakes him!

TIRESIAS: He comes! he comes! Victory! Conquest! Triumph!
But oh! Guiltless and Guilty: Murder! Parricide!

Incest; Discovery! Punishment——'tis ended,
And all your sufferings o're.

A Trumpet within; Enter Hæmon.

HÆMON: Rouze up ye Thebans; tune your Io Pæans!
Your King returns; the Argians are o'ercome;
Their Warlike Prince in single Combat taken,
And led in Bands by God-like Oedipus.
ALL: Oedipus, Oedipus, Oedipus.
CREON: *(aside)* Furies confound his Fortune!——
(to them) Haste, all haste;
And meet with Blessings our Victorious King;
Decree Processions; bid new Holy-days;
Crown all the Statues of our Gods with Garlands;
And raise a brazen Collumn, thus inscrib'd,
To Oedipus, now twice a Conquerour; Deliverer of his Thebes.
Trust me, I weep for joy to see this day.
TIRESIAS: Yes, Heav'n knows how thou weep'st:——go, Countrymen,
And as you use to supplicate your Gods——
So meet your King, with Bayes, and Olive-branches:
Bow down, and touch his Knees, and beg from him
An end of all your Woes; for only he
Can give it you. *(Exit Tiresias, the People following.)*

Enter Oedipus in triumph; Adrastus Prisoner; Dymas, Train.

CREON: All hail, great Oedipus;
Thou mighty Conquerour, hail; welcome to Thebes:
To thy own Thebes; to all that's left of Thebes:
For half thy Citizens are swept away,
And wanting to thy Triumphs:
And we, the happy remnant, only live
To welcome thee, and dye.
OEDIPUS: Thus pleasure never comes sincere to man;
But lent by Heav'n upon hard Usury:
And, while Jove holds us out the Bowl of Joy, [364]
E're it can reach our Lips it's dasht with Gall

By some left-handed God. O mournful Triumph!
O Conquest gain'd abroad and lost at home!
O Argos! now rejoyce, for Thebes lyes low;
Thy slaughter'd Sons now smile and think they won,
When they can count more Theban Ghosts than theirs.

ADRASTUS: No; Argos mourns with Thebes; you temper'd so
Your Courage while you fought, that Mercy seem'd
The manlier Virtue, and much more prevail'd:
While Argos is a People, think your Thebes
Can never want for Subjects: Every Nation
Will crowd to serve where Oedipus commands.

CREON: *(to Hæmon)* How mean it shews to fawn upon the Victor!

HÆMON: Had you beheld him fight, you had said otherwise:
Come, 'tis brave bearing in him, not to envy
Superiour Vertue.

OEDIPUS: This indeed is Conquest,
To gain a Friend like you: Why were we Foes?

ADRASTUS: 'Cause we were Kings, and each disdain'd an equal.
I fought to have it in my pow'r to do
What thou hast done; and so to use my Conquest;
To shew thee, Honour was my only motive,
Know this, that were my Army at thy Gates,
And Thebes thus waste, I would not take the Gift,
Which, like a Toy, dropt from the hands of Fortune,
Lay for the next chance-comer.

OEDIPUS: *(embracing)* No more Captive,
But Brother of the War: 'Tis much more pleasant,
And safer, trust me, thus to meet thy love,
Than when hard Gantlets clench'd our Warlike Hands,
And kept 'em from soft use.

ADRASTUS: My Conquerour.

OEDIPUS: My Friend! that other name keeps Enmity alive.
But longer to detain thee were a Crime;
To love, and to Eurydice, go free:
Such welcome as a ruin'd Town can give
Expect from me; the rest let her supply.

ADRASTUS: I go without a blush, though conquer'd twice,
By you and by my Princess. *(Exit Adrastus.)*
CREON: *(aside)* Then I am conquer'd thrice; by Oedipus,
And her, and even by him, the slave of both:
Gods, I'm beholding to you for making me your Image,
Would I could make you mine. *(Exit Creon.)*

Enter the People with branches in their hands, holding them up, and kneeling: Two Priests before them.

OEDIPUS: Alas, my People!
What means this speechless sorrow, down cast eyes,
And lifted hands! if there be one among you
Whom grief has left a tongue, speak for the rest.
1. PRIEST: O Father of thy Country!
To thee these knees are bent, these eyes are lifted,
As to a visible Divinity.
A Prince on whom Heav'n safely might repose
The business of Mankind: for Providence
Might on thy careful bosome sleep secure,
And leave her task to thee.
But where's the Glory of thy former acts?
Ev'n that's destroy'd when none shall live to speak it.
Millions of Subjects shalt thou have; but mute.
A people of the dead; a crowded desart.
A Midnight silence at the noon of day.
OEDIPUS: O were our Gods as ready with their pity,
As I with mine, this Presence shou'd be throng'd
With all I left alive; and my sad eyes
Not search in vain for friends, whose promis'd sight
Flatter'd my toyls of war.
1. PRIEST: Twice our deliverer.
OEDIPUS: Nor are now your vows
Addrest to one who sleeps:
When this unwelcome news first reach'd my ears,
Dymas was sent to Delphos to enquire
The cause and cure of this contagious ill:
And is this day return'd: but since his message

Concerns the publick, I refus'd to hear it
But in this general Presence: Let him speak.
DYMAS: A dreadful answer from the hallow'd Urn,
And sacred tripous did the Priestess give,
In these Mysterious words,
The Oracle. *Shed in a cursed hour, by cursed hand,*
Blood-Royal unreveng'd, has curs'd the Land.
When Lajus death is expiated well,
Your Plague shall cease: the rest let Lajus tell.
OEDIPUS: Dreadful indeed! blood, and a Kings blood too:
And such a Kings, and by his Subjects shed! [366]
(Else, why this curse on Thebes?) no wonder then
If Monsters, Wars, and plagues revenge such Crimes!
If Heav'n be just, it's whole Artillery,
All must be empty'd on us: Not one bolt
Shall erre from Thebes; but more, be call'd for more:
New moulded thunder of a larger size,
Driv'n by whole Jove. What, touch annointed Pow'r!
Then Gods beware; Jove would himself be next;
Cou'd you but reach him too.
2. PRIEST: We mourn the sad remembrance.
OEDIPUS: Well you may:
Worse than a plague infects you: y'are devoted
To Mother Earth, and to th'infernal Pow'rs:
Hell has a right in you: I thank you Gods,
That I'm no Theban born: how my blood cruddles!
As if this curse touch'd me! and touch'd me nearer
Than all this presence!——Yes, 'tis a Kings blood,
And I, a King, am ty'd in deeper bonds
To expiate this blood: but where, from whom,
Or how must I attone it? tell me, Thebans,
How Lajus fell? for a confus'd report
Pass'd through my ears, when first I took the Crown;
But, full of hurry, like a morning dream,
It vanish'd in the business of the day.
1. PRIEST: He went in private forth; but thinly follow'd;
And ne're return'd to Thebes.
OEDIPUS: Nor any from him? came there no attendant?
None to bring news?

2. PRIEST: But one; and he so wounded,
He scarce drew breath to speak some few faint words.
OEDIPUS: What were they? something may be learn'd from thence.
1. PRIEST: He said a band of Robbers watch'd their passage;
Who took advantage of a narrow way,
To murder Lajus and the rest: himself
Left too for dead.
OEDIPUS: Made you no more enquiry,
But took this bare relation?
2. PRIEST: 'Twas neglected:
For then the Monster Sphynx began to rage;
And present cares soon buried the remote;
So was it hush'd, and never since reviv'd.
OEDIPUS: Mark, Thebans, mark!
Just then, the Sphynx began to rage among you; [367]
The Gods took hold ev'n of th' offending minute,
And dated thence your woes: thence will I trace 'em.
1. PRIEST: 'Tis Just thou should'st.
OEDIPUS: Hear then this dread imprecation; hear it:
'Tis lay'd on all; not any one exempt:
Bear witness Heav'n, avenge it on the perjur'd.
If any Theban born, if any stranger
Reveal this murder, or produce its Author;
Ten attique Talents be his just reward:
But, if for fear, for favour, or for hire,
The murder'r he conceal, the curse of Thebes
Fall heavy on his head: Unite our plagues
Ye Gods, and place 'em there: from Fire and Water
Converse, and all things common be he banish'd.
But for the murderer's self, unfound by man,
Find him ye pow'rs Cœlestial and Infernal;
And the same Fate or worse, than Lajus met,
Let be his lot: his children be accurst;
His Wife and kindred, all of his be curs'd.
BOTH PRIESTS: Confirm it Heav'n!

Enter Jocasta; Attended by Women.

JOCASTA: At your Devotions! Heav'n succeed your wishes;

And bring th' effect of these your pious pray'rs
On you, and me, and all.
PRIEST: Avert this Omen, Heav'n!
OEDIPUS: O fatal sound, Unfortunate Jocasta!
What hast thou said! an ill hour hast thou chosen
For these fore-boding words! why, we were cursing.
JOCASTA: Then may that curse fall only where you laid it.
OEDIPUS: Speak no more!
For all thou say'st is ominous: we were cursing;
And that dire imprecation hast thou fastn'd
On Thebes, and thee, and me, and all of us.
JOCASTA: Are then my blessings turn'd into a curse?
O Unkind Oedipus. My former Lord
Thought me his blessing: be thou like my Lajus.
OEDIPUS: What yet again! the third time hast thou curs'd me?
This imprecation was for Lajus death,
And thou hast wish'd me like him.
JOCASTA: Horrour seizes me!
OEDIPUS: Why dost thou gaze upon me? prithee love,
Take off thy eye; it burdens me too much. [368]
JOCASTA: The more I look, the more I find of Lajus:
His speech, his garb, his action; nay his frown;
(For I have seen it;) but ne're bent on me.
OEDIPUS: Are we so like?
JOCASTA: In all things but his love.
OEDIPUS: I love thee more: so well I love, words cannot speak how well.
No pious Son e're lov'd his Mother more
Than I my dear Jocasta.
JOCASTA: I love you too
The self same way: and when you chid, me thought
A Mother's love start up in your defence,
And bad me not be angry: be not you:
For I love Lajus still as wives should love:
But you more tenderly; as part of me:
And when I have you in my arms, methinks
I lull my child asleep.

OEDIPUS: Then we are blest:
And all these curses sweep along the skyes,
Like empty clowds; but drop not on our heads.

JOCASTA: I have not joy'd an hour since you departed,
For publick Miseries, and for private fears;
But this blest meeting has o're-pay'd 'em all.
Good fortune that comes seldom comes more welcome.
All I can wish for now, is your consent
To make my Brother happy.

OEDIPUS: How, Jocasta?

JOCASTA: By Marriage with his Neece, Eurydice!

OEDIPUS: Uncle and Neece! they are too near, my Love;
'Tis too like Incest: 'tis offence to Kind:
Had I not promis'd, were there no Adrastus,
No choice but Creon left her of Mankind,
They shou'd not marry; speak no more of it;
The thought disturbs me.

JOCASTA: Heav'n can never bless
A Vow so broken, which I made to Creon;
Remember he's my Brother.

OEDIPUS: That's the Bar:
And she thy Daughter: Nature wou'd abhor
To be forc'd back again upon her self,
And, like a whirle-pool swallow her own streams.

JOCASTA: Be not displeas'd; I'll move the Suit no more. [369]

OEDIPUS: No, do not; for, I know not why, it shakes me
When I but think on Incest; move we forward
To thank the Gods for my success, and pray
To wash the guilt of Royal Blood away. *(Exeunt Omnes.)*

ACT II. SCENE I.

An open Gallery. A Royal Bed-Chamber being suppos'd behind. The Time, Night. Thunder, etc.

Enter Hæmon, Alcander, Pyracmon.

HÆMON: Sure 'tis the end of all things! Fate has torn
The Lock of Time off, and his head is now
The gastly Ball of round Eternity!
Call you these Peals of Thunder, but the yawn
Of bellowing Clouds? By Jove, they seem to me
The World's last groans; and those vast sheets of Flame
Are its last Blaze! The Tapers of the Gods,
The Sun and Moon, run down like waxen-Globes;
The shooting Stars end all in purple Gellies,
And Chaos is at hand.

PYRACMON: 'Tis Midnight, yet there's not a Theban sleeps,
But such as ne're must wake. All crow'd about
The Palace, and implore, as from a God,
Help of the King; who, from the Battlement,
By the red Lightning's glare, descry'd afar,
Atones the angry Powers. *(Thunder, etc.)*

HÆMON: Ha! Pyracmon look;
Behold, Alcander, from yon' West of Heav'n,
The perfect Figures of a Man and Woman:
A Scepter bright with Gems in each right hand,
Their flowing Robes of dazling Purple made,
Distinctly yonder in that point they stand,
Just West; a bloody red stains all the place:
And see, their Faces are quite hid in Clouds.

PYRACMON: Clusters of Golden Stars hang o're their heads,
And seem so crouded, that they burst upon 'em:

All dart at once their baleful influence,
In leaking Fire.
ALCANDER: Long-bearded Comets stick,
Like flaming Porcupines, to their left sides,
As they would shoot their Quills into their hearts.
HÆMON: But see! the King, and Queen, and all the Court!
Did ever Day or Night shew ought like this? *(Thunders again.)*

The Scene draws and discovers the Prodigies.

Enter Oedipus, Jocasta, Eurydice, Adrastus, all coming forward with amazement.

OEDIPUS: Answer, you Pow'rs Divine; spare all this noise,
This rack of Heav'n, and speak your fatal pleasure,
Why breaks yon dark and dusky Orb away?
Why from the bleeding Womb of monstrous Night,
Burst forth such Miriads of abortive Stars?
Ha! my Jocasta, look! the Silver Moon!
A setling Crimson stains her beauteous Face!
She's all o're Blood! and look, behold again,
What mean the mistick Heav'ns, she journeys on?
A vast Eclipse darkens the labouring Planet:
Sound there, sound all our Instruments of War;
Clarions and Trumpets, Silver, Brass, and Iron,
And beat a thousand Drums to help her Labour.
ADRASTUS: 'Tis vain; you see the Prodigies continue;
Let's gaze no more, the Gods are humorous.
OEDIPUS: Forbear, rash man——Once more I ask your pleasure!
If that the glow-worm-light of Humane Reason
Might dare to offer at Immortal knowledge,
And cope with Gods, why all this storm of Nature?
Why do the Rocks split, and why rouls the Sea?
Why these Portents in Heav'n, and Plagues on Earth?
Why yon' Gygantick Forms, Ethereal Monsters?
Alas! is all this but to fright the Dwarfs
Which your own hands have made? Then be it so.
Or if the Fates resolve some Expiation
For murder'd Lajus; Hear me, hear me, Gods!

Hear me thus prostrate: Spare this groaning Land,
Save innocent Thebes, stop the Tyrant Death;
Do this, and lo I stand up an Oblation
To meet your swiftest and severest anger,
Shoot all at once, and strike me to the Center.

The Cloud draws that veil'd the heads of the Figures in the Skie, and shews 'em Crown'd, with the names of Oedipus and Jocasta written above in great Characters of Gold.

ADRASTUS: Either I dream, and all my cooler senses [371]
Are vanish'd with that Cloud that fleets away;
Or just above those two Majestick heads,
I see, I read distinctly in large gold,
Oedipus and Jocasta.

ALCANDER: I read the same.

ADRASTUS: 'Tis wonderful; yet ought not man to wade
Too far in the vast deep of Destiny. *(Thunder; and the Prodigies vanish.)*

JOCASTA: My Lord, my Oedipus, why gaze you now,
When the whole Heav'n is clear, as if the Gods
Had some new Monsters made? will you not turn,
And bless your People; who devour each word
You breathe?

OEDIPUS: It shall be so.
Yes, I will dye, O Thebes, to save thee!
Draw from my heart my blood, with more content
Than e're I wore thy Crown. Yet, O, Jocasta!
By all the indearments of miraculous love,
By all our languishings, our fears in pleasure,
Which oft have made us wonder; here I swear
On thy fair hand, upon thy breast I swear,
I cannot call to mind, from budding Childhood
To blooming youth, a Crime by me committed,
For which the awful Gods should doom my death.

JOCASTA: 'Tis not you, my Lord,
But he who murder'd Lajus, frees the Land:
Were you, which is impossible, the man,

Perhaps my Ponyard first should drink your blood;
But you are innocent as your Jocasta,
From Crimes like those. This made me violent
To save your life, which you unjust would lose:
Nor can you comprehend, with deepest thought,
The horrid Agony you cast me in,
When you resolv'd to dye.

OEDIPUS: Is't possible?

JOCASTA: Alas! why start you so? Her stiff'ning grief,
Who saw her Children slaughter'd all at once,
Was dull to mine: Methinks I should have made
My bosom bare against the armed God,
To save my Oedipus!

OEDIPUS: I pray, no more.

JOCASTA: Yo've silenc'd me, my Lord.

OEDIPUS: Pardon me, dear Jocasta; [372]
Pardon a heart that sinks with sufferings,
And can but vent it self in sobs and murmurs:
Yet to restore my peace, I'll find him out.
Yes, yes, you Gods! you shall have ample vengeance
On Lajus murderer. O, the Traytor's name!
I'll know't, I will; Art shall me Conjur'd for it,
And Nature all unravel'd.

JOCASTA: Sacred Sir——

OEDIPUS: Rage will have way, and 'tis but just; I'll fetch him,
Tho' lodg'd in Air, upon a Dragon's wing,
Tho' Rocks should hide him: nay, he should be dragg'd
From Hell, if Charms can hurry him along:
His Ghost shall be by sage Tiresias pow'r,
(Tiresias, that rules all beneath the Moon)
Confin'd to flesh, to suffer death once more;
And then be plung'd in his first fires again.

Enter Creon.

CREON: My Lord,
Tiresias attends your pleasure.

OEDIPUS: Haste, and bring him in.

O, my Jocasta, Eurydice, Adrastus,
Creon, and all ye Thebans, now the end
Of Plagues, of Madness, Murders, Prodigies,
Draws on: This Battel of the Heav'ns and Earth
Shall by his wisdom be reduc'd to peace.

Enter Tiresias, leaning on a staff, led by his Daughter Manto, follow'd by other Thebans.

O thou, whose most aspiring mind
Know'st all the business of the Courts above,
Open'st the Closets of the Gods, and dares
To mix with Jove himself and Fate at Council;
O Prophet, answer me, declare aloud
The Traytor who conspir'd the death of Lajus:
Or be they more, who from malignant Stars
Have drawn this Plague that blasts unhappy Thebes.
TIRESIAS: We must no more than Fate commissions us
To tell; yet something, and of moment, I'll unfold,
If that the God would wake; I feel him now,
Like a strong spirit Charm'd into a Tree,
That leaps and moves the Wood without a Wind:
The rouz'd God, as all this while he lay [373]
Intomb'd alive, starts and dilates himself:
He struggles, and he tears my aged Trunk
With holy Fury, my old Arteries burst,
My rivel'd skin,
Like Parchment, crackles at the hallow'd fire;
I shall be young again: Manto, my Daughter,
Thou hast a voice that might have sav'd the Bard
Of Thrace, and forc'd the raging Bacchanals,
With lifted Prongs, to listen to thy airs:
O Charm this God, this Fury in my bosom,
Lull him with tuneful notes, and artful strings,
With pow'rful strains; Manto, my lovely Child,
Sooth the unruly God-head to be mild.

SONG to *APOLLO*

Phoebus, God belov'd by men;
At thy dawn, every Beast is rouz'd in his Den;
At thy setting, all the Birds of thy absence complain,
And we dye, all dye till the morning comes again,
Phoebus, God belov'd by men!
Idol of the Eastern Kings,
Awful as the God who flings
His Thunder round, and the Lightning wings;
God of Songs, and Orphean strings,
Who to this mortal bosom brings,
All harmonious heav'nly things!
Thy drouzie Prophet to revive,
Ten thousand thousand forms before him drive;
With Chariots and Horses all o' fire awake him,
Convulsions, and Furies, and Prophesies shake him:
Let him tell it in Groans, tho' he bend with the load,
Tho' he burst with the weight of the terrible God.

TIRESIAS: The wretch, who shed the blood of old Labdacides,
Lives, and is great;
But cruel greatness ne're was long:
The first of Lajus blood his life did seize,
And urg'd his Fate,
Which else had lasting been and strong.
The wretch who Lajus kill'd, must bleed or fly;
Or Thebes, consum'd with Plagues, in ruines lye.

OEDIPUS: The first of Lajus blood! pronounce the person; [374]
May the God roar from thy prophetick mouth,
That even the dead may start up, to behold:
Name him, I say, that most accursed wretch,
For by the Stars he dies:
Speak, I command thee;
By Phœbus, speak; for sudden death's his doom:
Here shall he fall, bleed on this very spot:
His name, I charge thee once more, speak.

TIRESIAS: 'Tis lost,
Like what we think can never shun remembrance;
Yet of a sudden's gone beyond the Clouds.
OEDIPUS: Fetch it from thence; I'll have't, where e're it be.
CREON: Let me intreat you, sacred Sir, be calm,
And Creon shall point out the great Offendor.
'Tis true, respect of Nature might injoin
My silence, at another time; but, oh,
Much more the pow'r of my eternal Love!
That, that should strike me dumb: yet Thebes, my Country——
I'll break through all, to succour thee, poor City!
O, I must speak.
OEDIPUS: Speak then, if ought thou know'st:
As much thou seem'st to know, delay no longer.
CREON: O Beauty! O illustrious Royal Maid!
To whom my Vows were ever paid till now,
And with such modest, chaste, and pure affection,
The coldest Nymph might read 'em without blushing;
Art thou the Murdress then of wretched Lajus?
And I, must I accuse thee, O my tears!
Why will you fall in so abhor'd a Cause?
But that thy beauteous, barbarous, hand destroy'd
Thy Father (O monstrous act!) both Gods
And men at once take notice.
OEDIPUS: Eurydice!
EURYDICE: Traytor, go on; I scorn thy little malice,
And knowing more my perfect innocence
Than Gods and men, then how much more than thee,
Who art their opposite, and form'd a Lyar,
I thus disdain thee! Thou once didst talk of Love;
Because I hate thy love,
Thou dost accuse me.
ADRASTUS: Villain, inglorious Villain
And Traytor, double damn'd, who dur'st blaspheme
The spotless virtue of the brightest beauty;
Thou dy'st: nor shall the sacred Majesty, *(Draws and wounds him.)*

That guards this place, preserve thee from my rage.
OEDIPUS: Disarm 'em both: Prince, I shall make you know
That I can tame you twice. Guards, seize him.
ADRASTUS: Sir,
I must acknowledge in another Cause
Repentance might abash me; but I glory
In this, and smile to see the Traytor's blood.
OEDIPUS: Creon, you shall be satisfy'd at full.
CREON: My hurt is nothing, Sir; but I appeal
To wise Tiresias, if my accusation
Be not most true. The first of Lajus blood
Gave him his death. Is there a Prince before her?
Then she is faultless, and I ask her pardon.
And may this blood ne're cease to drop, O Thebes,
If pity of thy sufferings did not move me
To shew the Cure which Heav'n it self prescrib'd.
EURYDICE: Yes, Thebans, I will dye to save your lives,
More willingly than you can wish my fate;
But let this good, this wise, this holy man
Pronounce my Sentence: for to fall by him,
By the vile breath of that prodigious Villain,
Would sink my Soul, tho' I should dye a Martyr.
ADRASTUS: Unhand me, slaves. O mightiest of Kings,
See at your feet a Prince not us'd to kneel;
Touch not Eurydice, by all the Gods,
As you would save your Thebes, but take my life:
For, should she perish, Heav'n would heap plagues on plagues,
Rain Sulphur down, hurl kindled bolts
Upon your guilty heads.
CREON: You turn to gallantry, what is but justice:
Proof will be easie made. Adrastus was
The Robber who bereft th' unhappy King
Of life; because he flatly had deny'd
To make so poor a Prince his Son-in-Law:
Therefore 'twere fit that both should perish.
1. THEBAN: Both, let both dye.
ALL THEBANS: Both, both; let 'em dye.

OEDIPUS: Hence, you wild Herd! For your Ring-leader here,
He shall be made Example. Hæmon, take him.

1. THEBAN: Mercy, O mercy.

OEDIPUS: Mutiny in my presence!
Hence, let me see that busie face no more. [376]

TIRESIAS: Thebans, what madness makes you drunk with rage?
Enough of guilty death's already acted:
Fierce Creon has accus'd Eurydice,
With Prince Adrastus; which the God reproves
By inward checks, and leaves their Fate in doubt.

OEDIPUS: Therefore instruct us what remains to do,
Or suffer; for I feel a sleep like death
Upon me, and I sigh to be at rest.

TIRESIAS: Since that the pow'rs divine refuse to clear
The mystick deed, I'll to the Grove of Furies;
There I can force th' Infernal Gods to shew
Their horrid Forms;
Each trembling Ghost shall rise,
And leave their grizly King without a waiter
For Prince Adrastus and Eurydice
My life's engag'd, I'll guard 'em in the Fane,
Till the dark mysteries of Hell are done.
Follow me, Princes: Thebans, all to rest.
O, Oedipus, to morrow——but no more.
If that thy wakeful Genius will permit,
Indulge thy brain this night with softer slumbers:
To morrow, O to morrow!——sleep, my Son;
And in prophetick dreams thy Fate be shown. *(Exit Tiresias, Adrastus, Eurydice, Manto, Thebans.)*

Remain Oedipus, Jocasta, Creon, Pyracmon, Hæmon, Alcander.

OEDIPUS: To bed, my Fair, my Dear, my best Jocasta.
After the toils of war, 'tis wondrous strange
Our loves should thus be dash'd. One moment's thought,
And I'll approach the arms of my belov'd.

JOCASTA: Consume whole years in care, so now and then
I may have leave to feed my famish'd eyes

With one short passing glance, and sigh my vows:
This, and no more, my Lord, is all the passion
Of languishing Jocasta. *(Exit.)*

OEDIPUS: Thou softest, sweetest of the World! good night.
Nay, she is beauteous too; yet, mighty Love!
I never offer'd to obey thy Laws,
But an unusual chillness came upon me;
An unknown hand still check'd my forward joy
Dash'd me with blushes, tho' no light was near:
That ev'n the Act became a violation.

PYRACMON: He's strangely thoughtful. [377]

OEDIPUS: Hark! who was that? Ha! Creon, didst thou call me?

CREON: Not I, my gracious Lord, nor any here.

OEDIPUS: That's strange! methought I heard a doleful voice
Cry'd Oedipus.——The Prophet bad me sleep;
He talk'd of Dreams, and Visions, and to morrow!
I'll muse no more on't, come what will or can,
My thoughts are clearer than unclouded Stars;
And with those thoughts I'll rest: Creon, good night. *(Exit with Hæmon.)*

CREON: Sleep seal your eyes, Sir, Eternal sleep.
But if he must sleep and wake again, O all
Tormenting Dreams, wild horrours of the night,
And Hags of Fancy wing him through the air:
From precipices hurl him headlong down;
Charybdis roar, and death be set before him.

ALCANDER: Your Curses have already ta'ne effect;
For he looks very sad.

CREON: May he be rooted, where he stands, for ever:
His eye-balls never move, brows be unbent,
His blood, his Entrails, Liver, heart and bowels,
Be blacker than the place I wish him, Hell.

PYRACMON: No more: you tear your self, but vex not him.
Methinks 'twere brave this night to force the Temple,
While blind Tiresias conjures up the Fiends,
And pass the time with nice Eurydice.

ALCANDER: Try promises, and threats, and if all fail,

Since Hell's broke loose, why should not you be mad?
Ravish, and leave her dead, with her Adrastus.
  CREON: Were the Globe mine, I'd give a Province hourly
For such another thought. Lust, and revenge!
To stab at once the only man I hate,
And to enjoy the woman whom I love!
I ask no more of my auspicious Stars,
The rest as Fortune please; so but this night
She play me fair, why, let her turn for ever.

Enter Hæmon.

  HÆMON: My Lord, the troubled King is gone to rest;
Yet, e're he slept, commanded me to clear
The Antichambers: none must dare be near him.
  CREON: Hæmon, you do your duty;——*(Thunder.)*
And we obey.——The night grows yet more dreadful!
'Tis just that all retire to their devotions; [378]
The Gods are angry: but to morrow's dawn,
If Prophets do not lye, will make all clear.

As they go off, Oedipus enters, walking asleep in his shirt, with a Dagger in his right hand, and a Taper in his left.

  OEDIPUS: O, my Jocasta! 'tis for this the wet
Starv'd Soldier lies all night on the cold ground;
For this he bears the storms
Of Winter Camps, and freezes in his Arms:
To be thus circled, to be thus embrac'd;
That I could hold thee ever!——Ha! where are thou?
What means this melancholly light, that seems
The gloom of glowing embers?
The Curtain's drawn; and see, she's here again!
Jocasta! Ha! what, fall'n asleep so soon?
How fares my love? this Taper will inform me.
Ha! Lightning blast me, Thunder
Rivet me ever to Prometheus Rock,
And Vultures gnaw out my Incestuous heart,
By all the Gods! my Mother Merope!

My Sword, a Dagger; Ha! who waits there? slaves,
My Sword: what, Hæmon, dar'st thou, Villain, stop me?
With thy own Ponyard perish. Ha! who's this?
Or is't a change of Death? By all my Honors,
New murder; thou hast slain old Polybus:
Incest and parricide, thy Father's murder'd!
Out thou infernal flame: now all is dark,
All blind and dismal, most triumphant mischief!
And now while thus I stalk about the room,
I challenge Fate to find another wretch
Like Oedipus. *(Thunder, etc.)*

Enter Jocasta attended, with Lights, in a Night-gown.

OEDIPUS: Night, Horrour, Death, Confusion, Hell, and Furies!
Where am I? O, Jocasta, let me hold thee,
Thus to my bosom, ages; let me grasp thee:
All that the hardest temper'd weather'd flesh,
With fiercest humane Spirit inspir'd, can dare
Or do, I dare; but, oh you Pow'rs, this was
By infinite degrees too much for man.
Methinks my deafn'd ears
Are burst; my eyes, as if they had been knock'd
By some tempestuous hand, shoot flashing fire:
That sleep should do this! [379]
JOCASTA: Then my fears were true.
Methought I heard your voice, and yet I doubted,
Now roaring like the Ocean, when the winds
Fight with the waves; now, in a still small tone
Your dying accents fell, as racking ships,
After the dreadful yell, sink murmuring down,
And bubble up a noise.
OEDIPUS: Trust me, thou Fairest, best of all thy Kind,
None e're in Dreams was tortur'd so before,
Yet what most shocks the niceness of my temper,
Ev'n far beyond the killing of my Father,
And my own death, is, that this horrid sleep
Dash'd my sick fancy with an act of Incest:

I dreamt, Jocasta, that thou wert my Mother;
Which tho' impossible, so damps my Spirits,
That I cou'd do a mischief on my self,
Lest I should sleep, and Dream the like again.
JOCASTA: O, Oedipus, too well I understand you!
I know the wrath of Heav'n, the care of Thebes,
The cries of its Inhabitants, war's toils,
And thousand other labours of the State,
Are all referr'd to you, and ought to take you
For ever from Jocasta.
OEDIPUS: Life of my life, and treasure of my Soul!
Heav'n knows I love thee.
JOCASTA: O, you think me vile,
And of an inclination so ignoble,
That I must hide me from your eyes for ever.
Be witness, Gods, and strike Jocasta dead,
If an immodest thought, or low desire
Inflam'd my breast, since first our Loves were lighted.
OEDIPUS: Oh, rise; and add not, by thy cruel kindness,
A grief more sensible than all my torments.
Thou think'st my dreams are forg'd; but by thy self,
The greatest Oath, I swear, they are most true:
But be they what they will, I here dismiss 'em;
Begon, Chimeras, to your Mother Clouds,
Is there a fault in us? Have we not search'd
The womb of Heav'n, examin'd all the Entrails
Of Birds and Beasts, and tir'd the Prophets Art?
Yet what avails? he, and the Gods together,
Seem like Physicians at a loss to help us:
Therefore, like wretches that have linger'd long,
Wee'll snatch the strongest Cordial of our love;
To bed, my Fair.
GHOST: *(within)* Oedipus!
OEDIPUS: Ha! who calls?
Didst thou not hear a voice?
JOCASTA: Alas! I did.
GHOST: Jocasta!

JOCASTA: O my love, my Lord, support me!
OEDIPUS: Call louder, till you burst your aiery Forms:
Rest on my hand. Thus, arm'd with innocence,
I'll face these babling Dæmons of the air.
In spight of Ghosts, I'll on,
Tho' round my Bed the Furies plant their Charms;
I'll break 'em, with Jocasta in my arms:
Clasp'd in the folds of love, I'll wait my doom;
And act my Joys, tho' Thunder shake the room. *(Exeunt.)*

ACT III. SCENE I.

A dark Grove. Enter Creon, Diocles.

CREON: 'Tis better not to be, than to be unhappy.
DIOCLES: What mean you by these words?
CREON: 'Tis better not to be, than to be Creon.
A thinking soul is punishment enough:
But when 'tis great, like mine, and wretched too,
Then every thought draws blood.
DIOCLES: You are not wretched.
CREON: I am: my soul's ill married to my body.
I wou'd be young, be handsom, be belov'd:
Cou'd I but breath my self into Adrastus——
DIOCLES: You rave; call home your thoughts.
CREON: I prithee, let my soul take air a while:
Were she in Oedipus, I were a King;
Then I had kill'd a Monster, gain'd a Battel;
And had my Rival pris'ner; brave, brave actions:
Why have not I done these?
DIOCLES: Your fortune hinder'd.
CREON: There's it: I have a soul to do 'em all: [381]
But fortune will have nothing done that's great,

But by young handsome fools: Body and brawn
Do all her work: Hercules was a fool,
And straight grew famous: a mad boistrous fool;
Nay worse, a Womans Fool.
Fool is the stuff, of which Heav'n makes a Hero.
DIOCLES: A Serpent ne're becomes a flying Dragon,
Till he has eat a Serpent.
CREON: Goes it there!
I understand thee; I must kill Adrastus.
DIOCLES: Or not enjoy your Mistress:
Eurydice and he are pris'ners here,
But will not long be so: this tell-tale Ghost,
Perhaps will clear 'em both.
CREON: Well: 'tis resolv'd.
DIOCLES: The Princess walks this way;
You must not meet her,
Till this be done.
CREON: I must.
DIOCLES: She hates your sight:
And more since you accus'd her.
CREON: Urge it not.
I cannot stay to tell thee my design;
For she's too near.

Enter Eurydice.

How, Madam, were your thoughts employ'd!
EURYDICE: On death, and thee.
CREON: Then were they not well sorted: life and me
Had been the better match.
EURYDICE: No, I was thinking
On two the most detested things in Nature:
And they are death and thee.
CREON: The thought of death to one near death is dreadful:
O 'tis a fearful thing to be no more.
Or if to be, to wander after death;
To walk, as spirits do, in Brakes all day;
And when the darkness comes, to glide in paths

That lead to Graves: and in the silent Vault,
Where lies your own pale shrowd, to hover o're it,
Striving to enter your forbidden Corps;
And often, often, vainly breathe your Ghost
Into your lifeless lips: [382]
Then, like a lone benighted Travellour
Shut out from lodging, shall your groans be answer'd
By whistling winds, whose every blast will shake
Your tender Form to Attoms.
EURYDICE: Must I be this thin Being? and thus wander!
No quiet after death!
CREON: None: you must leave
This beauteous body; all this youth and freshness
Must be no more the object of desire,
But a cold lump of Clay;
Which then your discontented Ghost will leave,
And loath it's former lodging.
This is the best of what comes after death,
Ev'n to the best.
EURYDICE: What then shall be thy lot!
Eternal torments, baths of boiling sulphur:
Vicissitudes of fires, and then of frosts;
And an old Guardian Fiend, ugly as thou art,
To hollow in thy ears at every lash.
This for Eurydice; these for her Adrastus.
CREON: For her Adrastus!
EURYDICE: Yes: for her Adrastus:
For death shall ne're divide us: death! what's death!
DIOCLES: You seem'd to fear it.
EURYDICE: But I more fear Creon:
To take that hunch-back'd Monster in my arms.
Th' excrescence of a man.
DIOCLES: *(to Creon)* See what you've gain'd.
EURYDICE: Death only can be dreadful to the bad:
To innocence, 'tis like a bug-bear dress'd
To fright'n Children; pull but off his Masque
And he'll appear a friend.

CREON: You talk too slightly
Of death and hell. Let me inform you better.
EURYDICE: You best can tell the news of your own Country.
DIOCLES: Nay now you are too sharp.
ERUYDICE: Can I be so to one who has accus'd me
Of murder and of parricide?
CREON: You provok'd me:
And yet I only did thus far accuse you,
As next of blood to Lajus: be advis'd,
And you may live.
EURYDICE: The means. [383]
CREON: 'Tis offer'd you
The Fool Adrastus has accus'd himself.
EURYDICE: He has indeed, to take the guilt from me.
CREON: He says he loves you; if he does, 'tis well:
He ne're cou'd prove it in a better time.
EURYDICE: Then death must be his recompence for love!
CREON: 'Tis a Fools just reward:
The wise can make a better use of life:
But 'tis the young mans pleasure; his ambition:
I grudge him not that favour.
EURYDICE: When he's dead,
Where shall I find his equal!
CREON: Every-where
Fine empty things, like him,
The Court swarms with 'em.
Fine fighting things; in Camps they are so common,
Crows feed on nothing else: plenty of Fools;
A glut of 'em in Thebes.
And fortune still takes care they shou'd be seen:
She places 'em aloft, o' th' topmost Spoke
Of all her Wheel. Fools are the daily work
Of Nature; her vocation: if she form
A man, she loses by't, 'tis too expensive;
'Twou'd make ten Fools: A man's a Prodigy.
EURYDICE: That is a Creon: O thou black detractor,
Who spitt'st thy venom against Gods and man!

Thou enemy of eyes:
Thou who lov'st nothing but what nothing loves,
And that's thy self: who hast conspired against
My life and fame, to make me loath'd by all;
And only fit for thee.
But for Adrastus death, good Gods, his death!
What Curse shall I invent?
DIOCLES: No more: he's here.
EURYDICE: He shall be ever here.
He wou'd give his life; give up his fame.——

Enter Adrastus.

If all the Excellence of woman-kind
Were mine; ——No, 'tis too little all for him:
Were I made up of endless, endless joyes.——
ADRASTUS: And so thou art:
The man who loves like me, [384]
Wou'd think ev'n Infamy, the worst of ills,
Were cheaply purchast, were thy love the price:
Uncrown'd, a Captive, nothing left, but Honour;
'Tis the last thing a Prince shou'd throw away;
But when the storm grows loud, and threatens love,
Throw ev'n that over-board, for Love's the Jewel;
And last it must be kept.
CREON: *(to Diocles)* Work him be sure
To rage, he's passionate;
Make him th' Agressor.
DIOCLES: O false love; false honour.
CREON: Dissembled both, and false!
ADRASTUS: Dar'st thou say thus to me?
CREON: To you; why, what are you, that I should fear you?
I am not Lajus: Hear me, Prince of Argos;
You give what's nothing, when you give your honour;
'Tis gone; 'tis lost in battel. For your love,
Vows made in wine are not so false as that:
You kill'd her Father; you confess'd you did:
A mighty argument to prove your passion to the Daughter!

ADRASTUS: *(aside)* Gods, must I bear this brand, and not retort
The lye to his foul throat?
DIOCLES: Basely you kill'd him.
ADRASTUS: *(aside)* O, I burn inward: my blood's all o' fire.
Alcides, when the poison'd shirt sate closest,
Had but an Ague fit to this my Feaver.
Yet, for Eurydice, ev'n this I'll suffer,
To free my love.——Well then, I kill'd him basely.
CREON: Fairly, I'm sure, you cou'd not.
DIOCLES: Nor alone.
CREON: You had your fellow-Thieves about you, Prince;
They conquer'd, and you kill'd.
ADRASTUS: *(aside)* Down swelling heart!
'Tis for thy Princess all——O my Eurydice!——*(to her)*
EURYDICE: *(to him)* Reproach not thus the weakness of my Sex,
As if I cou'd not bear a shameful death,
Rather than see you burden'd with a Crime
Of which I know you free.
CREON: You do ill, Madam,
To let your head-long Love triumph o're Nature:
Dare you defend your Fathers Murderer?
EURYDICE: You know he kill'd him not.
CREON: Let him say so.
DIOCLES: See he stands mute.
CREON: O pow'r of Conscience, ev'n in wicked men!
It works, it stings, it will not let him utter
One syllable, one, not to clear himself
From the most base, detested, horrid act
That e're cou'd stain a Villain, not a Prince
ADRASTUS: Ha! Villain!
DIOCLES: Eccho to him Groves: cry Villain.
ADRASTUS: Let me consider! did I murther Lajus,
Thus like a Villain?
CREON: Best revoke your words;
And say you kill'd him not.
ADRASTUS: Not like a Villain; prithee change me that
For any other Lye.

DIOCLES: No, Villain, Villain.
CREON: You kill'd him not! proclaim your innocence,
Accuse the Princess: So I knew 'twould be.
ADRASTUS: I thank thee, thou instruct'st me:
No matter how I kill'd him.
CREON: *(aside)* Cool'd again.
EURYDICE: Thou, who usurp'st the sacred name of Conscience,
Did not thy own declare him innocent;
To me declare him so? The King shall know it.
CREON: You will not be believ'd, for I'll forswear it.
EURYDICE: What's now thy Conscience?
CREON: 'Tis my slave, my Drudge, my supple Glove,
My upper Garment, to put on, throw off,
As I think best: 'Tis my obedient conscience.
ADRASTUS: Infamous wretch!
CREON: My Conscience shall not do me the ill office
To save a Rivals life; when thou art dead,
(As dead thou shalt be, or be yet more base
Than thou think'st me,
By forfeiting her life, to save thy own.——)
Know this, and let it grate thy very Soul,
She shall be mine: (she is, if Vows were binding;)
Mark me, the fruit of all thy faith and passion,
Ev'n of thy foolish death, shall all be mine.
ADRASTUS: Thine, say'st thou, Monster;
Shall my love be thine?
Oh, I can bear no more!
Thy cunning Engines, have with labour rais'd
My heavy anger, like a mighty weight, [386]
To fall and pash thee dead.
See here thy Nuptials; see, thou rash Ixion, (*Draws.*)
Thy promis'd Juno vanish'd in a Cloud;
And in her room avenging Thunder rowls,
To blast thee thus——Come both.——
CREON: 'Tis what I wish'd! *(Both Draw.)*
Now see whose Arm can lanch the surer bolt,
And who's the better Jove.——

EURYDICE: Help; Murther, help! *(Fight.)*

Enter Hæmon and Guards, run betwixt them and beat down their Swords.

HÆMON: Hold; hold your impious hands: I think the Furies,
To whom this Grove is hallow'd, have inspir'd you:
Now, by my soul, the holiest earth of Thebes
You have profan'd with war. Nor Tree, nor Plant
Grows here, but what is fed with Magick Juice,
All full of humane Souls; that cleave their barks,
To dance at Midnight by the Moons pale beams:
At least two hundred years these reverend Shades
Have known no blood, but of black Sheep and Oxen,
Shed by the Priests own hand to Proserpine.
ADRASTUS: Forgive a Stranger's ignorance: I knew not
The honours of the place.
HÆMON: Thou, Creon, didst.
Not Oedipus, were all his Foes here lodg'd,
Durst violate the Religion of these Groves,
To touch one single hair: but must, unarm'd,
Parle as in Truce, or surlily avoid
What most he long'd to kill.
CREON: I drew not first;
But in my own defence.
ADRASTUS: I was provok'd,
Beyond Man's patience: all reproach cou'd urge
Was us'd to kindle one not apt to bear.
HÆMON: 'Tis Oedipus, not I, must judge this Act:
Lord Creon, you and Diocles retire:
Tiresias, and the Brother-hood of Priests,
Approach the place: None at these Rites assist,
But you th' accus'd, who by the mouth of Lajus
Must be absolv'd, or doom'd.
ADRASTUS: I bear my fortune.
EURYDICE: And I provoke my tryal. [387]
HÆMON: 'Tis at hand.
For see the Prophet comes with Vervin crown'd,

The Priests with Yeugh, a venerable band;
We leave you to the Gods. *(Exit Hæmon with Creon and Diocles.)*

Enter Tiresias, led by Manto: The Priests follow; all cloathed in long black Habits.

TIRESIAS: Approach, ye Lovers;
Ill-fated Pair! whom, seeing not, I know:
This day your kindly Stars in Heav'n were join'd:
When lo, an envious Planet interpos'd,
And threaten'd both with death: I fear, I fear.
EURYDICE: Is there no God so much a friend to love,
Who can controle the malice of our fate?
Are they all deaf? Or have the Gyants Heav'n?
TIRESIAS: The Gods are just.———
But how can Finite measure Infinite?
Reason! alas, it does not know it self!
Yet Man, vain Man, wou'd with this short-lin'd Plummet,
Fathom the vast Abysse of Heav'nly justice.
What ever is, is in it's causes just;
Since all things are by Fate. But pur-blind Man
Sees but a part o' th' Chain; the nearest links;
His eyes not carrying to that equal Beam
That poizes all above.
EURYDICE: Then we must dye!
TIRESIAS: The danger's imminent this day.
ADRASTUS: Why then there's one day less for humane ills:
And who wou'd moan himself, for suffering that,
Which in a day must pass? something, or nothing——
I shall be what I was again, before
I was Adrastus.——
Penurious Heav'n canst thou not add a night
To our one day; give me a night with her,
And I'll give all the rest.
TIRESIAS: She broke her vow
First made to Creon: but the time calls on:
And Lajus death must now be made more plain.
How loth am I to have recourse to Rites

So full of horrour, that I once rejoice
I want the use of Sight.——

1. PRIEST: The Ceremonies stay.

TIRESIAS: Chuse the darkest part o'th' Grove; [388]
Such as Ghosts at noon-day love.
Dig a Trench, and dig it nigh
Where the bones of Lajus lye.
Altars rais'd of Turf or Stone,
Will th' Infernal Pow'rs have none.
Answer me, if this be done?

ALL PRIESTS: 'Tis done.

TIRESIAS: Is the Sacrifice made fit?
Draw her backward to the pit:
Draw the barren Heyfer back;
Barren let her be and black.
Cut the curled hair that grows
Full betwixt her horns and brows:
And turn your faces from the Sun.
Answer me, if this be done?

ALL PRIESTS: 'Tis done.

TIRESIAS: Pour in blood, and blood like wine,
To Mother Earth and Proserpine:
Mingle Milk into the stream;
Feast the Ghosts that love the steam;
Snatch a brand from funeral pile;
Toss it in to make 'em boil;
And turn your faces from the Sun;
Answer me, if all be done?

ALL PRIESTS: All is done.

Peal of Thunder; and flashes of Lightning; then groaning below the Stage.

MANTO: O, what Laments are those?

TIRESIAS: The groans of Ghosts, that cleave the Earth with pain:
And heave it up: they pant and stick half way.

The Stage wholly darkn'd.

MANTO: And now a sudden darkness covers all,
True genuine Night: Night added to the Groves;
The Fogs are blown full in the face of Heav'n.
TIRESIAS: Am I but half obey'd: Infernal Gods,
Must you have Musick too? then tune your voices,
And let 'em have such sounds as Hell ne're heard
Since Orpheus brib'd the Shades.

Musick first. Then Sing. (This to be set through.)

1. *Hear, ye sullen Pow'rs below:*
Hear, ye taskers of the dead. [389]
2. *You that boiling Cauldrons blow,*
You that scum the molten Lead.
3. *You that pinch with Red-hot Tongs;*
1. *You that drive the trembling Hosts*
Of poor, poor Ghosts,
With your Sharpen'd Prongs;
2. *You that thrust 'em off the Brim;*
3. *You that plunge 'em when they Swim:*
1. *Till they drown,*
Till they go
On a row
Down, down, down,
Ten thousand, thousand, thousand fadoms low.
CHORUS: *Till they drown,* etc.
1. *Musick for a while*
Shall your cares beguile:
Wondring how your pains were eas'd.
2. *And disdaining to be pleas'd;*
3. *Till Alecto free the dead*
From their eternal bands;
Till the snakes drop from her head,
And whip from out her hands.
1. *Come away,*
Do not stay,
But obey

While we play,
For Hell's broke up, and Ghosts have holy-day.
CHORUS: *Come away,* etc.

A flash of Lightning: the Stage is made bright; and the Ghosts are seen passing betwixt the Trees.

1. *Lajus!* 2. *Lajus!* 3. *Lajus!*
1. *Hear!* 2. *Hear!* 3. *Hear!*
TIRESIAS: *Hear and appear:*
By the Fates that spun thy thread;
CHORUS: *Which are three,*
TIRESIAS: *By the Furies fierce, and dread!*
CHORUS: *Which are three,*
TIRESIAS: *By the Judges of the dead!*
CHORUS: *Which are three*
Three times three.
TIRESIAS: *By Hell's blew flame:*
By the Stygian Lake:
And by Demogorgon's name,
At which Ghosts quake,
Hear and appear.

The Ghost of Lajus rises arm'd in his Chariot, as he was slain. And behind his Chariot, sit the three who were Murder'd with him.

GHOST OF LAJUS: Why hast thou drawn me from my pains below,
To suffer worse above: to see the day,
And Thebes more hated? Hell is Heav'n to Thebes.
For pity send me back, where I may hide,
In willing night, this ignominious head:
In Hell I shun the publick scorn; and then
They hunt me for their sport, and hoot me as I fly:
Behold ev'n now they grin at my gor'd side,
And chatter at my wounds.
TIRESIAS: I pity thee:
Tell but why Thebes is for thy death accurst,
And I'll unbind the Charm.

GHOST: O spare my shame.
TIRESIAS: Are these two innocent?
GHOST: Of my death they are.
But he who holds my Crown, Oh, must I speak!
Was doom'd to do what Nature most abhors.
The Gods foresaw it; and forbad his being,
Before he yet was born. I broke their laws,
And cloath'd with flesh his pre-existing soul,
Some kinder pow'r, too weak for destiny,
Took pity, and indu'd his new form'd Mass
With Temperance, Justice, Prudence, Fortitude,
And every Kingly vertue: but in vain.
For Fate, that sent him hood-winckt to the world,
Perform'd its work by his mistaking hands.
Asks thou who murder'd me? 'twas Oedipus:
Who stains my Bed with Incest? Oedipus:
For whom then are you curst, but Oedipus!
He comes; the Parricide: I cannot bear him:
My wounds ake at him: Oh his murd'rous breath
Venoms my aiery substance! hence with him,
Banish him; sweep him out; the Plague he bears
Will blast your fields, and mark his way with ruine.
From Thebes, my Throne, my Bed, let him be driv'n;
Do you forbid him Earth, and I'll forbid him Heav'n. *(Ghost descends.)* [391][1]

Enter Oedipus, Creon, Hæmon, etc.

OEDIPUS: What's this! methought some pestilential blast
Strook me just entring; and some unseen hand
Struggled to push me backward! tell me why
My hair stands bristling up, why my flesh trembles!
You stare at me! then Hell has been among ye,
And some lag Fiend yet lingers in the Grove.
TIRESIAS: What Omen saw'st thou entring?
OEDIPUS: A young Stork,
That bore his aged Parent on his back;
Till weary with the weight, he shook him off,

And peck'd out both his eyes.
ADRASTUS: Oh, Oedipus!
EURYDICE: Oh, wretched Oedipus!
TIRESIAS: O! Fatal King!
OEDIPUS: What mean these Exclamations on my name?
I thank the Gods, no secret thoughts reproach me:
No: I dare challenge Heav'n to turn me outward,
And shake my Soul quite empty in your sight.
Then wonder not that I can bear unmov'd
These fix'd regards, and silent threats of eyes:
A generous fierceness dwells with innocence;
And conscious vertue is allow'd some pride.
TIRESIAS: Thou know'st not what thou say'st.
OEDIPUS: What mutters he! tell me, Eurydice:
Thou shak'st: thy souls a Woman. Speak, Adrastus;
And boldly, as thou met'st my Arms in fight;
Dar'st thou not speak, why then 'tis bad indeed:
Tiresias, thee I summon by thy Priesthood,
Tell me what news from Hell: where Lajus points,
And who's the guilty head?
TIRESIAS: Let me not answer.
OEDIPUS: Be dumb then, and betray thy native soil
To farther Plagues.
TIRESIAS: I dare not name him to thee.
OEDIPUS: Dar'st thou converse with Hell, and canst thou fear
An humane name?
TIRESIAS: Urge me no more to tell a thing, which known
Wou'd make thee more unhappy: 'twill be found
Tho' I am silent.
OEDIPUS: Old and obstinate! Then thou thy self
Art Author or Accomplice of this murther, [392]
And shun'st the Justice, which by publick ban
Thou has incurr'd.
TIRESIAS: O, if the guilt were mine
It were not half so great: know wretched man,
Thou onely, thou art guilty; thy own Curse
Falls heavy on thy self.

OEDIPUS: Speak this again:
But speak it to the Winds when they are loudest:
Or to the raging Seas, they'll hear as soon,
And sooner will believe.
TIRESIAS: Then hear me Heav'n,
For blushing thou hast seen it: hear me Earth,
Whose hollow womb could not contain this murder,
But sent it back to light: and thou Hell, hear me,
Whose own black Seal has 'firm'd this horrid truth,
Oedipus murther'd Lajus.
OEDIPUS: Rot the tongue,
And blasted be the mouth that spoke that lye.
Thou blind of sight, but thou more blind of soul.
TIRESIAS: Thy Parents thought not so.
OEDIPUS: Who were my Parents?
TIRESIAS: Thou shalt know too soon.
OEDIPUS: Why seek I truth from thee?
The smiles of Courtiers, and the Harlots tears,
The Tradesmans oaths, and mourning of an Heir,
Are truths to what Priests tell.
O why has Priest-hood priviledge to lye,
And yet to be believ'd!——thy age protects thee.——
TIRESIAS: Thou canst not kill me; 'tis not in thy Fate,
As 'twas to kill thy Father; wed thy Mother;
And beget Sons, thy Brothers.
OEDIPUS: Riddles, Riddles!
TIRESIAS: Thou art thy self a Riddle; a perplext
Obscure Ænigma, which when thou unty'st,
Thou shalt be found and lost.
OEDIPUS: Impossible!
Adrastus, speak, and as thou art a King,
Whose Royal word is sacred, clear my fame.
ADRASTUS: Wou'd I cou'd!
OEDIPUS: Ha, wilt thou not: can that Plebeian vice
Of lying mount to Kings! can they be tainted!
Then truth is lost on earth.
CREON: The Cheats too gross: [393]

Adrastus is his Oracle, and he,
The pious Juggler, but Adrastus Organ.
OEDIPUS: 'Tis plain the Priest's suborn'd to free the Pris'ner.
CREON: And turn the guilt on you.
OEDIPUS: O, honest Creon, how hast thou been bely'd?
EURYDICE: Hear me
CREON: She's brib'd to save her Lover's life.
ADRASTUS: If Oedipus thou think'st——
CREON: Hear him not speak.
ADRASTUS: Then hear these holy men
CREON: Priests, Priests all brib'd, all Priests.
OEDIPUS: Adrastus I have found thee:
The malice of a vanquish'd man has seiz'd thee.
ADRASTUS: If Envy and not Truth——
OEDIPUS: I'll hear no more: away with him.

(Hæmon takes him off by force: Creon and Eurydice follow. To Tiresias.)

Why stand'st thou here, Impostor!
So old, and yet so wicked.——lye for gain;
And gain so short as age can promise thee!
TIRESIAS: So short a time as I have yet to live
Exceeds thy pointed hour; Remember Lajus:
No more; if e're we meet again, 'twill be
In Mutual darkness; we shall feel before us
To reach each others hand; Remember Lajus. *(Exit Tiresias: Priests follow.)*

Oedipus Solus.

Remember Lajus! that's the burden still:
Murther, and Incest! but to hear 'em nam'd
My Soul starts in me: the good Sentinel
Stands to her Weapons; takes the first Alarm
To guard me from such Crimes.——Did I kill Lajus?
Then I walk'd sleeping, in some frightful dream,
My Soul then stole my Body out by night;
And brought me back to Bed e're Morning-wake.

It cannot be ev'n this remotest way,
But some dark hint would justle forward now;
And goad my memory.——Oh my Jocasta!

Enter Jocasta.

JOCASTA: Why are you thus disturb'd?
OEDIPUS: Why, would'st thou think it?
No less than Murther? [394]
JOCASTA: Murder? what of Murder?
OEDIPUS: Is Murder then no more? add Parricide,
And Incest; bear not these a frightful sound?
JOCASTA: Alas!
OEDIPUS: How poor a pity is Alas
For two such Crimes!——was Lajus us'd to lye?
JOCASTA: Oh no: the most sincere, plain, honest man,
One who abhorr'd a lye.
OEDIPUS: Then he has got that Quality in Hell.
He charges me——but why accuse I him?
I did not hear him speak it: they accuse me;
The Priest, Adrastus, and Eurydice,
Of murdering Lajus——Tell me, while I think on't,
Has old Tiresias practis'd long this Trade?
JOCASTA: What Trade?
OEDIPUS: Why, this foretelling Trade.
JOCASTA: For many years.
OEDIPUS: Has he before this day accus'd me?
JOCASTA: Never.
OEDIPUS: Have you e're this inquir'd, who did this Murder?
JOCASTA: Often; but still in vain.
OEDIPUS: I am satisfy'd.
Then 'tis an infant lye; but one day old.
The Oracle takes place before the Priest;
The blood of Lajus was to Murder Lajus:
I'm not of Lajus's blood.
JOCASTA: Ev'n Oracles
Are always doubtful, and are often forg'd:
Lajus had one, which never was fulfill'd,

Nor ever can be now!
OEDIPUS: And what foretold it?
JOCASTA: That he shou'd have a Son by me, fore-doom'd
The Murderer of his Father: true indeed,
A Son was born; but to prevent that Crime,
The wretched Infant of a guilty Fate,
Bor'd through his untry'd feet, and bound with cords,
On a bleak Mountain, naked was expos'd:
The King himself liv'd many, many years,
And found a different Fate; by Robbers Murder'd,
Where three ways meet: yet these are Oracles;
And this the Faith we owe 'em.
OEDIPUS: Say'st thou, Woman?
By Heav'n thou hast awakn'd somewhat in me,
That shakes my very Soul!
JOCASTA: What, new disturbance!
OEDIPUS: Methought thou said'st,——(or do I dream thou said'st it!)
This Murder was on Lajus person done,
Where three ways meet?
JOCASTA: So common Fame reports.
OEDIPUS: Wou'd it had ly'd.
JOCASTA: Why, good my Lord?
OEDIPUS: No questions:
'Tis busie time with me; dispatch mine first;
Say where, where was it done!
JOCASTA: Mean you the Murder?
OEDIPUS: Cou'd'st thou not answer without naming Murder?
JOCASTA: They say in Phocide; on the Verge that parts it
From Daulia, and from Delphos.
OEDIPUS: So!——How long! when happen'd this!
JOCASTA: Some little time before you came to Thebes.
OEDIPUS: What will the Gods do with me!
JOCASTA: What means that thought?
OEDIPUS: Something: but 'tis not your turn to ask:
How old was Lajus, what his shape, his stature,
His action, and his meen? quick, quick, your answer——

JOCASTA: Big made he was, and tall: his port was fierce,
Erect his countenance: Manly Majesty
Sate in his front, and darted from his eyes,
Commanding all he viewed: his hair just grizled,
As in a green old age: bate but his years,
You are his picture.
OEDIPUS: *(aside)* Pray Heav'n he drew me not? am I his picture?
JOCASTA: So I have often told you.
OEDIPUS: True, you have;
Add that to the rest: how was the King
Attended when he travell'd?
JOCASTA: By four Servants:
He went out privately.
OEDIPUS: Well counted still:
One scap'd I hear; what since became of him?
JOCASTA: When he beheld you first, as King in Thebes,
He kneel'd, and trembling beg'd I wou'd dismiss him:
He had my leave; and now he lives retir'd.
OEDIPUS: This Man must be produc'd; he must, Jocasta.
JOCASTA: He shall——yet have I leave to ask you why? [396]
OEDIPUS: Yes, you shall know: for where should I repose
The anguish of my Soul, but in your breast!
I need not tell you Corinth claims my birth;
My Parents Polybus and Merope,
Two Royal Names; their only Child am I
It happen'd once; 'twas at a Bridal Feast,
One warm with Wine, told me I was a Foundling,
Not the Kings Son; I stung with this reproach,
Strook him: my Father, heard of it: the Man
Was made ask pardon; and the business hush'd.
JOCASTA: 'Twas somewhat odd.
OEDIPUS: And strangely it perplext me.
I stole away to Delphos, and implor'd
The God, to tell my certain Parentage.
He bade me seek no farther:—'twas my Fate
To kill my Father, and pollute his Bed,
By marrying her who bore me.

JOCASTA: Vain, vain Oracles!
OEDIPUS: But yet they frighted me;
I lookt on Corinth as a place accurst,
Resolv'd my destiny should wait in vain;
And never catch me there.
JOCASTA: Too nice a fear.
OEDIPUS: Suspend your thoughts; and flatter not too soon.
Just in the place you nam'd, where three ways meet,
And near that time, five persons I encounter'd;
One was too like, (Heav'n grant it prove not him)
Whom you describe for Lajus: insolent
And fierce they were, as Men who liv'd on spoil.
I judg'd 'em Robbers, and by force repell'd
The force they us'd: In short, four men I slew:
The fifth upon his knees demanding Life,
My mercy gave it.——bring me comfort now,
If I slew Lajus, what can be more wretched!
From Thebes and you my Curse has banish'd me:
From Corinth Fate.
JOCASTA: Perplex not thus your mind;
My Husband fell by Multitudes opprest,
So Phorbas said: this Band you chanc'd to meet;
And murder'd not my Lajus, but reveng'd him.
OEDIPUS: There's all my hope: Let Phorbas tell me this,
And I shall live again!——
To you, good Gods, I make my last appeal; [397]
Or clear my Vertues or my Crime reveal:
If wandering in the maze of Fate I run,
And backward trod the paths I sought to shun,
Impute my Errours to your own Decree;
My hands are guilty, but my heart is free. *(Exeunt Ambo.)*

ACT IV. SCENE I.

Pyracmon, Creon.

PYRACMON: Some business of import that Triumph wears,
You seem to go with; nor is it hard to guess
When you are pleas'd, by a malicious joy:
Whose Red and Fiery Beams cast through your Visage
A glowing pleasure. Sure you smile revenge,
And I cou'd gladly hear.
CREON: Would'st thou believe
This giddy hair-braind King, whom old Tiresias
Has Thunder-strook, with heavy accusation,
Tho' conscious of no inward guilt, yet fears;
He fears Jocasta, fears himself, his shadow;
He fears the multitude; and, which is worth
An Age of laughter, out of all mankind,
He chuses me to be his Orator:
Swears that Adrastus and the lean-look'd Prophet,
Are joint-conspirators; and wisht me to
Appease the raving Thebans, which I swore
To do.
PYRACMON: A dangerous undertaking;
Directly opposite to your own interest.
CREON: No, dull Pyracmon; when I left his presence,
With all the Wings with which revenge could imp
My flight, I gain'd the midst o'th' City;
There, standing on a Pile of dead and dying,
I to the mad and sickly multitude,
With interrupting sobs, cry'd out, O Thebes,
O wretched Thebes, thy King, thy Oedipus,
This barbarous stranger, this Usurper, Monster,
Is by the Oracle, the wise Tiresias,

Proclaim'd the murderer of the Royal Lajus.
Jocasta too, no longer now my Sister, [398]
Is found complotter in the horrid deed.
Here I renounce all tye of Blood and Nature,
For thee, O Thebes, dear Thebes, poor bleeding Thebes.
And there I wept, and then the Rabble howl'd,
And roar'd, and with a thousand Antick mouths
Gabbled revenge, Revenge was all the cry.
PYRACMON: This cannot fail: I see you on the Throne;
And Oedipus cast out.
CREON: Then strait came on
Alcander, with a wild and bellowing Croud,
Whom when he had wrought; I whisper'd him to join,
And head the Forces while the heat was in 'em:
So to the Palace I return'd, to meet
The King, and greet him with another story.
But see, he Enters.

Enter Oedipus, Jocasta, attended.

OEDIPUS: Said you that Phorbas is return'd, and yet
Intreats he may return, without being ask'd
Of ought concern'd what we have discover'd?
JOCASTA: He started when I told him your intent,
Replying, what he knew of that affair
Would give no satisfaction to the King;
Then, falling on his knees, begg'd, as for life,
To be dismiss'd from Court: He trembled too,
As if Convulsive death had seiz'd upon him,
And stammer'd in his abrupt Pray'r so wildly,
That, had he been the murderer of Lajus,
Guilt and distraction could not have shook him more.
OEDIPUS: By your description, sure as plagues and death
Lay waste our Thebes, some deed that shuns the light
Begot those fears: If thou respect'st my peace,
Secure him, dear Jocasta; for my Genius
Shrinks at his name.
JOCASTA: Rather let him go:
So my poor boding heart would have it be,

Without a reason.
OEDIPUS: Hark, the Thebans come!
Therefore retire: and, once more, if you lov'st me,
Let Phorbas be retain'd.
JOCASTA: You shall, while I
Have life, be still obey'd:
In vain you sooth me with your soft indearments, [399]
And set the fairest Countenance to view,
Your gloomy eyes, my Lord, betray a deadness
And inward languishing: that Oracle
Eats like a subtil Worm it's venom'd way,
Preys on your heart, and rots the noble Core,
How-e're the beauteous out-side shews so lovely.
OEDIPUS: O, thou wilt kill me with thy Love's excess!
All, all is well; retire, the Thebans come. *(Exit Jocasta.)*
GHOST: Oedipus!
OEDIPUS: Ha! again that scream of woe!
Thrice have I heard, thrice since the morning dawn'd
It hollow'd loud, as if my Guardian Spirit
Call'd from some vaulted Mansion, Oedipus!
Or is it but the work of melancholly?
When the Sun sets, shadows, that shew'd at Noon
But small, appear most long and terrible;
So when we think Fate hovers o're our heads,
Our apprehensions shoot beyond all bounds,
Owls, Ravens, Crickets seem the watch of death,
Nature's worst Vermine scare her God-like Sons.
Ecchoes, the very leavings of a Voice,
Grow babling Ghosts, and call us to our Graves:
Each Mole-hill thought swells to a huge Olympus,
While we fantastick dreamers heave and puff,
And sweat with an Immagination's weight;
As if, like Atlas, with these mortal Shoulders
We could sustain the burden of the World.

Creon comes forward.

CREON: O, Sacred Sir, my Royal Lord——
OEDIPUS: What now?

Thou seem'st affrighted at some dreadful action,
Thy breath comes short, thy darted eyes are fixt
On me for aid, as if thou wert pursu'd:
I sent thee to the Thebans, speak thy wonder;
Fear not, this Palace is a Sanctuary,
The King himself's thy Guard
CREON: For me, alas,
My life's not worth a thought, when weigh'd with yours!
But fly, my Lord, fly as your life is sacred,
Your fate is precious to your faithful Creon,
Who therefore, on his knees, thus prostrate begs
You would remove from Thebes that Vows your ruine.
When I but offer'd at your innocence,
They gather'd Stones, and menac'd me with Death,
And drove me through the Streets, with imprecations
Against your sacred Person, and those Traytors
Which justify'd your Guilt: which curs'd Tiresias
Told, as from Heav'n, was cause of their destruction.
OEDIPUS: Rise, worthy Creon, haste and take our Guard,
Rank 'em in equal part upon the Square,
Then open every Gate of this our Palace
And let the Torrent in. Hark, it comes, *(Shout.)*
I hear 'em roar: begon, and break down all
The dams that would oppose their furious passage. *(Exit Creon with Guards.)*

Enter Adrastus, his Sword drawn.

ADRASTUS: Your City
Is all in Arms, all bent to your destruction:
I heard but now, where I was close confin'd,
A Thundering shout, which made my Jaylors vanish,
Cry, Fire the Palace; where's the cruel King?
Yet, by th' Infernal Gods, those awful Pow'rs
That have accus'd you, which these ears have heard,
And these Eyes seen, I must believe you guiltless;
For, since I knew the Royal Oedipus,
I have observ'd in all his acts such truth

And God-like clearness; that to the last gush
Of bloud and Spirits, I'll defend his life,
And here have Sworn to perish by his side.
OEDIPUS: Be witness, Gods, how near this touches me, *(Embracing him.)*
O what, what recompence can glory make?
ADRASTUS: Defend your innocence, speak like your self,
And awe the Rebels with your dauntless virtue.
But hark! the Storm comes nearer
OEDIPUS: Let it come.
The force of Majesty is never known
But in a general wrack: Then, then is seen
The difference 'twixt a Threshold and a Throne.

Enter Creon, Pyracmon, Alcander, Tiresias, Thebans.

ALCANDER: Where, where's this cruel King? Thebans, behold
There stands your Plague, the ruine, desolation
Of this unhappy——speak; shall I kill him?
Or shall he be cast out to Banishment? [401]
ALL THEBANS: To Banishment, away with him.
OEDIPUS: Hence, you Barbarians, to your slavish distance;
Fix to the Earth your sordid looks; for he
Who stirs, dares more than mad-men, Fiends, or Furies;
Who dares to face me, by the Gods, as well
May brave the Majesty of Thundring Jove.
Did I for this relieve you when besieg'd
By this fierce Prince, when coop'd within your Walls,
And to the very brink of Fate reduc'd;
When lean-jaw'd famine made more havock of you
Than does the Plague? But I rejoyce I know you,
Know the base stuff that temper'd your vile Souls:
The Gods be prais'd, I needed not your Empire,
Born to a greater, nobler, of my own;
Nor shall the Scepter of the Earth now win me
To rule such Brutes, so barbarous a People.
ADRASTUS: Methinks, my Lord, I see a sad repentance,
A general consternation spread among 'em.

OEDIPUS: My Reign is at an end; yet e're I finish——
I'll do a justice that becomes a Monarch,
A Monarch, who, i'th' midst of Swords and Javelins,
Dares act as on his own Throne encompast round
With Nation's for his Guard. Alcander, you
Are nobly born, therefore shall lose your head: *(Seizes him.)*
Here, Hæmon, take him: but for this, and this,
Let Cords dispatch 'em. Hence, away with 'em.
TIRESIAS: O sacred Prince, pardon distracted Thebes,
Pardon her, if she acts by Heav'ns award;
If that the Infernal Spirits have declar'd
The depth of Fate, and if our Oracles
May speak, O do not too severely deal,
But let thy wretched Thebes at least complain:
If thou art guilty, Heav'n will make it known;
If innocent, then let Tiresias dye.
OEDIPUS: I take thee at thy word. Run, haste, and save Alcander:
I swear the Prophet, or the King shall dye.
Be witness, all you Thebans, of my Oath.
And Phorbas be the Umpire.
TIRESIAS: I submit. *(Trumpets sound.)*
OEDIPUS: What mean those Trumpets?
HÆMON: From your Native Country. [402]

Enter Hæmon with Alcander, etc.

Great Sir, the fam'd Ægeon is arriv'd,
That renown'd Favourite of the King your Father:
He comes as an Ambassador from Corinth,
And sues for Audience
OEDIPUS: Haste, Hæmon, fly, and tell him that I burn
T'embrace him
HÆMON: The Queen, my Lord, at present holds him
In private Conference; but behold her here.

Enter Jocasta, Eurydice, etc

JOCASTA: Hail, happy Oedipus, happiest of Kings?
Henceforth be blest, blest as thou canst desire,

Sleep without fears the blackest nights away;
Let Furies haunt thy Palace, thou shalt sleep
Secure, thy slumbers shall be soft and gentle
As Infants dreams
OEDIPUS: What does the Soul of all my joys intend?
And whither would this rapture?
JOCASTA: O, I could rave,
Pull down those lying Fanes, and burn that Vault,
From whence resounded those false Oracles,
That robb'd my Love of rest: if we must pray,
Rear in the streets bright Altars to the Gods,
Let Virgins hands adorn the Sacrifice;
And not a gray-beard forging Priest come near,
To pry into the bowels of the Victim,
And with his dotage mad the gaping World.
But see, the Oracle that I will trust,
True as the Gods, and affable as Men.

Enter Ægeon, Kneels.

OEDIPUS: O, to my arms, welcome, my dear Ægeon;
Ten thousand welcomes. O, my Foster-Father,
Welcome as mercy to a Man condemn'd!
Welcome to me,
As, to a sinking Marriner
The lucky plank that bears him to the shore!
But speak, O tell me what so mighty joy
Is this thou bring'st, which so transports Jocasta?
JOCASTA: Peace, peace Ægeon; let Jocasta tell him!
O that I could for ever Charm, as now, [403]
My dearest Oedipus: Thy Royal Father,
Polybus, King of Corinth, is no more.
OEDIPUS: Ha! can it be? Ægeon answer me,
And speak in short, what my Jocasta's transport
May overdo.
ÆGEON: Since in few words, my Royal Lord, you ask
To know the truth; King Polybus is dead.
OEDIPUS: O all you Pow'rs, is't possible? what, dead!

But that the Tempest of my joy may rise
By just degrees, and hit at last the Stars:
Say, how, how dy'd he? Ha! by Sword, by Fire,
Or Water? by Assassinates, or Poyson? speak:
Or did he languish under some disease?
  ÆGEON: Of no distemper, of no blast he dy'd,
But fell like Autumn-Fruit that mellow'd long:
Ev'n wonder'd at, because he dropt no sooner.
Fate seem'd to wind him up for fourscore years;
Yet freshly ran he on
Ten Winters more:
Till, like a Clock worn out with eating time,
The Wheels of weary life at last stood still.
  OEDIPUS: O, let me press thee in my youthful arms,
And smother thy old age in my embraces.
Yes Thebans, yes Jocasta, yes Adrastus,
Old Polybus, the King my Father's dead.
Fires shall be kindled in the mid'st of Thebes;
I'th midst of Tumults, Wars, and Pestilence,
I will rejoice for Polybus his death.
Know, be it known to the limits of the World;
Yet farther, let it pass yon dazling roof.
The mansion of the Gods, and strike 'em deaf,
With everlasting peals of Thundring joy.
  TIRESIAS: Fate! Nature! Fortune! what is all this world?
  OEDIPUS: Now, Dotard; now, thou blind old wizard Prophet,
Where are your boding Ghosts, your Altars now;
Your Birds of knowledge, that, in dusky Air,
Chatter Futurity; and where are now
Your Oracles, that call'd me Parricide,
Is he not dead? deep laid in's Monument?
And was not I in Thebes when Fate attack'd him?
Avant, begon, you Vizors of the Gods!
Were I as other Sons, now I should weep;
But as I am, I've reason to rejoice: [404]
And will, tho' his cold shades should rise and blast me.
O, for this death, let Waters break their bounds,

Rocks, Valleys, Hills, with splitting *Io*'s ring:
Io, Jacasta, Io pæan sing.

TIRESIAS: Who would not now conclude a happy end?
But all Fate's turns are swift and unexpected.

ÆGEON: Your Royal Mother Merope, as if
She had no Soul since you forsook the Land,
Waves all the neighb'ring Princes that adore her.

OEDIPUS: Waves all the Princes! poor heart! for what? O speak.

ÆGEON: She, tho' in full-blown flow'r of glorious beauty,
Grows cold, ev'n in the Summer of her Age:
And for your sake, has sworn to dye unmarry'd.

OEDIPUS: How! for my sake, dye, and not marry! O, dye unmarry'd.
My fit returns.

ÆGEON: This Diamond, with a thousand kisses blest,
With thousand sighs and wishes for your safety,
She charg'd me give you, with the general Homage
Of our Corinthian Lords.

OEDIPUS: There's Magick in it, take it from my sight;
There's not a beam it darts, but carries Hell,
Hot flashing lust, and Necromantick Incest:
Take it from these sick eyes, Oh hide it from me.
No, my Jocasta, tho' Thebes cast me out,
While Merope's alive, I'll ne're return!
O, rather let me walk round the wide World
A beggar, than accept a Diadem
On such abhorr'd conditions.

JOCASTA: You make, my Lord, your own unhappiness,
By these extravagant and needless fears.

OEDIPUS: Needless! O, all you Gods! By Heav'n I'd rather
Embrue my Arms up to my very shoulders
In the dear entrails of the best of Fathers,
Than offer at the execrable Act
Of damned Incest: therefore no more of her.

ÆGEON: And why, O sacred Sir, if Subjects may
Presume to look into their Monarch's breast,
Why should the chaste and spotless Merope

Infuse such thoughts as I must blush to name?
OEDIPUS: Because the God of Delphos did forewarn me,
With Thundring Oracles.
ÆGEON: May I entreat to know 'em?
OEDIPUS: Yes, my Ægeon; but the sad remembrance
Quite blasts my Soul: see then the swelling Priest!
Methinks I have his Image now in view;
He mounts the Tripos in a minutes space,
His clouded head knocks at the Temple roof,
While from his mouth
These dismal words are heard:
"Fly wretch whom Fate has doom'd thy Fathers Blood to spill,
"And with prepostrous Births, thy Mothers womb to fill.
ÆGEON: Is this the Cause
Why you refuse the Diadem of Corinth?
OEDIPUS: The Cause! why, is it not a monstrous one?
ÆGEON: Great Sir, you may return; and tho' you should
Enjoy the Queen (which all the Gods forbid)
The Act would prove no incest.
OEDIPUS: How, Ægeon?
Tho' I enjoy'd my Mother, not incestuous!
Thou rav'st, and so do I; and these all catch
My madness; look, they're dead with deep distraction:
Not Incest! what, not Incest with my Mother?
ÆGEON: My Lord, Queen Merope is not your Mother.
OEDIPUS: Ha! did I hear thee right? not Merope
My Mother!
ÆGEON: Nor was Polybus your Father.
OEDIPUS: Then all my days and nights must now be spent
In curious search, to find out those dark Parents
Who gave me to the World; speak then Ægeon,
By all the God's Celestial and Infernal,
By all the tyes of Nature, blood, and friendship,
Conceal not from this rack'd despairing King
A point or smallest grain of what thou know'st:
Speak then, O answer to my doubts directly.
If Royal Polybus was not my Father,

Why was I call'd his Son?
ÆGEON: He, from my Arms,
Receiv'd you as the fairest Gift of Nature.
Not but you were adorn'd with all the Riches
That Empire could bestow in costly Mantles
Upon its Infant Heir.
OEDIPUS: But was I made the Heir of Corinth's Crown,
Because Ægeon's hands presented me?
ÆGEON: By my advice,
Being past all hope of Children,
He took, embrac'd, and own'd you for his Son. [406]
OEDIPUS: Perhaps I then am yours; instruct me, Sir:
If it be so, I'll kneel and weep before you,
With all th' obedience of a penitent Chid,
Imploring pardon.
Kill me if you please,
I will not writhe my Body at the wound:
But sink upon your feet with a last sigh,
And ask forgiveness with my dying hands.
ÆGEON: O rise, and call not to this aged Cheek
The little blood which should keep warm my heart;
You are not mine, nor ought I to be blest
With such a God-like off-spring. Sir, I found you
Upon the Mount Cithæron.
OEDIPUS: O speak, go on, the Air grows sensible
Of the great things you utter, and is calm:
The hurry'd Orbs, with Storms so Rack'd of late,
Seem to stand still, as if that Jove were talking.
Cithæron! speak, the Valley of Cithæron!
ÆGEON: Oft-times before I thither did resort,
Charm'd with the conversation of a man
Who led a Rural life, and had command
O're all the Shepherds who about those Vales
Tended their numerous Flocks: in this man's Arms
I saw you smiling at a fatal Dagger
Whose point he often offer'd at your throat;
But then you smil'd, and then you drew it back;

Then lifted it again, you smil'd again:
Till he at last in fury threw it from him,
And cry'd aloud, the Gods forbid thy death.
Then I rush'd in, and, after some discourse,
To me he did bequeath your innocent life;
And I, the welcome care to Polybus.

OEDIPUS: To whom belongs the Master of the Shepherds?

ÆGEON: His name I knew not, or I have forgot,
That he was of the Family of Lajus,
I will remember.

OEDIPUS: And is your Friend alive? for if he be
I'll buy his Presence, tho' it cost my Crown.

ÆGEON: Your menial Attendants best can tell
Whether he lives, or not; and who has now
His place.

JOCASTA: Winds, bear me to some barren Island,
Where print of humane Feet was never seen, [407]
O're-grown with Weeds of such a monstrous height,
Their baleful tops are wash'd with bellying Clouds:
Beneath whose venomous shade I may have vent
For horrors that would blast the Barbarous World.

OEDIPUS: If there be any here that knows the person
Whom he describ'd, I charge him on his life
To speak; concealment shall be sudden death:
But he who brings him forth, shall have reward
Beyond Ambitions lust.

TIRESIAS: His Name is Phorbas:
Jocasta knows him well; but if I may
Advise, Rest where you are, and seek no farther.

OEDIPUS: Then all goes well, Since Phorbas is secur'd
By my Jocasta. Haste, and bring him forth:
My Love, my Queen, give Orders. Ha! what means
These Tears and Groans, and Struglings? speak, my Fair,
What are thy troubles?

JOCASTA: Yours; and yours are mine:
Let me Conjure you, take the Prophets Counsel,
And let this Phorbas go.

OEDIPUS: Not for the World.
By all the Gods, I'll know my birth, tho' death
Attends the search: I have already past
The middle of the Stream; and to return
Seems greater labour than to venture o're.
Therefore produce him.
JOCASTA: Once more, by the Gods,
I beg, my Oedipus, my Lord, my Life,
My love, my all, my only utmost hope,
I beg you banish Phorbas: O, the Gods,
I kneel, that you may grant this first request.
Deny me all things else; but, for my sake,
And as you prize your own eternal quiet,
Never let Phorbas come into your presence.
OEDIPUS: You must be rais'd, and Phorbas shall appear,
Tho' his dread eyes were Basilisks. Guards, haste,
Search the Queens Lodgings; find, and force him hither. *(Exeunt Guards.)*
JOCASTA: O, Oedipus, yet send,
And stop their entrance, e're it be too late:
Unless you wish to see Jocasta rent
With Furies, slain out-right with meer distraction,
Keep from your eyes and mine the dreadful Phorbas. [408]
Forbear this search, I'll think you more than mortal:
Will you yet hear me?
OEDIPUS: Tempests will be heard,
And Waves will dash, tho Rocks their basis keep,——
But see, they Enter. If thou truly lov'st me,
Either forbear this Subject, or retire.

Enter Hæmon, Guards, with Phorbas.

JOCASTA: Prepare then, wretched Prince, prepare to hear
A story, that shall turn thee into Stone,
Could there be hew'n a monstrous Gap in Nature,
A flaw made through the Center, by some God,
Through which the groans of Ghosts might strike thy ears,
They would not wound thee, as this Story will.

Hark, hark! a hollow Voice calls out aloud,
Jocasta: Yes, I'll to the Royal Bed,
Where first the Mysteries of our loves were acted,
And double dye it with imperial Crimson;
Tear off this curling hair,
Be gorg'd with Fire, stab every vital part,
And when at last I'm slain, to Crown the horrour,
My poor tormented Ghost shall cleave the ground,
To try if Hell can yet more deeply wound. *(Exit.)*
OEDIPUS: She's gon; and as she went, methought her eyes
Grew larger, while a thousand frantick Spirits
Seething, like rising bubbles, on the brim,
Peep'd from the Watry brink, and glow'd upon me.
I'll seek no more; but hush my Genius up
That throws me on my Fate.——Impossible!
O wretched Man, whose too too busie Thoughts
Ride swifter than the galloping Heav'ns round,
With an eternal hurry of the Soul:
Nay, there's a time when ev'n the rowling year
Seems to stand still, dead calms are in the Ocean,
When not a breath disturbs the drowzy Waves:
But Man, the very Monster of the World,
Is ne're at rest, the Soul for ever wakes.
Come then, since Destiny thus drives us on,
Let's know the bottom. Hæmon, you I sent:
Where is that Phorbas!
HÆMON: Here, my Royal Lord.
OEDIPUS: Speak first, Ægeon, say, is this the Man?
ÆGEON: My Lord, it is: Tho' time has plough'd that face [409]
With many furrows since I saw it first;
Yet I'm too well acquainted with the ground, quite to forget it.
OEDIPUS: Peace; stand back a while.
Come hither Friend; I hear thy name is Phorbas.
Why dost thou turn thy face? I charge thee answer
To what I shall enquire: Wert thou not once
The Servant of King Lajus here in Thebes?
PHORBAS: I was, great Sir, his true and faithful Servant;

Born and bred up in Court, no forreign Slave.
OEDIPUS: What Office hadst thou? what was thy Employment?
PHORBAS: He made me Lord of all his Rural Pleasures;
For much he lov'd 'em: oft I entertain'd
With sporting Swains, o're whom I had command.
OEDIPUS: Where was thy Residence? to what part o'th' Country
Did'st thou most frequently resort?
PHORBAS: To Mount Cithæron and the pleasant Vallies,
Which all about lye shadowing its large feet.
OEDIPUS: Come forth Ægeon. Ha! why starts thou, Phorbas?
Forward, I say, and Face to Face confront him;
Look wistly on him, through him if thou canst,
And tell me, on thy life, say, dost thou know him?
Did'st thou e're see him? converse with him;
Near Mount Cithæron?
PHORBAS: Who, my Lord, this man?
OEDIPUS: This Man, this old, this venerable Man:
Speak, didst thou ever meet him there?
PHORBAS: Where, sacred Sir.
OEDIPUS: Near Mount Cithæron; answer to the purpose:
'Tis a King speaks; and Royal minutes are
Of much more worth than thousand Vulgar years:
Did'st thou e're see this Man near Mount Cithæron.
PHORBAS: Most sure, my Lord, I have seen lines like those
His Visage bears; but know not where nor when.
ÆGEON: Is't possible you should forget your ancient Friend?
There are perhaps
Particulars which may excite your dead remembrance.
Have you forgot I took an Infant from you,
Doom'd to be murder'd in that gloomy Vale?
The Swadling-bands were purple, wrought with Gold,
Have you forgot too how you wept and begg'd
That I should breed him up, and ask no more.
PHORBAS: What e're I begg'd; thou, like a Dotard, speak'st
More than is requisite: and what of this?
Why is it mention'd now? and why, O why
Dost thou betray the secrets of thy Friend?

ÆGEON: Be not too rash. That Infant grew at last
A King: and here the happy Monarch stands.

PHORBAS: Ha! whither would'st thou? O what hast thou utter'd!
For what thou hast said, Death strike thee dumb for ever.

OEDIPUS: Forbear to Curse the innocent; and be
Accurst thy self, thou shifting Traytor, Villain,
Damn'd Hypocrite, equivocating Slave.

PHORBAS: O Heavens! wherein, my Lord, have I offended?

OEDIPUS: Why speak you not according to my charge?
Bring forth the Rack: since mildness cannot win you,
Torments shall force.

PHORBAS: Hold, hold, O dreadful Sir;
You will not Rack an innocent old man.

OEDIPUS: Speak then.

PHORBAS: Alas, what would have me say?

OEDIPUS: Did this old man take from your Arms an Infant?

PHORBAS: He did: And, Oh! I wish to all the Gods,
Phorbas had perish'd in that very moment.

OEDIPUS: Moment! Thou shalt be hours, days, years a dying.
Here, bind his hands; he dallies with my fury:
But I shall find a way——

PHORBAS: My Lord, I said
I gave the Infant to him.

OEDIPUS: Was he thy own, or given thee by another?

PHORBAS: He was not mine; but given me by another.

OEDIPUS: Whence! and from whom? what City? of what House?

PHORBAS: O, Royal Sir, I bow to the ground,
Would I could sink beneath it: by the Gods,
I do Conjure you to inquire no more.

OEDIPUS: Furies and Hell! Hæmon, bring forth the Rack;
Fetch hither Cords, and Knives, and Sulphurous flames:
He shall be bound, and gash'd, his skin flead off,
And burnt alive.

PHORBAS: O spare my age.

OEDIPUS: Rise then, and speak.

PHORBAS: Dread Sir, I will.

OEDIPUS: Who gave that Infant to thee?

PHORBAS: One of King Lajus Family.

OEDIPUS: O, you immortal Gods! But say, who was't?
Which of the Family of Lajus gave it?
A Servant; or one of the Royal-blood? [411]

PHORBAS: O wretched State! I dye, unless I speak;
And, if I speak, most certain death attends me!

OEDIPUS: Thou shalt not dye. Speak then, who was it? speak,
While I have sense to understand the horrour;
For I grow cold.

PHORBAS: The Queen Jocasta told me
It was her Son by Lajus.

OEDIPUS: O you Gods!—But did she give it thee?

PHORBAS: My Lord, she did.

OEDIPUS: Wherefore, for what?——O break not yet, my heart;
Tho' my eyes burst, no matter: wilt thou tell me,
Or must I ask for ever? for what end?
Why gave she thee her Child?

PHORBAS: To murder it.

OEDIPUS: O more than savage! murder her own bowels!
Without a Cause!

PHORBAS: There was a dreadful one,
Which had foretold, that most unhappy Son
Should kill his Father, and enjoy his Mother.

OEDIPUS: But, one thing more,
Jocasta told me thou wert by the Chariot
When the old King was slain: Speak, I conjure thee,
For I shall never ask thee ought again,
What was the number of th' Assassinates?

PHORBAS: The dreadful deed was acted but by one;
And sure that one had much of your resemblance.

OEDIPUS: 'Tis well! I thank you Gods! 'tis wondrous well!
Daggers, and Poyson; O there is no need
For my dispatch: and you, you merciless Pow'rs,
Hoord up your Thunder-stones; keep, keep your Bolts
For Crimes of little note. *(Falls.)*

ADRASTUS: Help, Hæmon, help, and bow him gently forward;
Chafe, chafe his Temples: how the mighty Spirits,

Half strangl'd with the damp his sorrows rais'd,
Struggle for vent: but see, he breathes again,
And vigorous Nature breaks through all opposition.
How fares my Royal Friend?
OEDIPUS: The worse for you.
O barbarous men, and oh the hated light,
Why did you force me back to curse the day;
To curse my friends; to blast with this dark breath
The yet untainted Earth and circling Air?
To raise new Plagues, and call new Vengeance down, [412]
Why did you tempt the Gods, and dare to touch me?
Methinks there's not a hand that grasps this Hell
But should run up like Flax all blazing fire.
Stand from this spot, I wish you as my friends,
And come not near me, lest the gaping Earth
Swallow you too——Lo, I am gone already.

Draws, and claps his Sword to his breast, which Adrastus strikes away with his foot.

ADRASTUS: You shall no more be trusted with your life:
Creon, Alcander, Hæmon, help to hold him.
OEDIPUS: Cruel Adrastus! wilt thou, Hæmon, too?
Are these the Obligations of my Friends,
O worse than worst of my most barbarous Foes!
Dear, dear Adrastus, look with half an Eye
On my unheard-of Woes, and judge thy self,
If it be fit that such a Wretch should live!
O, by these melting Eyes, unus'd to weep,
With all the low submissions of a Slave,
I do conjure thee give my horrours way;
Talk not of life, for that will make me rave:
As well thou may'st advise a tortur'd wretch,
All mangled o're from head to foot with wounds,
And his bones broke, to wait a better day.
ADRASTUS: My Lord, you ask me things impossible;
And I with Justice should be thought your Foe,
To leave you in this Tempest of your Soul.

TIRESIAS: Tho' banish'd Thebes, in Corinth you may Reign;
Th' Infernal Pow'rs themselves exact no more:
Calm then your rage, and once more seek the Gods.
OEDIPUS: I'll have no more to do with Gods, nor Men:
Hence from my Arms, avant. Enjoy thy Mother!
What, violate, with Bestial appetite,
The sacred Veils that wrapt thee yet unborn,
This is not to be born! Hence; off, I say;
For they who lett my Vengeance make themselves
Accomplices in my most horrid guilt.
ADRASTUS: Let it be so; we'll fence Heav'ns fury from you,
And suffer altogether: This perhaps,
When ruine comes, may help to break your fall.
OEDIPUS: O that, as oft I have at Athens seen
The Stage arise, and the big Clouds descend;
So now in very deed I might behold
The pond'rous Earth, and all yon marble Roof [413]
Meet, like the hands of Jove, and crush Mankind:
For all the Elements, and all the Pow'rs
Celestial, nay, Terrestrial and Infernal,
Conspire the rack of out-cast Oedipus,
Fall darkness then, and everlasting night
Shadow the Globe; may the Sun never dawn,
The Silver Moon be blotted from her Orb;
And for an Universal rout of Nature
Through all the inmost Chambers of the Sky,
May there not be a glimpse, one Starry spark,
But Gods meet Gods, and justle in the dark.
That jars may rise, and wrath Divine be hurl'd,
Which may to Atoms shake the solid World. *(Exeunt.)*

ACT V. SCENE I.

Enter Creon, Alcander, Pyracmon.

CREON: Thebes is at length my own; and all my wishes,
Which sure were great as Royalty e're form'd,
Fortune and my auspicious Stars have Crown'd.
O Diadem, thou Center of ambition,
Where all it's different Lines are reconcil'd,
As if thou wert the burning-glass of Glory!
PYRACMON: Might I be Counsellor, I wou'd intreat you
To cool a little, Sir:
Find out Eurydice;
And, with the resolution of a man
Mark'd out for Greatness, give the fatal Choice
Of death or marriage.
ALCANDER: Survey curs'd Oedipus,
As one who, tho' unfortunate, 's belov'd,
Thought innocent, and therefore much lamented
By all the Thebans; you must mark him dead:
Since nothing but his death, not banishment,
Can give assurance to your doubtful Reign.
CREON: Well have you done, to snatch me from the Storm
Of racking Transport, where the little Streams
Of Love, Revenge, and all the under passions,
As waters are by sucking Whirl-pools drawn,
Were quite devour'd in the vast Gulph of Empire: [414]
Therefore Pyracmon, as you boldly urg'd,
Eurydice shall dye, or be my Bride.
Alcander, Summon to their Master's aid
My Menial Servants, and all those whom change
Of State, and hope of the new Monarch's Favour,
Can win to take our part: Away. What now? *(Exit Alcander.)*

Enter Hæmon.

When Hæmon weeps, without the help of Ghosts,
I may foretel there is a fatal Cause.
HÆMON: Is't possible you should be ignorant
Of what has happen'd to the desperate King:
CREON: I know no more, but that he was conducted
Into his Closet, where I saw him fling
His trembling Body on the Royal Bed;
All left him there, at his desire, alone:
But sure no ill, unless he dy'd with grief,
Could happen, for you bore his Sword away.
HÆMON: I did; and, having lock'd the door, I stood;
And through a chink I found, not only heard,
But saw him, when he thought no eye beheld him:
At first, deep sighs heav'd from his woful heart,
Murmurs and groans, that shook the outward Rooms,
And art thou still alive, O wretch! he cry'd?
Then groan'd again, as if his sorrowful Soul
Had crack'd the strings of Life, and burst away.
CREON: I weep, to hear; how then should I have griev'd
Had I beheld this wondrous heap of Sorrow!
But, to the fatal period.
HÆMON: Thrice he struck,
With all his force, his hollow groaning breast,
And thus, with out-cries, to himself complain'd.
But thou canst weep then, and thou think'st 'tis well,
These bubbles of the shallowest emptiest sorrow,
Which Children vent for toys, and Women rain
For any Trifle their fond hearts are set on;
Yet these thou think'st are ample satisfaction
For bloodiest Murder, and for burning Lust:
No, Parricide; if thou must weep, weep bloud;
Weep Eyes, instead of Tears: O, by the Gods,
'Tis greatly thought, he cry'd, and fits my woes.
Which said, he smil'd revengefully, and leapt
Upon the floor; thence gazing at the Skies,

His Eye-balls fiery Red, and glowing vengeance;
Gods, I accuse you not, tho' I no more
Will view your Heav'n, till with more durable glasses,
The mighty Souls immortal Perspectives,
I find your dazling Beings: Take, he cry'd,
Take, Eyes, your last, your fatal farewel-view.
When with a groan, that seem'd the call of Death,
With horrid force lifting his impious hands,
He snatch'd, he tore, from forth their bloody Orbs,
The Balls of sight, and dash'd 'em on the ground.
CREON: A Master-piece of horrour; new and dreadful!
HÆMON: I ran to succour him; but, oh! too late;
For he had pluck'd the remnant strings away.
What then remains, but that I find Tiresias,
Who, with his Wisdom, may allay those Furies
That haunt his gloomy Soul? *(Exit.)*
CREON: Heav'n will reward
Thy care; most honest, faithful, foolish Hæmon!
But see, Alcander enters, well attended.

Enter Alcander, attended.

I see thou hast been diligent.
ALCANDER: Nothing these
For Number, to the Crowds that soon will follow;
Be resolute
And call your utmost Fury to revenge.
CREON: Ha! thou hast given
Th' Alarm to Cruelty; and never may
These eyes be clos'd, till they behold Adrastus
Stretch'd at the feet of false Eurydice.
But see, they're here! retire a while, and mark.

Enter Adrastus, Eurydice, attended.

ADRASTUS: Alas, Eurydice, what fond rash man,
What inconsiderate and ambitious Fool,
That shall hereafter read the Fate of Oedipus.
Will dare, with his frail hand, to grasp a Scepter?

EURYDICE: 'Tis true, a Crown seems dreadful, and I wish
That you and I, more lowly plac'd, might pass
Our softer hours in humble Cells away:
Not but that I love you to that Infinite height,
I could (O wondrous proof of fiercest Love!)
Be greatly wretched in a Court with you. [416]
ADRASTUS: Take then this most lov'd innocence away;
Fly from Tumultuous Thebes,
From blood and Murder,
Fly from the Author of all Villanies,
Rapes, Death, and Treason, from that Fury Creon:
Vouchsafe that I, o're-joy'd, may bear you hence,
And at your Feet present the Crown of Argos.

Creon and Attendants come up to him.

CREON: I have o're-heard thy black design, Adrastus.
And therefore, as a Traytor to this State,
Death ought to be thy Lot: let it suffice
That Thebes surveys thee as a Prince; abuse not
Her proffer'd mercy, but retire betimes,
Lest she repent and hasten on thy Doom.
ADRASTUS: Think not, most abject,
Most abhorr'd of Men,
Adrastus will vouchsafe to answer thee;
Thebans, to you I justifie my Love:
I have address'd my Prayers to this fair Princess;
But, if I ever meant a violence,
Or thought to Ravish, as that Traytor did,
What humblest Adorations could not win;
Brand me, you Gods, blot me with foul dishonour,
And let men Curse me by the name of Creon.
EURYDICE: Hear me, O Thebans, if you dread the Wrath
Of her whom Fate ordain'd to be your Queen,
Hear me, and dare not, as you prize your lives,
To take the part of that Rebellious Traytor.
By the Decree of Royal Oedipus,
By Queen Jocasta's order, by what's more,

My own dear Vows of everlasting Love,
I here resign to Prince Adrastus Arms
All that the World can make me Mistress of.

CREON: O perjur'd Woman!
Draw all; and when I give the word, fall on.
Traytor, resign the Princess, or this moment
Expect, with all those most unfortunate wretches,
Upon this spot straight to be hewn in pieces.

ADRASTUS: No, Villain, no;
With twice those odds of men,
I doubt not in this Cause
To vanquish thee.
Captain, remember to your care I give [417]
My Love; ten thousand thousand times more dear
Than Life, or Liberty.

CREON: Fall on, Alcander.
Pyracmon, you and I must wheel about
For nobler Game, the Princess.

ADRASTUS: Ah, Traytor, dost thou shun me?
Follow, follow
My brave Companions; see, the Cowards fly. *(Exit fighting: Creon's Party beaten off by Adrastus.)*

Enter Oedipus.

OEDIPUS: O, 'tis too little this, thy loss of Sight,
What has it done? I shall be gaz'd at now
The more; be pointed at, There goes the Monster!
Nor have I hid my horrours from my self;
For tho' corporeal light be lost for ever
The bright reflecting Soul, through glaring Opticks,
Presents in larger size her black Ideas,
Doubling the bloody prospect of my Crimes:
Holds Fancy down, and makes her act again,
With Wife, and Mother, Tortures, Hell, and Furies.
Ha! now the baleful off-spring's brought to light!
In horrid form they ranck themselves before me;
What shall I call this Medley of Creation?

Here one, with all th' obedience of a Son,
Borrowing Jocasta's look, kneels at my Feet,
And calls me Father; there a sturdy Boy
Resembling Lajus just as when I kill'd him,
Bears up, and with his cold hand grasping mine,
Cries out, How fares my Brother Oedipus?
What, Sons and Brothers! Sisters and Daughters too!
Fly all, begon, fly from my whirling brain;
Hence, Incest, Murder; hence, you ghastly figures!
O Gods! Gods, answer; is there any mean?
Let me go mad, or dye

Enter Jocasta.

JOCASTA: Where, where is this most wretched of mankind,
This stately Image of Imperial Sorrow,
Whose story told, whose very name but mention'd,
Would cool the rage of Feavers, and unlock
The hand of Lust from the pale Virgin's hair,
And throw the Ravisher before her feet? [418]
OEDIPUS: By all my fears, I think Jocasta's Voice!
Hence; fly, begon: O thou far worse than worst
Of damning Charmers! O abhorr'd loath'd Creature!
Fly, by the Gods, or by the Fiends, I charge thee,
Far as the East, West, North, or South of Heav'n;
But think not thou shalt ever enter there:
The golden Gates are barr'd with Adamant,
'Gainst thee, and me; and the Celestial Guards,
Still as we rise, will dash our Spirits down.
JOCASTA: O wretched Pair! O greatly wretched we!
Two Worlds of woe!
OEDIPUS: Art thou not gone then? ha!
How dar'st thou stand the Fury of the Gods?
Or com'st thou in the Grave to reap new pleasures?
JOCASTA: Talk on; till thou mak'st mad my rowling brain;
Groan still more Death; and may those dismal sources
Still bubble on, and pour forth blood and tears.
Methinks at such a meeting, Heav'n stands still;

The Sea nor Ebbs, nor Flows; this Mole-hill Earth
Is heav'd no more; the busie Emmets cease;
Yet hear me on——

OEDIPUS: Speak then, and blast my Soul.

JOCASTA: O, my lov'd Lord, tho' I resolve a Ruine
To match my Crimes; by all my miseries,
'Tis horrour, worse than thousand thousand deaths,
To send me hence without a kind Farewel.

OEDIPUS: Gods, how she shakes me! stay thee, O Jocasta,
Speak something e're thou goest for ever from me.

JOCASTA: 'Tis Woman's weakness, that I would be pity'd;
Pardon me then, O greatest, tho' most wretched,
Of all thy Kind: my Soul is on the brink,
And sees the boiling Furnace just beneath:
Do not thou push me off, and I will go
With such a willingness, as if that Heav'n
With all its glories glow'd for my reception.

OEDIPUS: O, in my heart, I feel the pangs of Nature;
It works with kindness o're: Give, give me way;
I feel a melting here, a tenderness,
Too mighty for the anger of the Gods!
Direct me to thy knees, yet oh forbear:
Lest the dead Embers should revive,
Stand off——and at just distance
Let me groan my horrours——here [419]
On the Earth, here blow my utmost Gale;
Here sob my Sorrows, till I burst with sighing:
Here gasp and Languish out my wounded Soul.

JOCASTA: In spight of all those Crimes the cruel Gods
Can charge me with, I know my Innocence;
Know yours: 'tis Fate alone that makes us wretched,
For you are still my Husband.

OEDIPUS: Swear I am,
And I'll believe thee; steal into thy Arms,
Renew endearments, think 'em no pollutions,
But chaste as Spirits joys: gently I'll come,
Thus weeping blind, like dewy Night, upon thee,

And fold thee softly in my Arms to slumber.

The Ghost of Lajus ascends by degrees, pointing at Jocasta.

JOCASTA: Begon, my Lord! alas, what are we doing?
Fly from my Arms! Whirl-winds, Seas, Continents,
And Worlds, divide us! O thrice happy thou,
Who hast no use of eyes; for here's a sight
Would turn the melting face of Mercy's self
To a wild Fury.
OEDIPUS: Ha! what seest thou there?
JOCASTA: The Spirit of my Husband! O the Gods!
How wan he looks!
OEDIPUS: Thou rav'st; thy Husband's here.
JOCASTA: There, there he Mounts,
In circling fire, amongst the blushing Clouds!
And see, he waves Jocasta from the World!
GHOST: Jocasta! Oedipus! *(Vanish with thunder.)*
OEDIPUS: What would'st thou have?
Thou know'st I cannot come to thee, detain'd
In darkness here, and kept from means of death.
I've heard a Spirit's force is wonderful;
At whose approach, when starting from his Dungeon,
The Earth does shake, and the old Ocean groans,
Rocks are remov'd, and Towers are Thundred down:
And walls of Brass, and Gates of Adamant,
Are passable as Air, and fleet like Winds.
JOCASTA: Was that a Raven's Croak; or my Sons Voice?
No matter which; I'll to the Grave, and hide me:
Earth open, or I'll tear thy bowels up.
Hark! he goes on, and blabs the deed of Incest.
OEDIPUS: Strike then, Imperial Ghost; dash all at once
This House of Clay into a thousand pieces:
That my poor lingring Soul may take her flight
To your immortal Dwellings.
JOCASTA: Haste thee then,
Or I shall be before thee: See, thou canst not see;
Then I will tell thee that my wings are on:

I'll mount, I'll fly, and with a port Divine
Glide all along the gaudy Milky soil,
To find my Lajus out; ask every God
In his bright Palace, if he knows my Lajus,
My murder'd Lajus!

OEDIPUS: Ha! how's this, Jocasta?
Nay, if thy brain be sick, then thou art happy.

JOCASTA: Ha! will you not? shall I not find him out?
Will you not show him? are my tears despis'd?
Why, then I'll Thunder, yes, I will be mad,
And fright you with my cries: yes, cruel Gods,
Tho' Vultures, Eagles, Dragons tear my heart,
I'll snatch Celestial flames, fire all your dwellings,
Melt down your golden Roofs, and make your doors
Of Chrystal flye from off their Diamond Hinges;
Drive you all out from your Ambrosial Hives,
To swarm like Bees about the field of Heav'n:
This will I do unless you shew me Lajus,
My dear, my murder'd Lord. O Lajus! Lajus! Lajus! *(Exit Jocasta.)*

OEDIPUS: Excellent grief! why, this is as it should be!
No Mourning can be suitable to Crimes
Like ours, but what Death makes, or Madness forms.
I cou'd have wish'd methought for sight again,
To mark the gallantry of her distraction:
Her blazing Eyes darting the wandring Stars,
T'have seen her mouth the Heav'ns, and mate the Gods,
While with her Thundring Voice she menac'd high,
And every Accent twang'd with smarting sorrow;
But what's all this to thee? thou, Coward, yet
Art living, canst not, wilt not find the Road
To the great Palace of magnificent Death;
Tho' thousand ways lead to his thousand doors,
Which day and night are still unbarr'd for all.

Clashing of Swords: Drums and Trumpets without.

Hark! 'tis the noise of clashing Swords! the sound
Comes near: O, that a Battel would come o're me!

If I but grasp a Sword, or wrest a Dagger,
I'll make a ruine with the first that falls. [421]

Enter Hæmon, with Guards. Tiresias, led by his Daughter Manto.

HÆMON: Seize him, and bear him to the Western-Tow'r.
Pardon me, sacred Sir; I am inform'd
That Creon has designs upon your life:
Forgive me then, if, to preserve you from him,
I order your Confinement.
OEDIPUS: Slaves, unhand me.
I think thou hast a Sword: 'twas the wrong side.
Yet, cruel Hæmon, think not I will live;
He that could tear his eyes out, sure can find
Some desperate way to stifle this curst breath:
Or if I starve! but that's a lingring Fate;
Or if I leave my brains upon the wall!
The Aiery Soul can easily o're-shoot
Those bounds with which thou strive'st to pale her in:
Yes, I will perish in despite of thee;
And, by the rage that stirs me, if I meet thee
In the other World, I'll curse thee for this usage. *(Exit.)*
HÆMON: Tiresias, after him; and, with your Counsel
Advise him humbly; Charm, if possible,
These feuds within: while I without extinguish,
Or perish in th' Attempt, the furious Creon;
That Brand which sets our City in a Flame.
TIRESIAS: Heav'n prosper your intent, and give a period
To all your Plagues: what old Tiresias can
Shall straight be done. Lead, Manto to the Tow'r. *(Exit Tiresias, Manto.)*
HÆMON: Follow me all, and help to part this Fray, *(Trumpets again.)*
Or fall together in the bloody broil. *(Exit.)*

Enter Creon with Eurydice, Pyracmon and his party giving ground to Adrastus.

CREON: Hold, hold your Arms, Adrastus Prince of Argos,
Hear; and behold; Eurydice is my Prisoner.

ADRASTUS: What would'st thou, Hell-hound?
CREON: See this brandish'd Dagger:
Forgo th' advantage which thy Arms have won,
Or, by the blood which trembles through the heart
Of her whom more than life I know thou lov'st,
I'll bury to the haft, in her fair breast,
This Instrument of my Revenge. [422]
ADRASTUS: Stay thee, damn'd wretch; hold, stop thy bloody hand.
CREON: Give order then, that on this instant, now,
This moment, all thy Souldiers straight disband.
ADRASTUS: Away, my Friends, since Fate has so allotted;
Begon, and leave me to the Villain's mercy.
EURYDICE: Ah, my Adrastus! call 'em, call 'em back!
Stand there; come back! O, cruel barbarous Men!
Could you then leave your Lord, your Prince, your King,
After so bravely having fought his Cause,
To perish by the hand of this base Villain?
Why rather rush you not at once together
All to his ruine? drag him through the Streets,
Hang his contagious Quarters on the Gates;
Nor let my death affright you.
CREON: Dye first thy self then.
ADRASTUS: O, I charge thee hold.
Hence, from my presence all: he's not my Friend
That disobeys: See, art thou now appeas'd? *(Exit Attendants.)*
Or is there ought else yet remains to do
That can atone thee? slake thy thirst of blood
With mine: but save, O save that innocent wretch.
CREON: Forego thy Sword, and yield thy self my Prisoner.
EURYDICE: Yet while there's any dawn of hope to save
Thy precious life, my dear Adrastus,
Whate're thou dost, deliver not thy Sword;
With that thou may'st get off, tho' odds oppose thee:
For me, O, fear not; no, he dares not touch me;
His horrid love will spare me. Keep thy Sword;
Lest I be ravish'd after thou art slain.

ADRASTUS: Instruct me, Gods, what shall Adrastus do?
CREON: Do what thou wilt, when she is dead: My Souldiers
With numbers will o're-pow'r thee. I'st thy wish
Eurydice should fall before thee?
ADRASTUS: Traytor, no:
Better that thou and I, and all mankind
Should be no more.
CREON: Then cast thy Sword away,
And yield thee to my mercy, or I strike.
ADRASTUS: Hold thy rais'd Arm; give me a moment's pause.
My Father, when he blest me, gave me this;
My Son, said he, let this be thy last refuge;
If thou forego'st it, misery attends thee:
Yet Love now charms it from me; which in all [423]
The hazards of my life I never lost.
'Tis thine, my faithful Sword, my only trust;
Tho' my heart tells me that the gift is Fatal.
CREON: Fatal! yes, foolish Love-sick Prince, it shall:
Thy arrogance, thy scorn,
My wounds remembrance,
Turn all at once the Fatal point upon thee.
Pyracmon, to the Palace, dispatch
The King: hang Hæmon up, for he is Loyal,
And will oppose me: Come, Sir, are you ready?
ADRASTUS: Yes, Villain, for what-ever thou canst dare.
EURYDICE: Hold Creon, or through me, through me you wound.
ADRASTUS: Off, Madam, or we perish both; behold
I'm not unarm'd, my ponyard's in my hand:
Therefore away.
EURYDICE: I'll guard your life with mine.
CREON: Dye both then; there is now no time for dallying *(Kills Eurydice.)*
EURYDICE: Ah, Prince, farewel; farewel, my dear Adrastus. *(Dyes.)*
ADRASTUS: Unheard of Monster! eldest-born of Hell!
Down, to thy Primitive Flames. *(Stabs Creon.)*
CREON: Help, Souldiers, help:

Revenge me.
ADRASTUS: More; yet more: a thousand wounds!
I'll stamp thee still, thus, to the gaping Furies. *(Adrastus falls, kill'd by the Souldiers.)*

Enter Hæmon, Guards, with Alcander and Pyracmon bound: the Assassins are driven off.

O Hæmon, I am slain; nor need I name
The inhumane Author of all Villanies;
There he lyes gasping.
CREON: If I must plunge in Flames,
Burn first my Arm; base instrument, unfit
To act the dictates of my daring mind:
Burn, burn for ever, O weak Substitute
Of that the God, Ambition. *(Dyes.)*
ADRASTUS: She's gone; O deadly Marks-man, in the heart!
Yet in the pangs of death she grasps my hand:
Her lips too tremble, as if she would speak
Her last farewel. O, Oedipus, thy fall
Is great; and nobly now thou goest attended!
They talk of Heroes, and Celestial Beauties, [424]
And wondrous pleasures in the other World;
Let me but find her there, I ask no more. *(Dyes.)*

Enter a Captain to Hæmon: with Tiresias and Manto.

CAPTAIN: O, Sir, the Queen Jocasta, swift and wild,
As a robb'd Tygress bounding o're the Woods,
Has acted Murders that amaze mankind:
In twisted Gold I saw her Daughters hang
On the Bed Royal; and her little Sons
Stabb'd through the breasts upon the bloody Pillows.
HÆMON: Relentless Heav'ns! is then the Fate of Lajus
Never to be Aton'd? How sacred ought
Kings lives be held, when but the death of one
Demands an Empire's blood for Expiation?
But see! the furious mad Jocasta's here.

Scene Draws, and discovers Jocasta held by her Women, and stabb'd in many places of her bosom, her hair dishevel'd, her Children slain upon the Bed.

Was ever such a sight of so much horrour,
And pity, brought to view!
JOCASTA: Ah, cruel Women!
Will you not let me take my last farewel
Of those dear Babes? O let me run and seal
My melting Soul upon their bubling wounds!
I'll Print upon their Coral mouths such Kisses,
As shall recall their wandring Spirits home.
Let me go, let me go, or I will tear you piece-meal.
Help, Hæmon, help:
Help, Oedipus; help, Gods; Jocasta Dyes.

Enter Oedipus above.

OEDIPUS: I've found a Window, and I thank the Gods,
'Tis quite unbarr'd: sure, by the distant noise,
The height will fit my Fatal purpose well.
JOCASTA: What hoa, my Oedipus! see, where he stands!
His groping Ghost is lodg'd upon a Tow'r,
Nor can it find the Road: Mount, mount my soul;
I'll wrap thy shivering Spirit in Lambent Flames! and so we'll sail.
But see! we're landed on the happy Coast;
And all the Golden Strands are cover'd o're
With glorious Gods, that come to try our Cause:
Jove, Jove, whose Majesty now sinks me down,
He who himself burns in unlawful fires,
Shall judge, and shall acquit us. O, 'tis done;
'Tis fixt by Fate, upon Record Divine:
And Oedipus shall now be ever mine. *(Dyes.)*
OEDIPUS: Speak, Hæmon; what has Fate been doing there?
What dreadful deed has mad Jocasta done?
HÆMON: The Queen her self, and all your wretched Off-spring,

Are by her Fury slain.
OEDIPUS: By all my woes,
She has out-done me, in Revenge and Murder;
And I should envy her the sad applause:
But, Oh! my Children! Oh, what have they done?
This was not like the mercy of the Heav'ns,
To set her madness on such Cruelty:
This stirs me more than all my sufferings,
And with my last breath I must call you Tyrants.
HÆMON: What mean you, Sir?
OEDIPUS: Jocasta! lo, I come.
O, Lajus, Labdacus, and all your Spirits
Of the Cadmean Race, prepare to meet me,
All weeping rang'd along the gloomy Shore:
Extend your Arms t'embrace me; for I come;
May all the Gods too from their Battlements
Behold and wonder at a Mortals daring;
And, when I knock the Goal of dreadful death,
Shout and applaud me with a clap of Thunder:
Once more, thus wing'd by horrid Fate, I come
Swift as a falling Meteor; lo, I flye,
And thus go downwards, to the darker Sky.

Thunder. He flings himself from the Window: The Thebans gather about his Body.

HÆMON: O Prophet, Oedipus is now no more!
O curs'd Effect of the most deep despair!
TIRESIAS: Cease your Complaints, and bear his body hence;
The dreadful sight will daunt the drooping Thebans,
Whom Heav'n decrees to raise with Peace and Glory:
Yet, by these terrible Examples warn'd,
The sacred Fury thus Alarms the World.
Let none, tho' ne're so Vertuous, great and High,
Be judg'd entirely blest before they Dye.

EPILOGUE

What Sophocles could undertake alone,
Our Poets found a Work for more than one;
And therefore Two lay tugging at the piece,
With all their force, to draw the pondrous Mass from Greece.
A weight that bent ev'n Seneca's strong Muse,
And which Corneille's Shoulders did refuse.
So hard it is the Athenian Harp to string!
So much two Consuls yield to one just King.
Terrour and pity this whole Poem sway;
The mightiest Machines that can mount a Play;
How heavy will those Vulgar Souls be found,
Whom two such Engines cannot move from ground?
When Greece and Rome have smil'd upon this Birth,
You can but Damn for one poor spot of Earth;
And when your Children find your judgment such,
They'll scorn their Sires, and wish themselves born Dutch;
Each haughty Poet will infer with ease,
How much his Wit must under-write to please.
As some strong Churle would brandishing advance
The monumental Sword that conquer'd France;
So you by judging this, your judgments teach
Thus far you like, that is, thus far you reach.
Since then the Vote of full two Thousand years
Has Crown'd this Plot, and all the Dead are theirs.
Think it a Debt you pay, not Alms you give,
And in your own defence, let this Play live.
Think 'em not vain, when Sophocles is shown,
To praise his worth, they humbly doubt their own.
Yet as weak States each others pow'r assure,
Weak Poets by Conjunction are secure.

Their Treat is what your Pallats relish most,
Charm! Song! and Show! a Murder and a Ghost!
We know not what you can desire or hope,
To please you more, but burning of a Pope. [427]

FINIS

Oedipus and the Sphinx

A Tragedy in Three Acts

Hugo von Hofmannsthal

Translated by Gertrude Schoenbohm

Hugo von Hofmannsthal (1874–1929) reinterpreted several of the great tragedies of Greek antiquity. Being acquainted with varied interpretations, he felt that each age and each individual must reckon with the past in order to achieve a valid self-comprehension and self-expression. Before him was the monumental task of synthesizing the vast dimensions of the ancient and modern worlds, the Orient and the Occident, Christianity and paganism, pre-existence and existence, being and becoming. This could—according to him—be best expressed in mythological works such as his Greek dramas. His dramas *Alkestis, Elektra, Oedipus und die Sphinx, Ariadne auf Naxos* and *Die ägyptische Helena* reflect the basic theme: How man can overcome the dichotomy of life and death, isolation and unification.

Few poets were as equipped for this task as Hofmannsthal with his rich Jewish-Silesian, German-Italian, aristocratic background. After legal training he turned to romance philology and held the position of army official and diplomatic representative. Hofmannsthal was editor of literary works and writer of literary and cultural criticism, co-founder of lasting cultural institutions such as the Salzburg Festival and the Austrian Antiquarian Library. In his lifelong part-

From Hugo von Hofmannsthal, "Oedipus und die Sphinx," *Dramen II.* (Frankfurt am Main: S. Fischer Verlag, 1954). Translation by Gertrude Schoenbohm.

nership with Richard Strauss he created libretti of considerable literary value. Together with Max Reinhardt and Richard Strauss he sought to establish a living stage.

As a lyricist, dramatist, essayist, and critic he was equally at home in the ancient culture, the Middle Ages, the Renaissance, and the Baroque. Because of his manifold spiritual heritage, Hofmannsthal was an esoteric poet with a universal vision of man. His refined, melodic lyrical dramas use the impressionistic, neo-romantic art of symbols, sounds, and colors. He admired perfected and disciplined style.

Hofmannsthal's attempt to transform and reinterpret ancient tragedy took place after what critics call the crisis in his creativity, documented in the famed "Chandos Letter."[1] This letter, written before his *Oedipus and the Sphinx,* shows that Hofmannsthal considered his poetic mission to be a serious effort toward reconciling our "contradictory existence." Like the criticism of many of Hofmannsthal's other literary works, that presented here shows the possibility of divergent interpretations of *Oedipus and the Sphinx*. Renewed confrontations with this drama reveal new and fascinating depths. Thus we realize once again that "Man is a manifold person." However, in trying to understand his work we may well keep in mind the remark by M. Hamburger in his work on Hofmannsthal: "It's yourself you should scrutinize to see whether you're center or periphery."

In this translation of *Oedipus und die Sphinx,* it was difficult, if not impossible, to reproduce the magic power of Hofmannsthal's lyricism. It was too great as well as too unnecessary a task for the purpose of this study to retain the iambic pentameter of the original. The translator has tried to remain faithful to the meaning and to do justice to the visionary quality of his choice of words.

[1] Hugo von Hofmannsthal, *Gesammelte Werke in Einzelausgaben,* edited by Herbert Steiner, Prosa IV, 1955, p. 412. A translation of the "Chandos Letter" can be found in Mary Hottinger and Tania and James Stern, *Hofmannsthal, Selected Prose* (New York: Pantheon Books, 1952).

The surge of the heart would never rise in such splendor and become spirit did not the reefs of fate stand mutely in its course. HÖLDERLIN

DRAMATIS PERSONAE

OEDIPUS
PHOENIX, ERMOS, ELATOS — his servants from Corinth
The ancestors' voices

LAIOS
The herald
The chariot driver
The first servant
The second servant
The third servant

JOCASTA, the queen
CREON, her brother
ANTIOPE, the queen, Laios' mother
TEIRESIAS
Creon's swordbearer
The seer
A man from the city
A child
A dying man
Messengers and couriers in the service of Creon
Maids of the palace
The people

ACT I

A three-way crossing in the land of Phocis. A wooded area in the mountains. Rocks and shrubbery. Plane trees and sycamores. A road, rising from the right, leads across the stage, descending on the left. In the center, a ravine plunges steeply down to the road.

Phoenix, Ermos, Elatos; others are standing on the left behind trees and bushes. Farther back a chariot and horses, barely visible.

VOICE:

from above

He is coming through the ravine! He is near, men!

ERMOS:

Let us bow down.

ELATOS:

Let us cover
our faces with dust of the road.

ERMOS:

His new-born anger is terrifying
like thunder and lightning. Phoenix—

Draws him closer.

PHOENIX:

It is not his anger
that crushes my weary heart
but something which I cannot name.
You gods, turn your wrath away—not from me—
but from the head of the one who approaches,
turn away, you gods!

Silence.

Oedipus, a staff in his hand, pale, dishevelled, like a fugitive, comes down the ravine as if he wanted to turn right. [273]

The three bow deeply. Oedipus does not recognize them and gropes past them as if sleepwalking.

PHOENIX:
jumps up, fearfully
Bar his way, fall at his feet!
Oedipus jumps back with a dull cry, shields his back and raises his heavy cane.

PHOENIX:
kneels before him
Would you raise your arm against yourself, my Lord,
and strike what is yours?

OEDIPUS:
Faithless servants, is this the way
from Delphi to Corinth?

PHOENIX:
This is one way from Delphi to Corinth.

OEDIPUS:
A roundabout way! And which road home
did my messenger
command you to choose?

PHOENIX:
The one that runs straight from Delphi
down to the sea like the string of a bow.

OEDIPUS:
Then why are you
here at this crossing?

PHOENIX:
We sought you
with anguished hearts, my Lord, and counting neither
hills nor valleys, regarding night [274]
as day and starlight as sunlight, we searched
until we found you here.

OEDIPUS:
Servants are wicked when they do
what is not commanded.

PHOENIX:
Oedipus,

I am the oldest and must defend them
when you are angry; I must open my mouth
and speak: My Lord, what you did to us
when we camped at Delphi you had never done before.
We seemed to feel an unfamiliar touch on the reins;
it was an unknown fist that
pressed a yoke upon us. For you always
ruled our actions with your heart—
not with lash and chain—yet the moment
we found shelter in this holy city
where the Oracle dwells, your words
grew harsh, your speech flared
like fire in the wind, and where it had been easy to obey,
it grew difficult.
On the ninth day you did not come back to us
at the inn. We waited for you in vain
at night, and the bed we prepared remained empty.

OEDIPUS:

My messenger came.

PHOENIX:
bows

He came. And we bowed when he said:
"I speak for Oedipus, my Lord,
and your Lord." But the words which came from his mouth
were too heavy for our hearts and too ominous. He said that we,
your servants, should leave you,
we your faithful, should travel
to Corinth alone. Then we said
to each other: "This cannot be; we cannot
believe that these were his words."

OEDIPUS:

The boy was authorized
by the ring he carried.

PHOENIX:
bows

And so we asked:
"Why do you carry this princely ring,

which our master never removed from his finger?"
He replied: "Take it with you and guard it
well, until you reach Polybos, the King;
give him the ring and say:
'Oedipus, your son, sends this to you and greets you
and greets his mother, our Queen,
and greets Corinth, our city; not you, O King, his father,
nor your Queen, his mother, nor your city, his home,
these three, will he ever see again.
This ring is the sign that your son Oedipus
will never return.' "

OEDIPUS:

My faithful messenger
spoke well. [276]

PHOENIX:

painfully

No!

OEDIPUS:

I, Oedipus, your Master,
command you, Phoenix,
you Elatos, you Ermos, and those
servants who are camped there with the horses and the chariot,
to rise quickly, harness the horses
to the chariot and fly like an arrow from a bow
straight down the road
to Corinth! And even if there is no other road
than the one gorged by a torrent,
yet go forward! Through the river bed! And
though men's limbs are broken and horses crippled—
no matter! Who told you to loiter day and night
in a foreign land? Who told you to stalk your Lord
like an animal and head him off in a ravine at sundown?
Now go your way!
Protect the ring and remember
my message! Begone!

PHOENIX:

My Lord!

OEDIPUS:

Begone, old man!

Phoenix grasps his robe

Let go, old man!

PHOENIX:

Master!

OEDIPUS:

Let go!

PHOENIX:

No, stay!

OEDIPUS:

pushes him away

Obey, old man!

PHOENIX:

My Lord, smash my old head
to pieces on this rock! Look at me!
If you can lay a crushing burden
upon my heart without wincing,
and if you gag my mouth
so that my sighs cannot putrify
the air around you, then
I am no more to you than an animal.

OEDIPUS:

moves his lips almost without a sound

I must.

PHOENIX:

kneeling

He who can do this to me,
can command me, an old man, to kneel
before another old man, a slave before his king,
and bring such news that
would cause death and give death as a reward, that man
dare not deny me a cloak
as payment; I demand a cloak of stones from you.
Seize a heavy stone in your right hand
and one in your left; hurl them at me;
and heap stones around me; then I shall have

a grave for my body and need not be buried
by anyone in Corinth.

OEDIPUS:
almost inaudibly
I must.

PHOENIX:
rising
O, my child—
my child—you do not know what it means to be old.

OEDIPUS:
with a gesture of refusal
My father
is strong; he still has many years before him.

PHOENIX:
Yes, if the gods are good, he will stand
like a mighty tree! My child, would you
be the merciless storm that
ravages his crown?

OEDIPUS:
Merciless—
it destroys us.

PHOENIX:
My Lord,
confine the cruelty of youth to battle
against the enemy; do not turn it against those who are yours.
If your heart were not so young, you could never have
conceived this; this could never
have come from your lips: how can the heart
of a father and mother endure such cruelty
without breaking?

OEDIPUS:
Phoenix! Phoenix! [279]

PHOENIX:
As a boy you often cried out like this in your
sleep. I would wake you quickly
from your dream.

OEDIPUS:

You can no longer wake me,
for now everything within me dreams. But all of you
have recognized me! You all called me by name . . .
Do I look as I did before?

PHOENIX:

My Lord,
you were only away from us for three days.

OEDIPUS:

fearfully

Three days?
three days, Phoenix?

PHOENIX:

My Lord, only three!

OEDIPUS:

looks at him strangely

Who are you that you speak to me
with such familiarity?

PHOENIX:

Who am I? Who am I to you?

OEDIPUS:

I can hardly remember.

PHOENIX:

Eternal gods!
He cannot remember who I am!

OEDIPUS:

hesitating

But yet—

PHOENIX:

But yet? Who first
lifted you into the chariot? Taught you
to lace the sandals on your feet
and comb your hair? Who hung your robe
night after night on the high nail,
and then bolted
your chamber door—do you know him no more?

OEDIPUS:

The gods infuse the blood
with a strange sap: for if this child's play has no meaning,
I am who was yesterday. Do you understand?
harshly
Go! Seek the boy you loved.

PHOENIX:

He stands before me.

OEDIPUS:

Hold your tongue.
The smell of Corinth that pours from your mouth disgusts me.
Yet, if you must serve, go and bring me
something to drink.
Phoenix goes to the left. Oedipus stands as if daydreaming.
Phoenix comes with the cup.

OEDIPUS:

looks toward the left. In a changed tone
O what are they doing over there?
There! With the horse—near the water.
The white horse is limping. [281]

PHOENIX:

nods
Nyssia, the mare.

OEDIPUS:

wants to rush toward it
Nyssia, my beautiful white mare!
Stops suddenly. Angrily knocks the cup from Phoenix's hand.
Does this please you?
What does that nag matter to me! See to it that
you get home. My road leads elsewhere.
Turns to go away.

PHOENIX:

Where does your road lead?

OEDIPUS:

Why do you care?
I go alone.
Goes toward the right.

PHOENIX:
follows
I will not leave you!
OEDIPUS:
O, go away!
Pushes him away.

PHOENIX:
in his way
This hair
is your father's hair, a mother lifts these hands
toward you. Will you
still push me away? [282]

OEDIPUS:
Clear the way!
PHOENIX:
There goes
the child who would kick his father and
cast stones upon his mother's heart.
Turn from him, you creatures of the forest
who dwell in caves and high upon cliffs,
hide yourselves lest the sight of
him turn you to stone.
Oedipus walks on unconcerned, slowly, with halting steps. He is already at the right between the trees. Phoenix, heartbroken, turns rigidly and moves away with an imploring gesture.

OEDIPUS:
turns as if coming out of a deep dream
O Phoenix!
Phoenix on the left; turns, stands trembling.

OEDIPUS:
gasping for breath, moves toward him, painfully
Help me, Phoenix!
He stumbles.
Phoenix catches him, kisses his hands, and gently lays him down. Oedipus tries to get up.

PHOENIX:
hovers close to him
Now you are yourself again!

OEDIPUS:

Do not search for him who was. Can't you understand,
finally understand, what my mouth is straining to say?
Go then, and leave me alone.
Understand just this! He spoke to me— [283]
through his priestess the god
spoke to me!

Exhausted from his tremendous effort to confess

I am thirsty. Bring me water.

PHOENIX:

wants to leave to fetch water. Reflects

And when I return, you will be gone.
I shall not leave. I will hold you back.

OEDIPUS:

weakly

I am thirsty.

I will not get up. I will continue
to talk with you.

Phoenix takes the cup, goes, looks around suspiciously.

OEDIPUS:

straining himself

I am talking to you. I am here.

Phoenix returns, hands him the cup.

OEDIPUS:

grabs the cup greedily, drinks

I will never again drink wine. The wine was black
and heavy as blood. We both drank, he and I,
each one to his death.

PHOENIX:

You speak of Lykos?

OEDIPUS:

That was the beginning.
I struck him with my hands; they fell upon him
like hammers. When they carried him away
everyone was stained with his blood.
Why were his lips chosen to speak?
The boy was not evil—but he was the instrument of evil;
hidden in the wine, it glided through his steeped senses

and puckered his lips disgustingly. . . .
How did it happen?

PHOENIX:

Are you asking?

OEDIPUS:

violently

I have forgotten.

PHOENIX:

My Lord!

OEDIPUS:

takes hold of him

I want you to repeat it.

PHOENIX:

Spare me!
At first he babbled on but no one
listened to him in the wine-blurred haze.

OEDIPUS:

Listened to what?
I want to know.

PHOENIX:

That many men
do not know whose blood is in their veins. . . .
Do I make you angry?

OEDIPUS:

Go on!

PHOENIX:

My Lord, will you be angry?

OEDIPUS:

I beg you. Go on! I have forgotten.

PHOENIX:

He raised himself above the table and looked
deliberately in the opposite direction.

OEDIPUS:

Right!—And . . .

PHOENIX:

And said sometimes foundlings
ascend the steps of a throne.

OEDIPUS:

And did I strike him then?

PHOENIX:

No; but you dug your fingernails into the table
so it could be heard
Everyone was silent; his glassy eyes were fixed
on you, and he shouted: "You,
Oedipus, tell me, are you the son
of Polybos?"

OEDIPUS:

gets up suddenly

Were those words, those words
alone, enough to seal the death of Lykos—of a living man?

PHOENIX:

You cannot see yourself when shaken with anger—
you grow black as death,
then white as foam. I have seen you like that.
It makes my soul tremble. [286]

OEDIPUS:

sinks down on a rock

That was the beginning.
What followed happened swiftly. I washed the blood
from my hands, put on another robe,
and went inside—it was not yet day
when I awoke them. How lightly my parents slept.
I barely reached their bed
and they awoke; my father
did not recognize me immediately, but my mother,
my mother—

shuddering

I will never see her again!—
Angry blood rushed through the veins
of my father's forehead; my mother's eyes were wet
with tears, and, half-sitting

in their marriage bed they swore
that I was their son. And then they both spoke
to me at once, exchanging lightning glances
of love and fear;
and King Polybos, my father, whom I had never touched,
threw his arms around my neck for the first time
in my life and pressed my head tightly
against his breast, and, from across the bed,
my mother grasped my hand.

PHOENIX:

And didn't this
convince you, unhappy man?

OEDIPUS:

I went away
but found no peace. [287]
When I rode my chariot,
or hunted, I thought of this,
even when I ate or drank.

PHOENIX:

You must have been ill!

OEDIPUS:

I was not ill. Yet there was something in me
which would give me no peace until I uncovered it.
I had to go to the place where truth burst
from the earth in streams of fire,
and pours from the lips of the priestess.
I had to journey to Delphi.
He shudders.

PHOENIX:

Woe, what have the priests
done to this child!

OEDIPUS:

How insignificant this all seems! It is as if I were standing
upon a high mountain and seeing life down there
like children's games in the street.
How small your life is, Phoenix!

PHOENIX:

My dearest Oedipus, how did the god

answer your question?

OEDIPUS:

The gods answer
our foolish questions wisely.
They scorn the question which spills from our lips,
but reveal with monstrous words [288]
what has slept unquestioned
in the deepest recesses of our being.
What a child I was to march forth,
bearing my question before me
like a banner! Suddenly the god seized me
by the hair and dragged me across the abyss
to confront him.

PHOENIX:

fearfully

Tell me, what did they do to you in the temple!

OEDIPUS:

O they are wise! They treated me both like a king
and a child. They gave me a chamber,
into which the stars shot down shafts
of flaming light.

PHOENIX:

The holy mountain rises high, close to the stars.
It is dangerous for men to live so close to the gods.

OEDIPUS:

Dangerous for men? Where mountain peaks join in a radiant
crown, gleaming in the light, carrying day and night
upon their august shoulders; where living cedars
are columns of a palace rising god-like,
in a golden haze; where in the forest's
evening, night and day embrace;
where in the night of sacrifice
the sparkling Milky Way bows heavily toward the soul
like a divining rod; and the soul,
surprised at its own strength, wishes to probe [289]
deeper within but senses that here no purpose
can be found: the universe
has a purpose—the soul has none—

PHOENIX:

My child, what did
the priests say to you?

OEDIPUS:

To me? The god
spoke to me through the woman in whom he dwells.

PHOENIX:

Did they consecrate you?

OEDIPUS:

They knew I had come to
learn the origin of my blood,
and they consecrated my blood
so that it might rise to the god by
its own power . . .

PHOENIX:

How did they consecrate your blood,
to life or to death?

OEDIPUS:

Why should
a servant concern himself about rituals! Night and day
did not interest me;
wiped away was the distinction between sleeping and waking;
and soon the one between death and life
had disappeared.

PHOENIX:

Oedipus!

OEDIPUS:

In the middle of the day I awoke from
a chain of forgotten dreams, but after each one
my spirit was renewed.
Beautiful creatures, everyone different,
surrounded me, then disappeared
in flames merging one with the other.
Can you understand? My sleepless soul roamed with
my ancestors.

PHOENIX:

But how could you

remember the dead whom you have never seen?

OEDIPUS:

No—they remembered me
and possessed me with more than desire,
more than boundless lust; theirs was
the desire and the pain of giants—

PHOENIX:

Kings
and gods, now you know!

OEDIPUS:

The flow of blood
is a dark, turgid flood into which the soul dives
and finds no bottom.
It was in me. No, it was me!
I was a wild king who heartlessly
embraced a woman in a burning city,
but was also dying, in flames, in the tower—
I was both the priest who swings the blade
and the sacrifice
Yet I could not die! I was not destroyed!
The flow of blood swept up from its channels
and with me on its crest rose to the gods.
Then it receded, swirling—
Now I lie here. [291]

PHOENIX:

How did the god speak to you?

OEDIPUS:

This is how he spoke to me: Surrounded by darkness
I lay with closed eyes, and everywhere
in the darkness living creatures were moving;
they were the priests; they stood silently
around my bed; enveloped by
the scent of strange herbs,
I sank always more deeply
into myself—

PHOENIX:

You were dreaming, my child!

OEDIPUS:

Don't question it!

I dreamed the dream of life and death.
In surging waves my future raced through me,—
suddenly my hands killed a man:
and my heart was drunk with the lust of anger.
I wanted to see his face, but it was hidden
by a cloth. The dream swept me away
and plunged me into a bed where
I lay with a woman—in whose arms
I felt like a god. Consumed with lust,
my body entwined with hers, I raised myself
to awaken her with a kiss—Phoenix, Phoenix!
A cloth lay upon her face, and with a sudden pain
the haunting memory of the man I had killed
pierced my heart and awoke me.
I was all alone. My heart beat heavily.
In the wall an invisible door opened
and a light crept in over the threshold, [292]
coming toward me.
A flowing gown glided
softly across the floor, toward my bed—
like a mother stepping to her child's bedside,
like a bride approaching the bridegroom,
so softly did it come.

PHOENIX:

In the name of our gods—
who?

OEDIPUS:

You still don't know? The woman.

PHOENIX:

The priestess?

OEDIPUS:

Names are meaningless! Woman and man
can become one: out of the woman glowed
the god, out of her distorted features
the god looked at me; it was her tongue
that stammered, yet it was the god who spoke!

PHOENIX:

To you—to you—

OEDIPUS:

Her face was as close to my mouth
as you are to me. How her stammering
tongue slashed into my wounded heart!

PHOENIX:

Say it! Say it! before your blood
hardens again. You are dying in my arms!

OEDIPUS:

I am still living and enduring it! I will tell you now: [293]
this is how the god spoke through the twisted mouth
of the enraptured woman: YOUR FATHER PAID
FOR YOUR LUST TO KILL, YOUR MOTHER PAID
FOR YOUR LUST TO LOVE; THIS IS THE DREAM,
AND THUS IT MUST HAPPEN.

PHOENIX:

Terrible!
But this was not the answer to your question!

OEDIPUS:

What, you madman?

PHOENIX:

Didn't you
ask the question then?

OEDIPUS:

I lay there and she slipped away
into the darkness.

PHOENIX:

You had to follow her!

OEDIPUS:

Follow her? A mountain lay upon my chest,
and weighed down every limb of my body! Follow her?

PHOENIX:

Unhappy man!
She did not answer your question!

OEDIPUS:

Phoenix, you are a fool! She did more than that!
What kind of a man are you! What was there left to ask?
What was left worth asking? Where was
the world! Swallowed by her stammering
tongue! After this prophecy there was nothing left [294]
but the three of us: father,
mother, and child welded body to body
with eternal, trembling chains of fate.

PHOENIX:

The prophecy was unclear!

OEDIPUS:

To the mind of a servant, yes,
not to me. God does not
speak twice. The one he chooses
understands him. Don't stare at me
so fearfully or I will say no more
and you will never see me again.
How could I ask anything more? How could I
chatter like a woman about this dreadful thing?
How could I fail to comprehend
what the frightful abyss had opened within me,
understand with unspeakable pain that
the oracle had spoken of my father and my mother?

PHOENIX:

Did you believe those ghastly words?
Didn't your mind cast them out?
Beloved! All this is still in you?

OEDIPUS:

It ate deeply into the marrow of my life.
It found food there—nothing but food.

PHOENIX:

You are good, you are pure,
there is not evil in your blood—
and no evil in your mind.
I know your breathing by night and day,
I know your face when it falls asleep and when it awakens.
Don't you see how calm I am

and can look straight into your eyes? [295]

OEDIPUS:

What do you know of me? What did I know of myself
before that hour
shook me from my childhood dream?
I will tell you something:
be quiet and listen.

PHOENIX:

Tell me, my child.

OEDIPUS:

You call me a child, yet I think I am a man.

PHOENIX:

A man! And a royal one! Who would dare deny it?

OEDIPUS:

Listen quietly, I'll tell you now:
I have never touched a woman.

PHOENIX:

What do you mean by that? You have never desired one?

OEDIPUS:

Of course I have felt the pain they call yearning.
How mild that pain seems now.
How small this all is: a child's pain and a child's joy.
When I slept near my hunting companions in their houses,
I could hear the latch being drawn in the silent night,
and hear the sighs that came from young breasts
among the noises of the night.
My pounding heart did not deceive me
I knew where surrender glowed in the dark— [296]
but it was as if a sword lay across my threshold.
When morning came it had all passed.

PHOENIX:

Child, the modesty and shyness
of your young blood restrained you.

OEDIPUS:

O no: it was a sword that barred my way.
And do you know why? Because of my mother.

PHOENIX:

What are you saying! You are drunk with a sorrow
inflicted upon you by a cruel god.
Your mind does not know what your lips are saying.

OEDIPUS:

It is not the way you think. I am telling you about my fate,
If you can't understand me—I won't say any more.
I wanted to show you how it all links together:
So that at least one man will understand, when I am gone forever.
You see, I could not bear the glances of virgins
once I was old enough to understand them.
I felt they could never satisfy my deepest longings.

PHOENIX:

Not one of all the young in the land?

OEDIPUS:

Not one. I could not have lain in their arms
without a deep and secret shame.
How can I explain it?
If a small glance could not transfix the depths of my soul,
if the world would not vanish,
if reverence and awe would not consume me— [297]
how could I give myself?
And to take a woman without giving myself,
to do this and not feel that my entire being
had been seized by a whirlwind—
to do this unspeakable thing, without emotion, boldly and brazenly
to press her against my breast and caress her hair,
to conceal myself shamelessly—waiting
like an adventurous beast to take one and then another—
would this not shame me even to death before the sea
and the shadows, before light, stars and wind,
before the stark presence of the living gods,
whose eyes are everywhere?
And so I restrained my desire
for body and hair, because not one was a queen . . . .
Now can you understand why I said: because of my mother?

Phoenix looks at him.

OEDIPUS:

Watching my mother, I had seen how a queen walks.

When I rode in my chariot
and saw her walking with her women,
carrying her body like a sacred vessel
to the sacred feasts by the river
where the gods, our ancestors, live in floating palaces,
then I descended from my chariot, knelt,
bending to the ground to greet her.
And I knew: I will beget children with one
who, with anointed hands, may offer sacrifices at sundown
in sacred woods, forbidden to all others: [298]
for the gods, her ancestors,
speak to her through dark branches in the night wind.
In such a sacred womb will I beget children
or die childless.

PHOENIX:

Noble youth! Pure child!
What have you to fear if your thoughts are so royal?

OEDIPUS:

The decree of the gods! Don't you understand yet? Is your soul so numb? Do you still not shudder?

PHOENIX:

There is not a breath of evil in you. Why do you torture yourself?

OEDIPUS:

Are you forever free from the powerful gods?
Do you not know what horror may come to us,
so that we will blindly stagger past each other?
You stare at my face as at death,
because a feast, of which we all partook, turned into a battle,
and the blood of brothers will flow in the streets
and women will kill themselves on rooftops
to avoid seeing how father and son, brother and brother
are strangling each other in the halls and chambers.

PHOENIX:

Those are just hideous delusions!

OEDIPUS:

All these things are in my blood.
Weren't there possessed men amongst my ancestors [299]
who caused streams of blood to flow?
Did not entire nations languish in their dungeons?

Didn't they fornicate with gods and demons?
And when their lust had swollen like sails in a raging storm,
could they spare even their own blood?
And who could ever restrain this rage?
Who could say to all this:
Go, and never return?

PHOENIX:

Those are ancient tales of horror.

OEDIPUS:

Distant things are brought close to him who feels them in his blood—
What happened long ago can happen again—
who knows who will cause them?

PHOENIX:

You must come! The chariot is ready to take you home!
You will see your parents and your dream will vanish, and
your horror will be dispersed like an evil fog.

OEDIPUS:

The god said it would happen thus; how he did not say.
But I sense the way.
It is forcing its way through me
as through flowing water

PHOENIX:

Get a hold of yourself! If only you were home in bed!

OEDIPUS:

I'd rather be dead in an abyss with vultures above me!

PHOENIX:

O son of my King!

OEDIPUS:

I wanted to ask my father to put me in a tower,
to give me a bed of straw and heavy chains—
but how could that save us?
I would lie near them like a villain in ambush;
and one day the walls of the tower would melt like fading snow,
or an arrow would fly in the window and throwing it back
it would pierce my father's neck.

They would come in crowds and break into my prison:
I should bring the message to my mother,
and then my arms would embrace her,
my lips linger upon hers.

PHOENIX:

Those are wild dreams! Can't you wake up—how you must suffer!
None of this is in your thoughts; your soul abhors it!

OEDIPUS:

There are no barriers;
Fate acts through us as through a void.
Yes, it sounds like an evil dream!
My mother is no longer young . . .
But, do you believe that this is enough to depend on?
When I think of the priestess, a woman—yet not a woman,
and her womb the dreadful dwelling of a god—
then there is nothing in this world my heart cannot believe.
Take away the hand that restrains me!
Let me go! He who hesitates is lost!

PHOENIX:

What will you do? [301]

OEDIPUS:

Only one sacrifice can save me:
offered ceaselessly
nourished by all I own,
flowing on, like time before the stars!

PHOENIX:

What sacrifice, my child?

OEDIPUS:

My life.
But I am not to die;
a dreadful sense of foreboding warns me;
I must linger without a dwelling,
restless, wrapped in deepest loneliness,
with only animals for company—
then I won't have to lose myself
to this unspeakable fate, to this living death.

PHOENIX:

But how can you ever be lonely?
The servants, or I,
we could grow like animals,
we could become one with the stones;
our hair could grow like vines and moss,
and our hands like claws.
We, cloaked in wickedness, could
lose ourselves in this world
and live with animals.
But you are a king,
all know your name;
wherever you ride the earth resounds
and men crowd around your horses;
your forefathers are on your side wherever you go. [302]
The gods, your ancestors, raise their heads and hands to you from the rivers—
at sea, the waves foam and rush to drive your ship forward.
You could not roam on the empty sea,
but a wind will rise to blow your sail and lead you on like a herald.
Stars will greet you kindly as they do at home,
and lands welcome you with open arms—
Untrodden paths are no wilderness to you,
and shores on which you land are not barren:
because you are a king!

OEDIPUS:

Well said: yet, all this I'll cast away!
Were it less, how could it possibly
balance that unspeakable fate.
Thus it may suffice.

PHOENIX:

This is a useless sacrifice pleasing no one.
Sorrow will turn your parents to stone!

OEDIPUS:

A cruel sacrifice indeed! Show me a king who will atone like this?
Phoenix! I never really saw you as I do now.
And over there—the others—how they crowd around the chariot!
I can see what they are thinking.

O god, I had such men to serve me!
They stare at me with aching hearts,
their hands heavy with the deeds
we would have done;
now those deeds have rolled into the abyss, never done.
Look at the horses! They paw the ground,
raise their nostrils and cry to me. [303]
Their eyes speak,
as if their dumb souls were trying to free themselves.
They are not ordinary horses.
They would have raced into battles with me
and fought beside me biting my enemies ferociously—
They would have crossed strange rivers with me—
but now everything has changed.
If the horses urge their master on,
the men must grab the reins and drag them down the hill,
should their dumb souls cling to me,
to me, who cannot ride with them.
But I must go; now it is enough!

PHOENIX:

Send one last message to your mother and father when they ask about their child!

OEDIPUS:

They must never expect word from me,
not from the fishermen on the shore, nor the pilgrims who travel through the land.
They must not hope for something that can never happen,
nor burden their lives with "perhaps."
They must lock my house, empty my coffers,
kill my dogs, so they won't howl for me at night.
I have cut a staff and that is enough,
I need nothing else, neither man nor beast,
nor bed at night, nor light in darkness:
but do not tell that to my father and mother.
Not even a tree is so alone, nor a stone.
Stones lie together one with the other,
always in the same place, so familiar they are to each other, [304]
so peaceful is their countenance,
as if each one were the threshold of a home.

The trees too—each has its companion;
together they stretch upward;
with their flourishing crowns
they praise their lives,
and are happy to dwell
for countless days
deeply rooted in the rock,
spreading their jagged branches—
in never-ending celebration!
But who would entwine his branches with mine
and lie with me as stone lies with stone?

Phoenix weeps.

OEDIPUS:

Tell my mother and my father that once each day
at this hour, when the earth trembles with fear
because the night has draped it heavily with darkness,
they should remember that I am still alive.
Then, wherever I am, I will kneel down;
and when the hands of the night wind shake the branches
like the breath of a heavy burdened man,
their faces will appear before me.
Not every day, but now and then,
they will feel something in the mighty wind;
it will stir and move gently before the window of their room:
and they will know that it is their child.
For my prayers will be stronger than my thoughts;
my life's breath will remain to guard its home, my body,
but my soul will wing above its nest
over the forests and rivers
like a shining god, a happy swan—

A gust of wind.

A storm is coming—take the chariot and the servants and leave!
They must not hurry or my horses will stumble.
Take charge! Farewell—everyone farewell!

He walks upward into the rocks.

PHOENIX:

They will ask what you were doing when I left you.

OEDIPUS:

Tell them the wind is my companion and darkness is my home.

PHOENIX:

I cannot bring them such a message!

OEDIPUS:

Are you too stupid to find words?
Tell them their son fares well in the desert,
that you saw him kneel down among rough stones
as others do in consecrated groves and sacred clearings
to offer prayer.
Now go!

PHOENIX:

My Lord, let your servants wait while you pray!

OEDIPUS:

Go away! your presence burdens me!

PHOENIX:

Son of my King!

OEDIPUS:

Enough! Enough! [306]

PHOENIX:

One more look!

OEDIPUS:

Do you want to torture me?
When you are gone, only then will I be free
to pray for myself and mine.

Pitch darkness, strong gusts of wind.

Phoenix off to the left, looking back in pain.

Oedipus above, at the highest point of the ravine, lays down his staff, kneels. The servants step out from behind the bushes, stretch out their arms toward him. Then they leave. The chariot drives off.

VOICES out of the storm:

We are the dead kings—
We dwell in the winds—
we who so mighty were
the storm drags us by the hair,
and this is our son.

OEDIPUS:

his head bent to the ground, his hands stretched out

Earth, now you alone must be my mother.
The silent clouds and the loud winds are my brothers.
I have given up all I own.
To be your child is life alone.

VOICES:

Our strain and toil
created him.
Body and soul,
lust and pain—
he must repay
because with gifts [307]
we blessed him.
He is a king and must atone—
and were a naked stone his throne:
he is of our blood the son.

OEDIPUS:

Not a word—not a light,
yet somehow I am aware
that not in vain did I forsake
father and mother, world and fame
and what delights my heart.
I feel it weaving about me: I shall live.
The storm rises.

HERALD of Laios:
comes up from the right
Wicked storm, tricky darkness,
I can scarcely see the path before my feet!
Why, strange land, such a hostile welcome for my master?
The way is so steep—a rock lies here, and a tree trunk bars the way.
Oedipus raises his hands in prayer.

HERALD:
closer to him
A man! Get out of my way! Be gone!
Clear the path! Can't you hear?

OEDIPUS:
looking up as from a dream
That ugly tone! Angry voice!
When a man prays, you must not disturb him—
should his soul not return

he can never be healed. [308]

HERALD:

Don't you hear the chariot wheels, you creature of the night?
Be off!

OEDIPUS:

Solitude, stay!

HERALD:

Out of my way, you!
Why are you twisting on the ground?
Are you a dog? I'll take a stone!

OEDIPUS:

raises himself against the slope

Cruel man! Disgusting words!

HERALD:

For the last time, get out of my way!

OEDIPUS:

(reluctantly)

You dog, not so loud!

HERALD:

Shall I use a staff?

OEDIPUS:

(bends down)

I too have a staff!
I'll go—only wait—wait till I am over there.
Keep your distance!

HERALD:

Go on!
Get away, or—

OEDIPUS:

Don't strike me! [309]

HERALD:

Why not?

OEDIPUS:

There, you dog, take that!

The herald falls with a dull thud.

OEDIPUS:

It is quiet now. Are you dead?

Lightning.

No trace of blood—he is white as stone—
by my staff—my hand?

A chariot has stopped close by. Enter Laios, the driver, and servants from the right.

DRIVER:

groping

Here is the path.

A flash of lightning.

The herald! He's murdered!

Oedipus has dropped his staff, stands on the left, staring at the dying man.

Raging storm.

SERVANT:

My Lord! Bandits!—back to the chariot!

LAIOS:

a knotty staff in his hand

My herald!

HERALD:

recognizes the voice, moves

My Lord, it is enough to die near you!

LAIOS:

You must not die!—Bring water!

OEDIPUS:

A spring is over there.

DRIVER:

Master, there are too many of them: they are lurking in the darkness.

OEDIPUS:

I am alone.

Strong lightning.

LAIOS:

Ah, seize the murderer!

SERVANTS:

softly

Get ropes from the chariot to bind him!

One servant leaves.

OEDIPUS:

What do you want? You did not see how it happened.
He struck at me, he came too close!

LAIOS:

Silence, ruffian! Your breath desecrates the dead man's peace!

OEDIPUS:

If he belongs to you, close his eyes.

LAIOS:

bends toward the dead man

You did belong to me;
we can no longer count the years . . . can we?

OEDIPUS:

Let me be your servant in the dead man's place—I am young!

Laios whispers to the servants who all stand in groups behind him. One of them steps in back of Oedipus. [311]

OEDIPUS:

I will humble myself day and night—I will sleep at your feet on the ground—
I will tend your horses—take me with you!

LAIOS:

You will be taken along
but bound hand and foot—that's how you will come.

OEDIPUS:

What do they want?

Backs up against a tree.

LAOIS:

Together!—All three of you!

One of them raises a rope-sling behind Oedipus' back during a flash of lightning.

OEDIPUS:

reaches swiftly for his staff on the ground

I? bound? What do you want with me?

LAIOS:

You will soon find out: your blood is too young
to atone for his blood; his was aged and heavy,
your hair is no price for his graying hair,
to send you with him to rest,
that punishment is far too mild.
I am not so generous.

OEDIPUS:

Where are you taking me?

LAIOS:

I want to see suffering on your insolent face,
but in daylight.
Until, bound and beaten with whips, [312]
your voice fails you.
You will be executed in a public place
before old men and young men, women and children.
They shall stand and watch—
The sun will hear your cries.

OEDIPUS:

You reach out into the world with murderous hands! Who are you?

LAIOS:

An old man, who had to see another die
like a dog by your hands.
But you must pay!
You will die, draped in pain,
and he will meet you among the dead,
and be happy, and he will bless me.

OEDIPUS:

Your voice is filled with hate and torment. You never had a child;
you are unfruitful;
day and night your sad wife lay before the gods,
dust on her hair: there is no blessing upon your house!
Let me pass, let me go!

LAIOS:

He wants to escape!

OEDIPUS:

If you knew who I am, you would have pity on me.
My life is more bitter than death.
What can your old heart know of my horrible distress?

LAIOS:

You dare to brag?—Grab him, drag him here! [313]
I will make him drink my heart's bitter sap!
I have been drinking it for years. I have had enough—
he will drink it all in one draught!
Quickly, you three!

OEDIPUS:

Let me go!

LAIOS:

Servants!

OEDIPUS:
to himself

There is no other way but this!

LAIOS:

Here I stand!

He lifts the knotty staff.

OEDIPUS:

Make way, you villain!

Strikes at him.

LAIOS:
falling

My curse upon your heart!

Oedipus runs off to the right.

SERVANTS:

Down there! After him! Catch him! Kill him!

Rush after him, wrestle.—Storm.

VOICES out of the air:

I am thrust down out of the heavens,
I am cast out of my royal tomb;

age-old rage grips my dead bones—
Ayee! Our blood runs from the dead man's veins! [314]

A SERVANT:

has reached the upper cliff from the rear, hurries across, flees
Ah, a demon pursues us—he will kill us all!
Flees.

OEDIPUS:

comes back from lower right. Silence. He stands still.
How ominously the water helped me,
as with a hundred arms!
Shuddering
They touched me and then drowned.
Here he must lie. I still remember
it was a strange, old man;
why does this hideous delusion come over me
to believe that it was my father?
I must creep near enough to touch him!
A moonbeam penetrates the clouds.
A light is falling on his lifeless face!
Give me but enough courage, enough strength to look,
for it cannot be he!
He drags himself closer
Strange! Strange! Pale, strange and evil!
No, not evil—only strange—ice cold, pale, and strange.
The gods are good—good! My heart rests easy now!
Raises his hands toward the moon
Thank you, eternal wing,
sent from the night to comfort me!
I raise my hands with ease! The deed I have done weighs lightly!
What does all this mean? Why did this
happen to me? Have you merely warned me. Fate?
Why am I now at ease? Shall I do deeds for you?
And may the homeless Oedipus [315]
find shelter now in his deed—?
Pale dawn from the right below.
A new day is breaking. The world unfolds before me. My heart
is new again! No blood on my staff,
no blood on me! Night take away your dead!
The moon disappears. Signs of daylight. Rustling in the branches.

VOICES:

See there the youth
to whom we sang:
he flies as though pursued
to meet the dawn—
He sits upon the old man's throne—
he is of our blood the son!

Curtain. [316]

ACT II

Entrance Hall of Creon's palace. On a step, on the right, Creon's young swordbearer lies asleep. The Guard and the Keeper of dogs stand together.

BOY:

stirs in his sleep

My Lord and King, I want to see you fight your first battle.

KEEPER:

Who is speaking?

GUARD:

The boy.

KEEPER:

Like a hunting dog he dreams out loud.

GUARD:

But he's sleeping as sound as a dead man.

BOY:

My King, can't you hear them? Listen to their cries!
The people are all shouting: "Thebes to Creon!"

KEEPER:

To whom does he speak?

GUARD:

To our Master, I suppose. Get up, and leave him alone.

KEEPER:

He calls him king.

GUARD:

What's that to you!

KEEPER:

Will our Master be King of Thebes? Of course I know he'd like to be. There's enough talk of it everywhere. [317]

GUARD:

Do you talk to your dogs this much?

KEEPER:

I have only to open my mouth and they wag their tails with joy.

GUARD:

I don't, as you can see.

KEEPER:

Yesterday there was a fight between our men and the servants of the Queen. Haven't you heard, or are you just pretending you haven't?

Guard looks at him angrily.

KEEPER:

You look like my vicious Thessalonians with their split noses. You are a fine one to guard the door. They are saying: "Though she is ten times a woman, she still is the Queen and should keep the crown and the scepter." But our men are shouting: "The crown belongs to Creon!" What confusion!

GUARD:

Swine!

BOY:

in his sleep

My King, I want to stand in your chariot
and hand you the arrows. I want to revel
when you sow death with a king's hand.

KEEPER:

Listen to him, he is fighting already.

GUARD:

I tell you, get out of here! [318]

KEEPER:

Why does he act as he does? Why does he want the crown so much? Isn't he the richest Lord in the land and brother to the Queen? Isn't his kennel of dogs the finest in Greece? I can't understand what is driving him; if I were him I would forget it.

GUARD:

He would forget about it, too, if he were you.

SERVANT:

comes running

They are bringing the Seer—
Half dragging and half carrying him!
His eyes are closed, they are leading him.

The Seer, Anagyrotidas, led by two men. His face disturbed and pale, his heavy-lidded eyes closed. Creon, dressed in robes of a prince, enters from the palace.

SERVANT:

to the Seer

You are standing before Creon, old man.

CREON:

Are you the Seer?

SEER:

with closed eyes

His bleeding body stands here. Torn by a sword
from the womb of the night. Curse on your slaves
who dragged it here.

CREON:

Did they seize you while you slept?
They did as I commanded. [319]

SEER:

Curses on him who commanded it. The night was good.
The night was beyond compare. I lay on the dying body
of the sacrifice and quivered with each of its spasms.
I mixed my breath with the blood dripping from its throat:
my soul was released and freed from my body,
and it plunged downward
carried by the beast to Hecate, our Queen.
O, how my limbs ache!

CREON:

Let them ache.
I will scatter turmalin and amethyst
upon you!

SEER:

They thrust the divine body
naked into the cold darkness above.

CREON:

I shall wrap your limbs in purple and byssus.

SEER:

Cursed be their breath that came over me.

CREON:

I shall cover you day and night with clouds of amber
and the scent of myrrh, if you will help me!

SEER:

opens his eyes

What do you demand of me?

CREON:

Need I explain
to a seer? Make my spirit strong, Anagyrotidas,
then claim whatever you want.

SEER:

You are caught in a great struggle
for a high prize.

CREON:

Yes, you are right.

SEER:

By day
and by night you wrestle ceaselessly.
You dug me from my grave, where
I lay alive. You could wait no longer:
because the force which opposes you is more powerful
than you.

CREON:

Once again you are right.

SEER:

But this fight is not fought
by the light of day: something from the darkness works
a spell against you.

CREON:

So it seems.

SEER:

It begins with someone in your family.

CREON:

Seer, you are very wise!

SEER:

Before my eyes
each man is an open book, [321]
and each soul reveals signs of its fate
before me.

CREON:

Can you name my enemy?

SEER:

His power is great.
That I can see.
Because of him your face quivers like that of a
tortured man. Your spirit drains from you.
He robs you of your essence. You never know
where you are. When you awake in the morning
your day is not really day, nor your night really night;
they resemble only vaguely former days and nights.
Endlessly you wander as on a foreign star;
strange things are sweeping through you; your strength,
the crown of your soul, is taken from you;
and the mountains, seas and valleys of the earth are only pillows
tossed about in pain by your soul
to wrench you from a wild and feverish nightmare.

CREON:

How great you are; you see me for the first time
and yet you know my sickness! Free
my soul, Seer, and I shall have you
led home on a white horse with a golden bridle.

SEER:

The enemy who wrestles with you has a mighty soul.

CREON:

I will tell you who it is, Anagyrotidas,
but then you must help me! It is my sister!
Reconcile me with my sister that she may
free my soul and let me be King! [322]
Once she loved me, but she hates me now.
Yes, my sister! Do you hear? She is the demon
who drains the soul from my body:
because I have done a hideous thing to her;
and now she is repaying me.
On their wedding night, you understand,
the night when King Laios
was wedded to Jocasta, the high priests
sent a message by me, then only a boy.
Let me tell you what it was.
I must also reveal this! The message said:
"Be careful, Laios. Beware, before you sleep with her,
for if the womb
of your shining Jocasta ever should bear your son,
you will die by this son's hand.
Now choose!" A dreadful message, Seer,
from the mouth of a child! It was
the wedding night of the King, the night
when he came to his virgin wife.
When such a royal child is conceived, doesn't
Queen Hecate hover near the earth?
Curses on the priests who did this to a boy,
who let his innocent mouth drip
poison and death into life's seed!
And like the poisonous salve Medea sent
to Creusa on her wedding day: it
destroyed its vial.

SEER:

The poison destroyed
the child's soul?

CREON:

Yes, you understand me well;
now help me, Seer! [323]

SEER:

Through swirling mist, I see,
glows the nakedness of your heart;
pour your soul out to me,
like black sacrificial blood!

CREON:

I will, great Seer!
The unspeakable knowledge of my inmost destiny
will fill you! Do not forsake me, Seer,
for today my fate will be decided.
Since that day, this knowledge has gnawed at
my heart and mind: "You are to be a king; but until that day
you will be the unborn phantom
of a king!" O mortal, from that hour on
before life had begun, life's opportunities
were denied me. What could I do?
No act of mine could wrench the crown
from Laios' head; everything was useless.
My hands did nothing more.
I wandered everyhere, but the land repulsed me;
I went to the sea, and it was barren.
My desire for women was exhausted: it was
as if I had already possessed each one naked in my dreams
and then abandoned her.
Everything in the world, yes, even murder,
listen, Seer, even murder was empty of meaning
as if I had tasted it and spit it out.
Seer, the gods burned out like old torches!
The universe was sucked dry, are you listening?
Jocasta did all that to me.
Her glance hardened me to all life:
because I had strangled her unborn child, [324]
thus she repaid me; she emasculated my will
and drove me to unrealizable, powerless dreams.
I dreamt too much. Take a knife and
cut out my dreams, Seer!
For Laios is dead, now,
and my strength must soar
to tear, and seize
the crown and sword. I must cast away my dreams:
a king does not merely dream; the dreams of a king
issue from him and become deeds,

and rule in the world. I must bloom now,
else I decay! This is my morn of fate, Sorcerer;
and even should it cause your death, tear something
from the night which I can grasp—something, even anguish,
or merely what the sparkle of dice, not yet cast,
promising heaven or hell, what that means to a player!
Seer, conjure for me from a stone-hard world
just one such view of life.
Then I shall be King, Seer; then demand
the world from me! What do your eyes see?
Don't look at me as if I were a stranger.
I must have power over Jocasta! Shall I burn incense for you?
Would you drink of a cup
in which pearls are dissolved? Would you bathe in blood,
even in human blood? It is yours.
How can I master my sister?

SEER:

Bring sacrifices, Creon,
bring sacrifices!

CREON:

What shall I sacrifice? All my herds, Seer?
My house? Command it and flames will devour it,
the jewels, the robes, everything?

SEER:

O Creon, what you did not buy, Creon,
what is untouched by your soul's greed
and yet belongs to you, sacrifice that
immediately!

DWARF:

jumps on stage

You lie!
Such a thing does not exist on earth, Seer!
Creon is such a mighty prince there is nothing
in the world that Creon could not buy;
did he not buy me, a handsome dwarf,
me, whom Ethiopia bore?
To Creon, the world is for sale. Creon cannot sacrifice
an unbought thing.

CREON:

You smack your lips
and sputter mockery upon me? Bring the whip!
Dwarf runs away

CREON:

(to the Seer)
Why do you stretch your arms into the air?

SEER:

My demon seizes me. Curses on the hands
that tore me from my sacred sleep. Curses on
the greed in my heart that made me come!

CREON:

Though it should kill you, I demand you answer!
What must I sacrifice? [326]

SEER:

Creon, curses on you,
from my death's agony be cursed
for your greed and mine.
And should I not die now, be cursed
that I had this foretaste of death.

CREON:

Answer me!

SEER:

I am dying.

CREON:

grabs him
How can I master my fate?
Seer falls down.

CREON:

Servants!
Servants approach.
Take him away.

A SERVANT:

He is not dead.
He was lying this way when we found him: his brother
bade us on his knees to spare him, until his soul

had returned to his body.
But you had commanded it: this morning!
And we dragged him here.
Two servants carry the Seer away.

CREON:
Into the house, get out of my sight!
The world is a sham. It is my luck [327]
that before my eyes it rends apart and ghastly progenies
gush forth. Must I yet lay that corpse
against my breast? How long did I sleep
this morning?

SERVANT:
You did not sleep, my Lord, you rode in
your chariot to the city.

CREON:
You dog, do you think I have forgotten
how long I slept after my bath?

SERVANT:
You barely
rested after your bath, you scarcely closed
your eyes.

CREON:
turns his back to him. The servant leaves, bowing.
Scarcely closed my eyes. And yet
I dreamt of such horror. I was old,
and heavy limbed
and yet not King, yet not King of Thebes!
What was I? Something like a servant
to the new man who then was King.
I believe I stood before him as a messenger
and was reproached. O might I only rid my ear
of the ugly tone with which I replied,
a loathsome tone. I believe I humbly touched his gown
with my hands. Cursed dream!
I cannot recall the face of this strange man.
When I think I do, it bears the traits of Laios,
a kind of younger Laios, [328]
a Laios who has returned! Who am I,

that I am so full of stuff for dreams?
I am a bottomless pit, for the fount of my mind
is poisoned with such feebleness
and breathes out such odious dreams
that it makes me sick with disgust.

BOY:
rising quickly
Lord, what do you command?

CREON:
Sleep on; young blood
needs its sleep.

BOY:
No. Today I did not sleep.

CREON:
You were not sleeping?

BOY:
No, my Lord, I was standing here:
You walk like a panther but I heard you
coming from your bath.
Did I sleep standing?

CREON:
Ah, was no one here?

BOY:
Not a soul.

CREON:
Well!

BOY:
Lord, do you sigh? [329]

CREON:
to himself
What a night!

BOY:
How could I sleep
after such a night! How pale you are, my Lord,
after that night!

CREON:

What do you know, boy,
of my nights?

BOY:

Wasn't I with you?
O what a night, my Lord! She raised
a king and knew it, and sparkling
and shining she boasted that she knew it.
When you entered houses, my Lord,
the darkness covered you like a mane.
And in the darkness a wind arose
and murmured and kept her secret. The stars
wanted to break from their spheres
to fall into your diadem. Delirious with fever
I lay before the houses
near your chariot.

CREON:

Boy, when I am King,
I shall drink at night
from a golden chalice into which
your name is carved.

BOY:

I listened to the rustling
and murmuring of the wind as it
wove your royal fate; and when dull sounds
issued from the houses then I knew
that princely men were falling to the ground
before you paying homage to their King.
With this night you already paid
for the arrow which shall pierce my heart, Lord,
in your first battle; and when it strikes
I'll sink before the chariot and die
laughing as the swimmer does who slips
from the boat into the water because
he has lost the desire to row.

CREON:

O, that I might drink
his words as morning-draught
for my soul! Ah, but the cup is broken,
and I thirst.

BOY:

My Lord, I hear someone running.
A messenger, Lord. Look here, over here!

CREON:

to himself

What can happen? Has a conqueror ever
had such dreams on his coronation morn?

FIRST MESSENGER:

rushing in

Who can lead me to the Prince? Where in this house
can I find Creon who will be King today?

CREON:

stepping forward

What are you bringing him?

MESSENGER:

falls down before him

Tremendous fortune. [331]
Great Prince, words are barren.
I have rushed in from the plains:
Your herdsmen and servants
gather from vineyards and fields;
they reach for their knives,
and tie sickles to their staffs:
messengers are everywhere.

CREON:

Messengers?

MESSENGER:

On foaming horses, covered with dust.

CREON:

Sent by me?

MESSENGER:

By you! Spurred on by gods, it seems,
and spewn from the earth!
They say the Dioscuri themselves were seen racing
through one of your villages shouting: Arm yourselves for Creon,
men! Arm yourselves and go to the city,
fight for him!

SECOND MESSENGER:
coming up quickly
My reward, great Prince!
I am Agathocles, the day-courier.
I bring you
the crown of Thebes, Creon.

CREON:
Let it fall, friend.

SECOND MESSENGER:
The city is up in arms, the harbor section is aflame, [332]
and as the naked and screaming
crowd onto the river and beaches
shouts rise from the bridges:
let your houses burn, sailors,
Creon will give you new houses!
You with no houses rise up for Creon
who shall be King!

CREON:
And what are the people doing?

SECOND MESSENGER:
Within the hour thousands will move
through the Lion's Gate
to call for you at yonder castle, Lord!

THIRD MESSENGER:
steps forward
Whatever they say, King Creon,
tell them to stand aside and wait: I
alone am worthy to be heard.

CREON:
Lad,
you honor me too soon.

THIRD MESSENGER:
No, my greeting is right,
for I come gasping from the sacred road:
an enormous throng is moving there,
an immeasurable throng of priests, Creon,

and this is what they chant: Look to your King,
sacred Thebans, who will drive
the Sphinx from her cave at Harma,
your King who is called Creon. [333]

BOY:

O my King, I can feel
how the throngs are meeting!
Three of them are merging
like roaring rivers
in my heart, beloved Lord!
Are you turning pale?

CREON:

Out of disgust for you,
flattering toad! Liar!

BOY:

I,
lie to you?

CREON:

Could this ever happen,
could these sleek skills
so poorly and painfully wrought,
gain power, and force the people to come to the castle,
to make me their King,
me whose heart they know less than
the cliffs of the Cytharon mountain over there?

BOY:

to the messenger
Depart, I beg you; our Lord, you see, is not well.
Go into the house friends, and wait, be so good.
You will be called back.

SECOND MESSENGER:

Lord, I swear,
I spoke the truth.

BOY:

Just go. Leave.
No one doubts you! [334]

FIRST MESSENGER:

still in the doorway, to Creon

It is as I said, my Lord, your servants
swarm in numbers up from the plains,
armed.

CREON:

The maids as well?

FIRST MESSENGER:

What, my Prince?

CREON:

I mean did the Dioscuri
call the stable-maids to arms as well
to seize the crown for me?

BOY:

Away, go, they are calling for you.

Pushes them into the house.

CREON:

Why do you stare at me like that: you know
I planned all this,
you know its source?
How can you rejoice, snake,
to learn that now the sun
must witness what rises from the bottomless pit
to give birth to my faded dreams!
All this came from my desire.
Curses on all that which drags itself up so wretchedly!
I will strangle it before the sun reveals it.
I shudder, I cannot step to the mirror
for there I must see myself!

BOY:

My King!

CREON:

Do you grow pale? Will all
that I look upon grow pale? Must I with each glance
see corpses in whitened sepulchres?
Begone!

BOY:

Lord, you tempt me terribly,
and yet you do not wound my soul.
When my blood freezes at your words,
I think: just as horror rises up in dreams,
you must descend dreaming. And should
I see you with your own hands do a hideous crime,
or should I see you writhe in pain and shame,
yet my heart would cry
that thus kings must weigh their diadem;
and I would fall at your feet.

CREON:

How cleverly you lie.

BOY:

Go on, despise me!
What have you ever seen me do?

CREON:

Ah! Do you adorn yourself
with tears?
One can adorn oneself with deeds, then
why not with tears? Tell me, with what
did I buy you then? Was it the gleam
of a royal sword which you want to bear
before me? Was it a place by my side
in my chariot? Has all this filled your soul
to the brim? [336]

BOY:

You did not buy me,
unless you did it by being Creon,
born a king. Look, I can
prove that, my Lord, by a script
written on my breast.

CREON:

A scar
above your heart?

BOY:

Yes! This is from the night

when we knelt at Thebes,
and the priests sang to the gods in the darkness.
Did not the night wind bear it up to you?
It was all for you.

CREON:

Was it the night
I went to conquer the Sphinx?

BOY:

That night.
Suddenly all lights went out,
all singing ceased and everyone prayed for you;
but my prayer seemed too weak,
made up of thoughts. Thoughts,
though ardent, are tarnished
by the emptiness of words.
So I seized the small knife, which I
carried in my belt, and let my blood flow
for you.

CREON:

And I returned [337]
before dawn; my effort was futile,
and your sacrifice for nought.
Didn't it disgust you?

BOY:

The gods did not will it
that night. They gave you a sign:
they made the torchbearer's foot
slip and he plunged into the abyss,
and you had to return. But look, I
did not know that my eyes would open
and I would live again, nor did I know
that your swordbearer lay where only vultures
would find him!

CREON:

I am Midas, Midas,
what I touch changes hideously!
I bought you, too, ignorant boy.

It was not the gods who hurled
my torchbearer into the abyss.

BOY:

One does not stumble on such a path
without cause.

CREON:

My dagger is sticking from his back.

BOY:

Deny it!
Say that you are only testing me! If you despised him,
would you let him bear your sword?

CREON:

Boy,
I don't know whether I hated or [338]
loved him. But as he walked before me that day
I felt that his heart did not believe
in my victory. Do you understand?
I sensed it in his step. I could
see it on his back—then I stabbed him.

The boy buries his face.

CREON:

When he walked before me as my torchbearer
but within had lost faith in me, wasn't he
a traitor?

The boy trembles.

CREON:

You are silent? You believe that he only could judge
who knew that his heart had betrayed me—
perhaps that his heart was suffering
from doubt. Look, I tell you,
one like that is better off dead.
The simple souls should live, boy.
Now, do you still want to be Creon's swordbearer?

BOY:

on the ground

Leave me, Lord.

CREON:

bent over him

I taught you fear, and yet you always
walked like one unthreatened from behind.
I envy you! . . .

Silence.

Bought none the less,
bought by the life of him who first
bore my sword. . .

Silence.

I felt that something
led my hand when I silently stabbed him:
perhaps it was your demon, boy. My boy,
was it not an ambitious game you played
with your blood that night?

Goes to the door.

BOY:

raising himself

Alas, if I stay with you,
your heart will think that you bought me
with the splendor of your sword and a place on your chariot.

CREON:

at the door

Can you hear the ancient songs mourning
for Laios, resounding through every wall?
The Queen is strong; leave me, boy;
a wise man leaves a sinking ship.

BOY:

gets up, broken

As never before your eyes are sad, my Lord.
They look at me across an abyss of pain.
How little I know of your heart! I feel
you can be both here and somewhere else. My King,
where are you?

CREON:

O simple soul, wherever
I don't care to be. What would I not give
to be with you, whom I have bought,

yet I believe I am with him who is dead [340]
and decays in yonder pit.

BOY:

Your soul
is sick, my King.

CREON:

And still I could
love you more than I ever loved him.
Though I believe he gave me greater strength
when he was with me. Were he with me now,
I think, I would not stand here
shaking with weakness; were he with me, I think,
I would now lie asleep and they would
come to wake me from that sleep
and place the crown upon my bed.

BOY:

At your first battle,
my Lord and King, I want to ride upon your chariot,
with no armor shielding my neck and head;
for you I will give myself to the first arrow.

CREON:

Is that my path to victory?
O how she sends the gruesome dirges
over here to mock me!

BOY:

The songs are
for Laios who was King before you.

CREON:

True enough, but why did Laios depart,
leaving his spear-bearers at home?
For whom does that woman keep the castle? For whom does she save
the crown and sword? [341]

BOY:

The people of Thebes are knocking
at the gate for you.

CREON:

Cursed echo
of impotent desires. Help descends
from nowhere, be it only
a breath, only a touch. How sterile is
the universe! Did he not depart as though
to make way for another? For whom? I must ask her.
Wants to leave.

BOY:

In one hour, Creon, you will be the King;
then ask.

CREON:

I must know now, stupid boy,
now or never. She rules, and she is a demon
full of power who mocks me with her dirges;
she holds my naked fate in her hands.

BOY:

Your fate lies in your own hands, Creon.

CREON:

Silence! Why did Laios seek his death?
This is the only thought in the world that matters.

BOY:

Because Laios went away to die,
because of this you can be King,
before the sun sets.

CREON:

Idiotic boy, it is just [342]
because this smiles upon my fate,
that it proves my undoing!
Dashes off.

BOY:

Creon! Creon!
He doesn't hear me—I am nothing to him. The universe
stands silent about him, and he believes in no man.
There is no way to reach him. Only one remains: One—
which makes me shudder, but this is mine,
my only choice,—else I am nothing, rejected,
shattered.
Draws a knife

Creon,
O my King, from the void of space a demon shall swing down
to you and breathe strength into your soul! . . .
Men can be adorned with their deeds. How hideous
that I should think of this. Away, that turmoil
must not grip me. I must be strong.
Now I can sacrifice myself quickly.
Enters the house.

FOURTH MESSENGER:
enters quickly
Creon! Creon!

FIFTH MESSENGER:
enters
The wharf is in flames; ten thousand are crying
for their king. Where is Creon?

FOURTH MESSENGER:
Creon! [343]

FIFTH MESSENGER:
No time for that, inside!

FOURTH MESSENGER:
in the doorway
A man!

FIFTH MESSENGER:
near him
His boy? He is sleeping here?

FOURTH MESSENGER:
I am full of blood.

FIFTH MESSENGER:
The boy is dead!

FOURTH MESSENGER:
He is still warm; this is not
the time to report it.

SIXTH MESSENGER:
enters quickly
Creon!

Room in the palace, drapes drawn. Half-darkness. Steps lead on the left to an opening into a higher and more distant room.

Jocasta enters. At the same time Antiope appears above on the threshold of the neighboring room. Her old face is without color; her dark gown trails off into the dimness of the room. She leans on a staff.

When Jocasta enters, the loud wail of the mourning women is heard in the house. Then it is muffled immediately as if doors had fallen shut. [344]

JOCASTA:

Are you asleep, Mother?

ANTIOPE:

from above, where she remains

My eyes sleep, but my heart is awake.
What are they singing?

JOCASTA:

The dirges, Mother,
for Laios, your son.

ANTIOPE:

And you are not mourning?
You are not lying on the ground? Your gown
is not torn?

JOCASTA:

My women have beaten
their breasts. Don't you hear
the hollow arches echo their laments?
Their mournful bodies writhe upon the ground for me;
my whole being knows only death and sorrow—
do I need signs?
Of what use are gestures?

ANTIOPE:

angrily

Such great strength is in your blood,
O Queen, great priestess—
who can fathom your royal mind!
Why should you honor the dead!

JOCASTA:

What do you want of me, Mother?

ANTIOPE:

Woe to those who are barren! [345]

JOCASTA:

Mother, you have lived too long—
you were fruitful once, but are no longer.
Your blessed hands are empty now,
your womb childless again.
And the wind blows past you
as it does past me.

ANTIOPE:

Woe to you that it is so!
While you yet utter them,
your words betray you.

JOCASTA:

What do you want from me, Mother?

ANTIOPE:

Laios, my son, I want my son from you!
Give him back to me!

JOCASTA:

Mother, if your son, still he was my husband. Who is to help me?

ANTIOPE:

When they brought my husband and brothers
back from honored battles I stood erect.
Kings must not die as Laios died:
his hair had turned white before his time;
I saw destruction weave its sedulous net about him.
Give him back to me!

JOCASTA:

Mother, you're raving! He was my husband.

ANTIOPE:

He who takes to himself a fruitless woman [346]
is looked upon with anger by the gods.
He sleeps with her, and shares with her his bread,—

thus nourishing his own slow death.
He cleaves to the curse by his own blood;
it robs him of all joy—
woe!

JOCASTA:

Mother, of whom do you speak?

ANTIOPE:

You were his wife? Then hear me;
I also am a queen.
I know the laws and customs and their meaning.
Kings take wives
so that what'ere was royal in them,
in their souls and features,
in their thoughts and actions,
should live on among the people.
Where can I find such a likeness from your womb,
that I may see my son again, regal and great?
Bring back his image in a son
that I may rejoice at his presence!

JOCASTA:

Mother, let us go each to our own chamber
and weep for the dead.
All things upon this earth are not
as they seem.

Antiope silent, full of hate, turns away supporting herself

JOCASTA:

raising her hands to her

O Mother of my King, most noble, [347]
how my husband resembled you in face and eyes!
I bow before you who bore him for me.

ANTIOPE:

Why did Laios
go away? I know you cannot lie,
so tell me. Could he not bear the childless house?
Did he so abhor your fruitless bed
to leave with few servants, as
one who did not want to avoid death?

JOCASTA:

Who can avoid his own death? Your son went to Delphi
to the god—

ANTIOPE:

What request
was murdered together with him
before it was uttered?

JOCASTA:

Must you ask?
The Sphinx! What king could endure that?

ANTIOPE:

You shared his bed; and still you say that was the reason?

JOCASTA:

Ever since the demon chose yonder pit
for her nest and, singing, strangled men,
night after night, no sleep reached our eyes.
We sat and listened.
And it was awful to hear—more awful still
the silence. We avoided each other's glances [348]
and our lips remained shut—but
we thought of that one thing only.

ANTIOPE:

But why did
the King never go to bring sacrifice
and perform sacred rites before the cave
where she rages?

JOCASTA:

This—perhaps—was done—
perhaps Laios did offer one very great sacrifice
on that dark sacrificial night.

ANTIOPE:

In what place?

JOCASTA:

The gods themselves chose
the place.

ANTIOPE:

Yet the demon still lives and murders!
The sacrifice was not enough.

JOCASTA:

So it seems.
to herself
That's what I think—now she says it too.
aloud
Farewell.

ANTIOPE:

Farewell? But you remain. And I—I do too—.
Is it that you believe I will die soon after my son,
and are bidding me farewell? No, I shall live.
If this did not cast me into the grave,
then I stand fast: age-old gods nourish
my blood, the Night and others,
to whom you do not pray enough. I [349]
have no need for sleep. My eyes see
the Night even in the day, just as one who descends
deep enough into an old well
can see the stars at high noon.
I live half in life and half in death.
Those I have borne are gone.
The first was a handsome child:
a sparkling, bright, innocent stream,
a lovely stream, drew him down,—and he was dead.
The second was a wild and daring boy:
he set the city of his enemies aflame,
and fire consumed his own body with it. The third—
Reflects
the third was your husband, he took the road
through unknown mountain passes, through night and wind,
and never did return. Yet I live on.
What I gave to the light of day
returned to me at night in secret.
I feel that I will outlive even you.

JOCASTA:

to herself
That may well be.

ANTIOPE:

There you stand
glowing from within, bearing the signs
of life—just as Laios bore the marks
of death.—Yet what sustains me
is as mysterious as the life
within the ruby, the only jewel in the royal crown,
which glows more vividly by night than by day.
Should I, one day, refuse all food and drink, [350]
and hover in darkness, I might live on
for years and years, sustained by the dull gleam
of the royal sword that hangs there on the wall.
Death will not tear my hands
from this staff: a god and destiny must come
to wrest it from me.

JOCASTA:

Yes, you speak to gods
as to familiar blood. You wrestle with them
like a giant torch with a storm.

to herself

I burn with so weak a flame—if a
child should come, standing somewhere in the shadow,
he could blow it out. Mother—Mother—
how your hands resemble Laios' hands when
they clasp the staff! Mother—
he truly was your son! He held the royal sword
with such hands; with such hands
he clasped the diadem—embraced my body—

to herself, not fully aware

with such hands he seized the child—
Alas, Mother, can you hear me?

ANTIOPE:

I hear you—
you spoke of Laios, of my child.

JOCASTA:

I spoke
of Laios and a child!

ANTIOPE:

You did not [351]

bear his child. Woe to the barren!
They are cursed!

JOCASTA:

Does it not make you shudder
to realize what you have borne?

ANTIOPE:

I bore kings for a king!
Away from their beds, you childless!

JOCASTA:

I would shudder in my heart to know
I were the mother of a man.
Alas! Mother of demons! You heap up endless
guilt and pain! Do you know no limits? How
can you atone for it? How can you chain
raging desire? When will this fire
burn out which leaps and spreads, consuming
all it touches! Beg for an end!
Man can endure pain beyond measure!
You should bless the gods for having mercifully
stamped out the fire around you, the consuming
fire that lay in your body, and made us alike!
Now pure air surrounds you,
and now should you die, you would find peace at last.
It would be well for you and me!

ANTIOPE:

Curses on your tongue!
My sons, arise! Arise, you, out of the water—
you, out of the fire—you, from your fresh grave!
Arise! Come to me! And drive this woman away!
She boasts, she who bore no son, and
mocks me that I was fruitful. [352]

JOCASTA:

I gave birth to a son.

ANTIOPE:

angrily

Almost. But you did not
give him the breath of life. That you forgot.

He was born dead and but exchanged
one grave for another.

JOCASTA:
somber
He did live.

ANTIOPE:
That audacious child! For how long?
Not an hour.

JOCASTA:
He did live,
as long as those hands would
grant him life.

ANTIOPE:
My hands?

JOCASTA:
Or those
of your son; it is the same.

ANTIOPE:
What kind of
words are these?—Dark ones at least.

JOCASTA:
The deed was darker still. It poured
eternal night for ever over me
and over him. [353]

ANTIOPE:
I will listen if you wish,
or go away.
My head is too old for mysterious words.

JOCASTA:
You, ancestress of all this evil,
you could not reach your grave
until even this last, deeply hidden thing,
from where it lay, heaped with
the agony of years and irresistibly
twisting toward the light, crept back

into your womb as snakes
creep to their holes at night.
No longer able to force it back,
I feel it break free—as if death already deep
in my soul silently, irresistibly,
were arising like dark waters and chasing
all that lives there into the light of day.

ANTIOPE:

I shall stay and listen.

JOCASTA:

The child from my womb, a beautiful child,
with deep and shining eyes, and the breath
of life surging through its body—the strong,
living child—Laios took it in his hands
and strangled it!

ANTIOPE:

She is mad!
Jocasta, come to your senses!

JOCASTA:

I am in my right mind. [354]
Does it matter whether he strangled it
with his own hands or gave it
to a servant to kill?
Alas! I can still see
how he seized it—then darkness fell—darkness!
And when I came to myself, Laios stood there
at my bedside,—then
it was over.

Antiope is silent.

JOCASTA:

Can you hear me, Mother?
My living child was dead!

Antiope is silent.

JOCASTA:

Are you cast in stone?

After silence

ANTIOPE:

Why did my son, Laios the King, have to
execute the child of your womb
with his own hand?
Had it not been his,
he would have condemned you as well as the child.
Speak! It is dark, I cannot see.

JOCASTA:

Do you wish to drink truth to its dregs?
You are strong. The day I wed Laios
my womb was blessed—or
rather cursed—with a child. Then
the King sent this command to the priests:
that they should come to perform the rites
and bless the unborn child that lay in my womb.
They did not come. They sent a message
back, not by a herald—no!
But in the mouth of a child, my brother Creon,
the hideous priests sent
their message: The King should take care
and stand at the bedside of his wife,
armed with a naked sword
as before a cave in which his worst enemy
lurks to attack. If the Queen
bears his son, that son,
when he becomes a man, will kill his father
and set himself upon the throne.

ANTIOPE:

You stood near by,
when Creon, then a child, brought this message
to your husband?

JOCASTA:

No. I was so happy
about what lay before me, I lived
and bathed in sacred waters;
and did not notice that the King
grew pale and sullen. Then suddenly one night
he came to my bed, and his breath

was like that of a strange man
that in fear I called his name:
then he told me.

ANTIOPE:
And then?

JOCASTA:
I prayed
that it would be a girl. Day and night
I fought within myself with what is dark,
and has no name. Yet [356]
All this agony was for nought. Alone,
on a mountain cliff stands a tower—there
I brought to the light of day what was not to remain in the light.

ANTIOPE:
You say he gave it to a servant to kill?
The servant was a witness too. He certainly would
not be allowed to live. What happened to him?

JOCASTA:
That I do not know. Yet I believe
he sent another to follow,
one who was stronger, to strangle him
and to bury him, secretly somewhere.
He who did this deed
could do more, he would not shrink from shedding blood.

ANTIOPE:
What Laios did was wise
and befitting to a king.
Even a king wrestles with his fate,
breast to breast.

JOCASTA:
No! No! No! You—you, yes!
You would do that! With terrifying hands you reach
into the world. But it does not help.
What good is the bloody sacrifice? Did we not—
the two of us, he who was my Lord and King
and I, still a child, both of us
of the blood of gods, did we not then

sacrifice to life as never had
been done before—And because of that
life stared at us as if we had
stunned it by our deed and it would [357]
punish us with stares that froze our marrow
for serving it too ardently.
O, had Laios only listened to me
and consecrated himself and me to death, in
the child's stead—O, I could have given him
all that has now remained buried!—the stars
would have trembled in us, the dark, sacred rivers
rushed through us, we would have been
all alone in this silent world—
alone!—how I could have given myself!
Like a goddess to a god!—But he,
he was your son and struggled with his life,
he struggled and struggled; I saw him grow more pale
and somber, I saw him suffer—and didn't I
suffer with him? I hardly know. I withdrew
from life as one steps
from a bath, with one foot remaining—
I was already separate,
I did not think: I must suffer thus;
nay: I thought, the world suffers thus,
so a queen must suffer;
it was as though another sang and I listened.

ANTIOPE:

That is a sign that the gods
enfolded you in a cloud
to spare you for what is still to come.
Jocasta, I see you now as
I never did before.

JOCASTA:

Now nothing more can happen. No, Mother,
the gods do not deceive! Even so it was
the child who brought death to his father. [358]
Of course, not by his own hand,
for the poor child—does not dwell in the light.
He sent a messenger to hover about

so that his songs would always
reach his father and mother, especially
when they desired to sleep.

ANTIOPE:
Are you speaking
of the Sphinx?

JOCASTA:
I speak of the Sphinx.
A mother knows those messengers her child
sends from the gloomy world below.

ANTIOPE:
Robbers slew the King,
the Sphinx did not.

JOCASTA:
But it was the Sphinx who drove
Laios onto yonder unknown mountain passes,
where his sad fate overtook him. The robber
was but a malformed, lowly pawn
for the one who stood in darkness. And so the child
slew his father. But his messenger
waits there still. The message he was to take
down there is not complete.

ANTIOPE:
How she interprets all the signs—
how right and yet how wrong!

JOCASTA:
Do you hear me, Mother?
Where are you? [359]

ANTIOPE:
How the dawn glows
from her blood! How strong the flame of life
is rising!

JOCASTA:
What are you saying, Mother?

ANTIOPE:
How you shine!

How you draw the god to you!

JOCASTA:

What god?
Whom do you see stepping out of the darkness, Mother?

ANTIOPE:

The god who is to marry you
and raise out of your womb
an heir to the dead Laios.

JOCASTA:

Be silent, Mother!
You do not live where men can breathe—
I will not listen to you.

ANTIOPE:

I feel he is coming;
he tears himself out of a forest.
Do eagle wings carry him? Are dark clouds
blowing along with him? I hear rustling—
is it his cloak?

JOCASTA:

Mother, it is my death, so soon to be upon me,
which makes you tremble as a storm moves a flame.

ANTIOPE:

It is not death but life, your coming life, it blows
toward me and overwhelms me like humid air
from a rushing cascade on my old
bones.

JOCASTA:

The signs of death are all about me—
Do you believe I cannot feel it? My life no longer
stares at me like stone; I see
all things as if I had
loved them and now must weep for them:
I feel as if my dead child were hidden
behind them all.

ANTIOPE:

The unborn
hide in bushes and shrubs; they nod

from the air and the waters.

JOCASTA:

Laios, my husband,
where are you now? I can no longer find you—
not here in my heart and not in the house!
I can no longer hear the sound of your voice!
Do not walk so fast ahead—
wait for me!—Do help me, Mother!
For three days I could not envision my husband;
now he moves away like a strange, faded
shadow, so far; he leaves me
so alone!

ANTIOPE:

Leave the dead to the dead—
happy you are to be alive!
Look, the vessels are aglow, and the house
cannot contain its joy, the air
is filled with it. [361]

JOCASTA:

No, no, it is death that greets this way.
Soon a sign will come. My body feels
as it never felt before: neither light nor heavy—
it feels as if I were air
flowing around it, bidding it farewell.

ANTIOPE:

descends the steps

Forgive this mouth that cursed and called you barren.
Look, these hands will make
amends and consecrate you. Womb of my daughter,
be blessed!

Touches Jocasta, blessing her, walks around her solemnly,

JOCASTA:

What are you doing, Mother?—Mother—
I am the dead Laios' wife! For whom
are you blessing me?

ANTIOPE:

For the one who is to come.

JOCASTA:

Death—death!

ANTIOPE:

You, blood from the blood of gods,
once I consecrated you for Laios' bed;
now I consecrate you for the one for whom Laios had to die
to make room.

JOCASTA:

Open the doors!
O death laments, envelop me! [362]

ANTIOPE:

walking and blessing

The gods
do not forsake their blood; they send one:
he wings out of the air, steps out of flames,
the waters surrender him, he is coming—
his is the sword, his the diadem, now
his is King Laios' bed.

JOCASTA:

Be silent and stand still!

A mighty, dull roar outside.

I hear it roar. Is the river, the old sacred river,
swelling toward us, across the mountain,
to wash this house away and me as well?
Then I bless the river: he is my ancestor
and comes for me.

They both stand still, listening. The dirge has suddenly stopped. The roar swells louder.

JOCASTA:

Now all dreams come true: this is
the end.

ANTIOPE:

What dreams?

JOCASTA:

As I was lying
half asleep, they came toward me,
with dragging feet—there were many—

with bare hands they beat against the wall.

ANTIOPE:

Who came? Who beat against the house? [363]

JOCASTA:

The mothers.

ANTIOPE:

Mothers?

JOCASTA:

Those whose dead, unburied children
lie over yonder.

ANTIOPE:

With the Sphinx?
Jocasta nods.

ANTIOPE:

The dead—
let them remain dead.

JOCASTA:

Yet mothers—to the one mother—
mothers draw everything along with them.
Blood is strong; all depends on mothers.
Dull knocks at the gate.

ANTIOPE:

What have we to do with the people?

JOCASTA:

Death came over them from my womb!

ANTIOPE:

From your womb?

JOCASTA:

fearfully
The Sphinx—I know it, Mother,
I know it—Laios knew it too—
he went out—but his sacrifice alone
was not enough. [364]
knocks
I must go out!

ANTIOPE:
calling
Bar
the gate with stones!

JOCASTA:
No, I want to go out!

ANTIOPE:
Who would rise against a mountain torrent?
It can be mastered by a wall, never by a man.

JOCASTA:
They want me!

ANTIOPE:
Who are they to dare
and stretch out hands to demand your blood?
You are the Queen.

JOCASTA:
They ask for me!

ANTIOPE:
Their cries resemble water when it roars.

JOCASTA:
I want to go to them!
Stronger knocks. Outside the maids cry out.

ANTIOPE:
Call to the gods.
Thus it had to be. With lightning
in his fists a flaming god descends,
with one hand embracing you
and with the other spreading death.
Hear us, Bacchus, we are
of your golden blood! Jocasta, come hither!
Off with this dress! Why drape your body in sorrow,
a god is coming to marry you!

JOCASTA:
Mother, yes, to a god I will soon be wed.
Bring the dress, bring the sash
of the priestess who holds the sacrifice!

She ascends the steps, stands still, and calls back.

Who silenced
the death lament? Here in this house
the death feast is not yet ended!

In front of the palace. The people push against the gate. Creon stands half-hidden in the sacred wood.

PEOPLE:

Open the gate! Bring out the sword! Bring out the crown!
Creon is King! Open for the King! Open the house!
Creon! Creon!

THE WOMEN:

Open the gate! Be quick, sons of the city!
Open the gate!

PEOPLE:

For Creon! For Creon!

They push harder.

THE FIRST IN THE CROWD:

They are coming. They are lifting the bolt.

THE LAST IN THE CROWD:

Move on! Go in! Creon! Creon! [366]

THE FIRST IN THE CROWD:

Lances and swords! They are breaking through!

They move back; all cry out.

The gate opens slowly. Jocasta steps out, Antiope behind her. At that moment the death songs sound very strong, then fade away.

PEOPLE:

softly

The Queens!

ANTIOPE:

What do you want, People? Why are you panting and howling
before this royal house. Answer, People.

PEOPLE:

We want to be without a king no longer.

The earth gives us the sword, the gods give us
royal blood. We want to see the royal sword
flash in a king's hand.
Laios is dead. Give the sword to Creon.
Let Creon be King: a consecrated king
must stand between the Sphinx and us.
We will no longer remain naked, bare, and without protection,
while the demon hovers over us like a cloud of death
from the mountain to the plain.
Creon must be King!

ANTIOPE:

You want him,
that man of shadows, that foppish rascal?
Shame! Your own wish damns you,
like a misbegotten, sickly child.

PEOPLE:

Don't give us evil words, give us a king!
That's why we are here. [367]

ANTIOPE:

From this womb? It is too old.

PEOPLE:

The young woman who stands alongside you, ask her
why she bears no king for us.

JOCASTA:

Silence, People! No mortal shall ever again touch me.

PEOPLE:

Then give up the crown, give up the sword, and Creon,
whom the gods want, shall be King!

ANTIOPE:

That one?

PEOPLE:

Yes, woman, the priests have told us so.

ANTIOPE:

The priests! What are priests that they
can speak to me of gods! You, priests, can crouch upon the ground
inhaling fumes until your limbs twitch;

when birds croak, you can mimic their message.
But do not speak to a queen
of gods, for they are our companions
at bed and board. They do not speak to you
except by storms or floods or lightning.
Have you ever heard the song of Tantalus,
of Niobe?

ELDERS:

She speaks magic words.
Woe to us, this woman is strong!

ANTIOPE:

You are like dogs, crude and full of fear. [368]
Creep back to your houses! Fill
the land with children, so that they swarm
over the sea as on firm ground! We expect
nothing else of you.

PEOPLE:

Why do you scorn us?
You are a woman, we want a king.

ANTIOPE:

You want the one that cowers there in the dark?
Did he buy himself a royal prophecy?
For anything can be bought, even murder.

CREON:

She mocks you as she mocks me. Do you hear her, People?

PEOPLE:

We hear what she says; she speaks of murder.
Whose murder?

CREON:

She is mad:
She cries that I murdered Laios.

ANTIOPE:

Murdered, no! You were always here,
not in the forest there. But who knows? Perhaps you
bought his killers.

CREON:

You lie, woman.

PEOPLE:

Who knows the truth? We want a king
with clean hands. Clear yourself,
Creon! Creon! [369]

VOICES:

calling from the flat roof over the gate

There, over there! He is stepping out of
the forest. He comes, led by a child, he comes!
Teiresias, Teiresias!

PEOPLE:

Teiresias!—What is hidden from our eyes
is revealed to the Seer. He is coming! He steps up to us:
Already we are half redeemed! He pulls
the blindfold from our eyes, and we no longer
stand waiting like the bull that is led to sacrifice: he will tell us
who will drive you from your throne of cruelty,
you Sphinx! He will hold a mirror for us that we may see
the savior who comes for us! He will reveal
what kind of a king the gods have chosen!
We greet you, O holy one, Seer!
Teiresias, led by a child, enters from the right. The people move back with respect.

TEIRESIAS:

Where am I?

CHILD:

Where you asked me to lead you;
I do not know these people.
We stand by a large house.

PEOPLE:

The house of Laios. Laios who is dead.
Two queens stand upon the threshold.

TEIRESIAS:

I am surrounded.

PEOPLE:

We are all here, the children of the city. [370]

ANTIOPE:

We greet you, Teiresias.

PEOPLE:

The Queens are greeting you.
Teiresias is silent.

PEOPLE:

He does not listen to them, he does not heed their word.

CHILD:

He sleeps and yet does not sleep.
He has neither eaten, nor drunk since the last moon.
He sits before his cave and sees what is not there.
Birds nest on his head; a snake sleeps in his lap: but he pays no heed.
Today he rose and said: lead me below;
then I led him. He told me the way.

PEOPLE:

His sleep is sacred. From it he sees into the soul of the world.

CREON:

Teiresias, here stands one innocently
accused. Help me, great Seer, help!

ANTIOPE:

Teiresias, here stands the King's mother,
lamenting a king. Help me, Seer!

PEOPLE:

Teiresias, here we stand, we of Thebes who
still live! From our city walls
we have come running with fear
in our hearts, and cry of our need:
the Sphinx, the Sphinx pursues us! [371]
Help us, Teiresias!

TEIRESIAS:

Here great suffering cries out to the gods.

PEOPLE:

He is turning around; he has heard our cry.

BOY:

They called for you there.

TEIRESIAS:

No, here, not there.

Pointing in the direction where Jocasta stands.

PEOPLE:

The Queen.

TEIRESIAS:

My sleep is too deep. I am too far from
the outer door where they cry.
Is it one or many? "Queen"!
Once it made sense. Now it has no meaning.

PEOPLE:

He is talking to himself.

TEIRESIAS:

Why don't you help me if you need me?
Your fear drew me here,
so help me out of this depth.

ANTIOPE:

Bring the robe of the dead King!

JOCASTA:

Mother, what do you want of him?

They bring the robe. Antiope goes to the edge of the platform with those who carry the robe. [372]

ANTIOPE:

Worthy Seer, who slew the man
that wore this on his body?

TEIRESIAS:

turns away

Why do they hold
the scent of blood before me? They spill blood
and more blood; the son slays his father;
they strangle life as it creeps
new from her womb!

JOCASTA:

O, Mother, let me go!

TEIRESIAS:

They cannot dwell content
with the blood of their bodies:
it rages in them and their veins swell
like snakes around their bodies; they don't
feel powerful enough; their hands
are too weak to root in the world;
they cannot taste of every fruit;
even in death their lustful eyes woo and cannot be satisfied:
so they conceive children, conceive again
lustful lips, new savage hands
and limbs, which can reach,
out of their blood and clasp, until blood
meets with blood in dark forests,
hate meets with hate, eyes askew, and limb
contorts with limb.

ANTIOPE:

Now he will reveal the murderer. [373]

TEIRESIAS:

O sacred blood!
They do not know your force,
they never plunged into your living depths
where pain and illusions die, and love,
hate, hunger, thirst,
age, and death do not dwell.

ANTIOPE:

Seer, we are waiting
for you to reveal the murderer.

WOMEN:

No! No!
The dead are gone! We want life.
A monstrous horror weighs on us.
The Sphinx! The Sphinx!

TEIRESIAS:

You must not tremble, my boy.
It is the suffering of man that, from without,
shakes my body with its dark touch;

within, in my blood, the world blooms,
the stars rise and fall. Stand up;
soon you will lead me home.

ANTIOPE:

I want the murderer!

PEOPLE:

Show us our savior! Our king!
Help us in our need!

ANTIOPE:

with the robe of Laios

Who slew Laios! Does he perhaps stand near?
Here, near us? [374]

TEIRESIAS:

moves back

The king lies stretched out in death;
the servants lie dead with open staring eyes.
The golden gifts for the god
sparkle upon the chariot
and the horses snort.

ANTIOPE:

Who is the murderer? And the others, his companions?
Who lurks in the dark behind the dead?

PEOPLE:

Silence,
the Seer pays you no heed.

TEIRESIAS:

absorbed in his vision

The boy
is of royal blood.

PEOPLE:

jubilant

He sees our savior
in his vision!

ANTIOPE:

Who is the boy?
Even boys can kill.

PEOPLE:
Be silent and listen.
Show us our savior!

ANTIOPE:
Don't let the murderer
out of your sight.

TEIRESIAS:
He steps from the forest
with the sun upon him.

ANTIOPE:
And blood?

PEOPLE IN THE REAR:
He sees
the one who is coming to save us.

OTHERS:
Does he see the god?

PEOPLE IN FRONT:
He is half god, illuminated by the sun.
He can still see him. Is he coming closer?

OTHERS:
Alas,
perhaps he knows nothing of us; knows nothing of the city
which awaits him!

ANTIOPE:
Don't let the boy
out of your sight.

PEOPLE:
Have mercy! Where is he,
where did our savior go?

Teiresias pays no heed to them; his blind eyes stare into the distance.

WOMEN:
He pushes us back
into night and death; we will cast

our children at your feet! But tell us which road
does our savior take? [376]

TEIRESIAS:

overcome by the magnitude of his vision, throws his arms up in the air

Ah, what takes form there! The abyss of pain,
a pit, world-wide, heaped with sorrow!
Final night. Vast pit! Ah, beyond
lies a new day and a new world;
below, a world, still hidden,
leads into a pit of suffering; deep
in the abyss of horror, its glare bursts forth.
A god-like man is rising up out of anguish without measure.
Tongue, be silent; flesh, bow down.

He goes toward Jocasta and prostrates himself before her

It is for your sake
that I have come.

JOCASTA:

Are you blessing me?

TEIRESIAS:

No, Mother,
it is you who bless me.

PEOPLE:

The Seer has cast himself down at the feet,
not of the old woman; he honors the young one like a goddess!

TEIRESIAS:

Away, my boy, return home.

BOY:

To the cave?

TEIRESIAS:

To the cave. [377]

PEOPLE:

surge toward him

We will not let you! Tell us of our savior! What road does he take?
When will he come?

TEIRESIAS:

walks through the crowd

He strides past the gate! He is in the city!
Go, my boy, let us go!

PEOPLE:

Woe, should he wander
past us and not hear us!
How can our cries be heard?
Seer, how can we call him?

TEIRESIAS:

Ask that of the Mother.

He leaves.

PEOPLE:

The Mother? Whom does he mean? He means Jocasta.
Jocasta! Mother!

ANTIOPE:

For her sake a god comes that
he will be wed to her.

JOCASTA:

Who speaks of a god?

PEOPLE:

It is for you that he comes, the one to whom
the crown belongs.

CREON:

from the rear

The poison of madness is spreading. Who [378]
comes? Do you wish to cast
crown and kingdom to a foreign thief?

PEOPLE:

If he is a thief
yet saves us, he is a god and
shall be king. Call to him, Jocasta.

forcefully

Jocasta, call to him!

JOCASTA:

How can I call to him

who is a stranger?

PEOPLE:

Swear by the air,
the fire, and the earth, that the diadem
shall be his, and his the sword.

JOCASTA:

That I swear.

PEOPLE:

And you!

JOCASTA:

What, more?

PEOPLE:

The Queen, too, belongs
to our savior. Swear you too will be his.

JOCASTA:

The stranger's wife?

PEOPLE:

Were he a thief,
a runaway slave, even a murderer,
swear you will be his if he saves us.
Swear, woman! [379]

WOMEN:

O loved one, swear!

JOCASTA:

I have vowed to myself.

CREON:

Her bed is still warm from Laios.

PEOPLE:

Swear aloud!

JOCASTA:

I swear, if a stranger comes and
redeems Thebes from the Sphinx, my house
will be open to him, the sword free for
his hand, the diadem for his head and Laios' bed—

and he will find me in my chamber.

CREON:

Thus queens keep their troth!

JOCASTA:

to herself

That he will find me alive, that I did not swear.

ANTIOPE:

Now shout it loud to the four winds! The one
the Seer saw in his vision was near;
he breathes the same air as we;
a call will reach him.

JOCASTA:

Mother, come into the house.

The Queens enter the palace. The gate closes behind them.

CREON:

steps forward

Why do you stay, People? Why this madness?

PEOPLE:

We await the savior. Leave us, Creon.
We do not know you. The Seer did not
point to you. Go away.

CREON:

O People! The waters
are more steady than you. Whoever holds even the dirt
from the ground holds something;
he who holds you has nothing.
Like a goat you lust for novelties.
You jump about at the words
of an old buffoon!
He who rules you
but does not beat you with scorpions, let him be shamed
and disgraced! When I am your king
I will tread upon your neck!

He disappears on the right.

A MAN:

from the city looking back at the people

A hero has entered our city.

He walks as kings walk, bearing
a staff in his hand, he comes from afar!
A hero!

PEOPLE:

What are the signs? Does he come with a unicorn
by his side? Or does a star shine above him?

MESSENGER:

There are stars in the hollow of his eyes, and the strength [381]
of the unicorn is girded about his loins!
Where houses stood aflame he rushed in
breaking doors with the power of his kick;
he tore the living free
from burning beams and held
his deeds as nothing: half the Thebans are falling
before his feet: he is pushing them aside
and climbing up here,
O sacred Thebans.

MANY VOICES:

from the rear

There he is, our hero.

Oedipus within sight, his back turned.

OTHER VOICES:

murmuring

The hero, look.

OEDIPUS:

People of the city,
why do you stand here pawing the ground before a closed gate
and rearing up like a horse without a rider?
Where is your King that he may bridle you?

PEOPLE:

Our King is dead, stranger.

OEDIPUS:

Why do the houses of your city burn?
Why do your fields lie fallow,
and why do you howl and wail?

PEOPLE:

You don't know?

This is Thebes. Did you come [382]
from the heavens? Are you Perseus?
Perseus?

OEDIPUS:

I came down
from the mountain, I have no name.

PEOPLE:

You came from the mountain? Didn't you see
the camp of the homeless and hear the air full
of wailing?

OEDIPUS:

I pay no heed to voices
in the air.

PEOPLE:

Then you are not
the savior who is sent to us?

OEDIPUS:

To save you from what?

PEOPLE:

You are not the savior. You don't
come as our King? Then who are you?

OEDIPUS:

People, speak sensibly! What need
makes you call to the heavens? I pity you,
that you have no king.

PEOPLE:

The Sphinx,
he knows nothing of the Sphinx.

OEDIPUS:

What? [383]

PEOPLE:

That word means pain and death. It lives over there.
It roams over cliffs like a vulture,
and watches Thebes; and we of Thebes
are like fallen cattle trembling in fear,

with panting flanks and eyes
filled with blood.

OEDIPUS:

Has no one gone to slay
the Sphinx?

The Women cry out in torment.

WOMEN IN THE FOREGROUND:

In a gorge before the cave—
our dead are lying.

THE WOMEN:

Alas!

OEDIPUS:

to himself

You great, holy gods!
What a task do you ask of me! Do you create
such tasks for the homeless man,
do such sparkling palaces lie before his feet,
where he can stay for one night,
and yet another? Did you bless me,
thus, with your curse? For I sense
I will not die today, strangled
by hideous limbs, by polyp arms: I can perform
your task and then go on.

PEOPLE:

Perseus,
do not leave us! [384]

OEDIPUS:

Arise, point out the path
where the demon lurks. But then I will
go alone. Do not ask for me.

PEOPLE:

Are you not Heracles, or Orpheus,
young god?

OEDIPUS:

Show me the way.

PEOPLE:

The Queen!
He must see the Queen before he leaves!

OEDIPUS:

See,
see whom?

PEOPLE:

The Queen, young god.
Jocasta! Open the gate!

JOCASTA:

steps out alone

Who calls?

PEOPLE:

Our savior, see, there, our savior, the youth!

JOCASTA:

spontaneously

Laios!

PEOPLE:

What does she say?

JOCASTA:

No, no, a dream.

OEDIPUS:

petrified at the sight of her

Who is this woman?

JOCASTA:

almost simultaneously

Who is this youth?

PEOPLE:

jubilant

Perseus! Orpheus! Heracles!

OEDIPUS:

startled

Who is this woman?

PEOPLE:

The Queen.

OEDIPUS:

What does
she want?

PEOPLE:

She is yours, young god, yours,
if you are victorious! He does not believe us.

to Jocasta

You have sworn: tell him.

JOCASTA:

You must not do it!
It means your death! For your mother's sake,
do not do it.

OEDIPUS:

For my mother's sake, woman?
O, for her I would do it.

PEOPLE:

Look there, the hero; [386]
see! Entreat the gods, woman;
then he will be your husband.

OEDIPUS:

to himself

The Queen.

PEOPLE:

She swore to it!

OEDIPUS:

in disbelief

Impossible!

restraining himself

I am out of my mind:
the King is her husband.

JOCASTA:

My husband
is dead.

OEDIPUS:

And I—O gods, help me
that I do not perish now.

JOCASTA:

Do you have
more to ask, young man?

OEDIPUS:

I—You will take me
as your husband?

JOCASTA:

I am like the diadem
and the sword: they belong to him
who saves the city.

OEDIPUS:

Don't leave, not yet! [387]
The King, he who was your husband, did he
who died beget children from this womb?
I will protect them and be their guardian.
Those born within the law are holy.

Meanwhile, the maids have stepped forth behind Jocasta. The death lament has stopped.

JOCASTA:

with a weak voice

There was a child, and then no longer.

CREON:

from behind

How this vagabond behaves!
He already plays the King!

OEDIPUS:

with dignity

If there is anyone
who received gold, goods,
cattle or land from the former King, he need not fear;
I ask that nothing be returned.

PEOPLE:

You are a king!
You have always been a king.

CREON:

rends his robe

Curses on you, charlatan!

Disappears among the trees. Dusk is falling.

OEDIPUS:

I would offer a sacrifice before I go, [388]
but I have nothing.

JOCASTA:

turning to her maids, with a completely changed tone of voice

They shall sacrifice
anything that lives in the house. All animals that are dear to me.
They shall kill the horses,
shoot the sacred birds with arrows
and the dogs, even the bitch,
who has slept before my chamber since she was a pup,
even she must die. Hurry, hurry, nothing must live
if he goes out to die.

With the force of her commands she chases all the maids into the house and now stands there all alone.

OEDIPUS:

Have I nothing then?
Am I so poor? No, my staff;
I must face the demon without a weapon:
take the staff and lay it upon the sacred fire.
Let it be sacrificed.

Several take the staff and carry it to the sacred wood. Tumult in the palace.

Jocasta, does not turn around; watches Oedipus, completely absorbed; he stands now before the steps to the sacred wood and is suddenly aglow in the reflection of strong flames.

PEOPLE:

pushing toward the sacred wood

The flame, see the flame!
The gods approve his sacrifice!
The staff lies upon the altar and the flame
leaps to the heavens! [389]

MAIDS:

bursting out of the palace door

The Queen Antiope!

JOCASTA:

What has happened
to her?

MAIDS:

She is motionless. She sits and
the staff has fallen from her hands.
We are afraid that she is dead.
Do you hear us, Queen?

Jocasta is silent, staring at Oedipus.

OEDIPUS:

Now all of you
pray for victory with me.

JOCASTA:

reaches into the air; then she suddenly sinks down with both hands over her heart

I have never lived!

The maids catch her in their arms.

PEOPLE:

The Queen is falling!

OEDIPUS:

She is not dead.

The gate closes while the maids carry the Queen inside. No light except the reflection of the large flame from the sacred wood.

OEDIPUS:

I know she is not dead. I hold the world
in my blood: no star falls, no bird
tumbles from its nest without me.
My dead rest peacefully:
My father and mother whom I shall never see again
are well at home; the man at the quiet
crossroads is at peace; the magnificent woman
in her deathlike sleep is well. For my sake
all this has come to pass that the strength
of the sleeping might rise into me
as water gushes from a spring. Arise! Now show me
the steep path. Where there is none, a mighty
cypress from the cliff will bow down to me,
that I may kiss her crown

and entwine my limbs with hers; she
will lift me up to the cave:
there the monster lurks waiting to die by my hand!
My hand is heavy like a world,
my blood has wings, and my soul
ascends like the water of a spring.
He turns to leave.

PEOPLE:
pushing after him
Perseus you are! Perseus!

Curtain. [391]

ACT III

Steep cliffs. Sparse trees rooted in rocks. At the right the land rises. At the left it drops off into an abyss where a path between rocks ends.
From below a torch glows. Creon is climbing up, disguised in a dark cloak. Carrying a torch he leads Oedipus.

CREON:
We have reached our goal.

OEDIPUS:
upward
Where is it?

CREON:
From here you must go
on alone. This path leads
to the cave.
A moaning is heard from the darkness. Creon raises the torch.

OEDIPUS:
Is it the demon? Step back.
Let me go.

CREON:

You are wrong. He sends
his chamberlain to greet you.

A man drags himself up from the rocks. He is half naked; death is on his face, although one cannot see a wound on him. He seems hardly human.

OEDIPUS:

Who are you?
What do you want?

DYING MAN:

I can't see you. I am blind [392]
from pain. Crush me
with a stone! Strangle me! Have mercy,
strangle me! Throw me into the pit.

Oedipus and Creon stand close together.

OEDIPUS:

It makes me shudder.

CREON:

Hurry on, night is almost over!

OEDIPUS:

Who is this man?

CREON:

in mocking triumph

Your predecessor.

OEDIPUS:

We must hurry!

DYING MAN:

Aren't you human? Put me to death!
The others have all died—they were lucky!
Vultures sit on them—why can't I
die? I climbed down
over countless corpses, and yet I live.
Is it night? Is it day? Does it storm?
Will this hideous gruesome night never end?
Has a murderess torn off the roof
from the world; does night envelop

everything? Speak! Or you are nothing?
Is nothing left in this crumbled world
but my agony? O Mother, why was I born!

OEDIPUS:

I shall help you
find death. Come. I too am born of a woman. [393]
I cannot bear hearing your cries
for death. Embrace me. I shall cast
you down.

CREON:

Watch out! He will drag you with him.

OEDIPUS:

Not me.

DYING MAN:

raising himself up on Oedipus

Blessed be the breast
on which I lean.

OEDIPUS:

Leaned!

Quickly pushes him down. A dull thud.

Alas, what is man!
Whoever mourns over this one will be destroyed. Come on!

He climbs up.

One thing more. Man from Thebes, can you hear?

CREON:

below him

What is it that you want, adventurer?

OEDIPUS:

remains standing above, turned sideways or with his back to the audience

Do not leave
me lying like that man below. When you find me
burn my body. I am the son of a king!
Can you still hear me? Stay near me. This
will be quickly decided—should I then be alive—
O Man, do you see that majestic tree above us,

crowning the barren cliff? If I triumph [394]
then I must use your torch
to make that tree my sign of fire: then the Queen
will rise from her sleep,
and they will bring the crown and sword,
then your effort will be repayed, man from Thebes!
Guard the torch for me!

CREON:

That I will do.

He pushes the torch against the rock, extinguishing it.

OEDIPUS:

has climbed higher, out of sight

What are you doing?

CREON:

Your vulture is so greedy
that he beats out the flame with his wings,
son of a king.

OEDIPUS:

above, out of sight

There, take your reward!

A heavy stone falls, missing Creon.

CREON:

My reward
will come when I hear your death cry.
Don't keep me waiting, adventurer!
Already I feel the dawn breaking. O Fate,
you ancient huntress of the dark,
now you will reveal how your nets are cast.
He brought his insolent,
his greedy blood to market, to bargain
with it for the crown of Thebes;
he climbs thinking he bought it from you; [395]
drawing the dying man to his breast
he thinks that he is a god,
that he gives life and death; he lets
death drip through his locks
like consecrated oil—and I stand here,
untouched by oil, wet with the cold dew

of night, alone, benumbed and regal.
I did not bargain with you, for I am Creon;
I know you, and as a body can know another
I sense your rule in the darkness: show me now
that you still want to probe deeper!
I do not call upon my ancestor who roars below
to rise enraged from his bed
and drag the adventurer down for me:
I do not speak to the mountain: O old throne
of Cadmos, crush this thief to bits
in your final pit–to you alone I speak,
to you, O Fate: it was for me that you have
created this night, which brings death to the cliffs,
and death upon the naked peaks in the star-crowned air,
not for this migrant boy. I know this quickly-angered youth,
this child with his acts, has no part
in this game–O Fate!
Was Creon not a royal youth?
And did you not transform his heart to
the heart of an old man and sear the deeds
from his hands with fiery air,
that they fell to the ground like smoldering embers,
unaccomplished! Nothing can be bought from you by deeds.
You want my soul; you let deeds
fall to the ground and decay,
mocking those who woo you with deeds! [396]

VOICE OF THE BOY SWORD-BEARER:

I gave my young blood
for naught, woe!

CREON:

startled by the voice, he moves back to the right

What, do threads from everywhere
intermesh to strangle me?
I do not want to hear a voice in the night wind;
I only want to hear the death-cry of this man,
nothing else in the world!

He gropes toward the right, climbing in the rocks.
The scene changes immediately.

Another place in the mountain. Open platform, all sides fall off abruptly, only loose stones and cliffs on the left. No tree, no brush. Darkness. A few stars in the sky. Only large shapes can be seen. From the left, driven by consuming impatience, climbing over loose rocks, comes Creon listening expectantly for a sound from above. He stands still.

CREON:

I want to hear the death-cry of this stranger
and be king in Thebes!

Silence.

Do you mock me,
you gods? I am strong—unyielding I stand
like a beast driven to the farthest recess of his cave!
Do not force me from the world!

Silence.

No? Only silence? You don't choose me, but ally yourself
with a thief? Curses upon the nights of sacrifice, [397]
when I dedicated the flower of my youth
to you! Curse on the water that washed me,
curse on the trembling of my young soul!

Desperately imploring, he stretches out his hands.

I call you, murderess, you, great Sphinx,
I debase myself before you
as no one ever did upon the naked peak of life:
O eternal one, cast down to me the cry,
the death-cry of the stranger! O that my soul
might rise to you like burning sacrifice!

From above, towards the side, close by, a horrible death cry is heard.

At first Creon drinks in the cry voluptuously, then—as the cry becomes gruesomely louder—with horror

This is no mortal cry!
O ruin! That was not the stranger's cry!

Oedipus comes, staggering down the rocky path on the left. Creon hides in the deep shadow of a huge rock in the foreground on the left.

OEDIPUS:

Face distorted, unable to control himself, holds onto stones, then staggers to the ground.

It called me by my name! It said to me "Oedipus,

dreamer of such deep dreams,
I greet you!" KNOWN!
Known here! For me the world has no shelter,
no place that is not cursed. There is no
place where I can hide. Here, in this foreign land of Thebes
is a cave where I am known.
shaken by horror
That demon,
that gruesome demon, communed
with me! Its dying breath raised [398]
the locked cover of my heart.
It knows my dreams—ah, there is but one,
the dream of Delphi, alas, the dream of the father,
the mother and the child!
He cowers on the ground.
Why
did I not shatter when the woman
of Delphi approached my bed? Why
does the wild dream of those last days still remain?
The world is breaking apart. My eyes are fixed in spasm. I hate
those who bore me. Father! Mother!
You are lucky not to know this.
His confused, wandering glance falls upon the stars.
O gods, gods!
You sit above in golden lofts
and feast because he whom you hunt with dogs
from morning till night lies now in your net.
Oedipus stands ominous, tall.
The world is your net, life
is your net, and our deeds strip
us naked before your ever-waking eyes,
eyes that watch us through that net:—Here I lie
and wanted to act but I did nothing
but betray myself to Death!
Now end it all! Have you no lightning!
Am I not worthy of the rock which would roll down
to crush me—below there foams a river:
Raise it up! Are your servants so lazy?
Cruel ones, are you thus silent when Oedipus
raises his hands to you begging for death?
Must I kill myself? Must I be both priest

and sacrifice? I shudder.
I shudder before you, gods; no longer do I [399]
want to look into your eyes; cast
darkness over me, cast death
upon my face like a cloak, O gods!
stretching out his arms
I want only death!

CREON:
springs out of the dark with a raised dagger
It is yours!

OEDIPUS:
falls back, grasps Creon
Does the darkness have arms?

CREON:
wrestles in order to free the arm holding the dagger
In Thebes, yes, and daggers too!

OEDIPUS:
wrestling with him
Give me the dagger.
I shall kill myself.
gets the upper-hand; pushes Creon to the ground
But you shall die first.
The sacrifice I want to make cannot tolerate
another's presence.
He raises the dagger to strike.
Down, and
announce my coming below.

CREON:
Adventurer, you don't know
whom you slay!

OEDIPUS:
raises the dagger again
All the world is dark;
no creature needs a name! [400]

CREON:
lying under him
I am the brother
of the Queen.

OEDIPUS:

stares at him from above

What speaks out of the night?
Who are you who wrestles with me upon the threshold
of eternal death?

CREON:

I am the brother
of the Queen, royal prince.

OEDIPUS:

without letting him go

Brother
of the wonderful woman who was
startled to death when she saw my face?
He draws him out of intense darkness to the foreground where the glimmer of stars creates a weak light. He looks into his face.
And are you not also the guide who climbed through the night
with me? Did you not extinguish the
torch and intend me to die before my time?

He lets go of him. Creon rises quickly to his feet.

OEDIPUS:

takes one step backward

The brother! O how monstrously you chain
mortals to one another with night
and death and lust, O gods, how monstrously!

He holds out the dagger to Creon.

There, take the sacrificial knife! Kill me!
It is your right! [401]

CREON:

backing away from him without taking the dagger

Dreadful
stranger, who are you that you play such ominous games
with your own life and mine?

OEDIPUS:

One cursed
by his father's seed! There, take the knife
and make the sacrifice!
Again urges him to take the dagger; again Creon moves back.
Quickly! this strange, cursed beast
would have desecrated your sister's bed.

Emphatically

Avenge the Queen, man!

CREON:

moves his hands back, makes a strong gesture of silence

You are
the victor! The scream was not yours! It was
the demon who screamed in death! You are
the victor!

OEDIPUS:

No, I am accursed
at home and abroad.

CREON:

unable to comprehend him

O Man, do you carry death
in your body? Why do you stand erect, writhe
before my feet! Let me put my hands
into your wounds! Quickly!

OEDIPUS:

My body is sound [402]
and bristles with indestructible strength.
I could not perform my deed:
the creature fled from me!

CREON:

Why do you still torture me,
masked god, when the victory is yours?

OEDIPUS:

with growing haste

Victory! Chaos lies upon me and
gnaws me to death.

CREON:

O puzzling, mysterious man,
what has the Sphinx done to you?

OEDIPUS:

in flying haste

At the entry of her cave
the woman arose and bowed to earth
before me, and when I came near, she stepped
humbly back and bowed low

to the ground as if I were the guest
for whom she had waited a hundred years.
In silence she reeled back,
raised her face and looked at me.
Then I saw her face, and my eyes
bulged from their sockets; I felt the flesh
falling from my bones like tinder
in terror and fear: My heart beat as in death,
my breast throbbed; then from her sallow, ugly lips
she offered her greeting to my
throbbing heart: "Ah, there you are,"
these words she said; "you for whom [403]
I have been waiting, hail Oedipus!
Hail to you, dreamer of deep dreams."
My breast torn apart, her dying eyes,
filled with repulsive tenderness
fixed upon me, she threw herself backwards
into the stony abyss which no eye can measure;
and in her fatal plunge she uttered an unequaled,
most terrible cry in which triumph
and death's agony were wed, and plunged down
in front of me, and hit deep below with a
dull sound. Have you turned to stone? If you
wanted to slaughter me in the dark, sacrifice me in the light!
Holds the dagger out to him.

CREON:
overcome by hidden terror
I will not raise my hand against you!
You are a god and a son of gods!

OEDIPUS:
urgently
Kill me!
I am the King of Corinth's son
and dreamt a dream that would rise
to strangle me even if I would cover it
with half the mountains in the world!

CREON:
You are the victor, Oedipus, you are
the victor! Now you are King of Thebes!
Intent to flee from him, afraid because he does not understand, halfway turned for flight. [404]

OEDIPUS:

more urgently

Then kill me! Can't you sense that I am
weighed down with curses, and spotted with misfortune
like a panther's skin! Take the knife
and sacrifice me while I can still restrain myself:
for I want to live, I want to be King,
I want to take the Queen for my wife
upon this naked throne of rocks!
I am both king and monster
in one body; quickly, strangle both!
The gods cannot separate one from the other; kill me!
I could believe that this night
I did the deed which tears the flower of life
from the trembling plains of heaven
with happy hands! I could imagine
that I am the greatest of all men,
the chosen son of fortune. Here, take it.
Kill me! Quickly!

He lowers himself before Creon like one who is ready to offer up his life.

CREON:

as if intoxicated from this unbelievable turn of fate, raises the dagger above Oedipus who cowers before him like a bound beast of sacrifice

Thank you, O gods!

When he is about to stab him, something from within paralyses his arm.

I cannot do it!

He raises the dagger once more, wrestling with fate.

What makes him stronger even now? He is nothing.
It is my dream that makes him stronger. My dream
has set its foot upon my neck!

Seized by terror he throws the dagger away so that it falls with a clatter. At this moment lightning strikes. At once the tree on the cliff catches fire invisibly, and a strong light breaks in from the upper left.

CREON:

blinded by the lightning, cries out

Ah!

He flees from Oedipus, covering his face with his cloak. Oedipus jumps up.

CREON:

afraid, five paces away from him

You are a god! Spare me!

OEDIPUS:

as if waking from a deep dream

The light of the gods!
What do you want of me?

CREON:

bowed down, ready to worship him

You are a god! The tremendous
light came down behind you
from the blue night like a golden eagle!

OEDIPUS:

lost in amazement

The light!

CREON:

The thousand-year-old tree perched
upon the barren cliff is aflame!
You are a god! I kiss the stones
before your feet. The gods kindle
your wedding torch with their own hands. [406]

OEDIPUS:

as above

With their own hands!

CREON:

The eagles circle
the mountains as your fiery messengers!
My King, let me touch your garment;

He throws himself down before him.

and then raise me up!

OEDIPUS:

stretches both arms into the air

O my parents, O Phoenix!
Corinth! be gone! . . . Rise and tell me
the name!

CREON:

I am Creon.

OEDIPUS:

You? Who asks for you?
I ask but one name in this world:
that name reveal to me!

CREON:

The name of the Queen
is Jocasta.
The tree has burned down. The faint dawn soon changes into the first greenish glimmer of morning.

OEDIPUS:

drinking in the name
How shallow dreams are: I
never dreamt of such a name.
From far below comes the sound of kettle drums. Slowly coming closer. Solemn singing can be heard on a high mountain top as if drifting up [407] *from a deep valley, gradually rising.*
Even though approaching, it remains far below and distant.
Yet now that I heard it,
it seems to me as if the dull thundering
pulse of the world, the restless sea,
were rising and falling, wedded in lust with the surges
of the blood in my veins.

CREON:

Oedipus,
those are the sacred drums which you hear, beating
in your honor!

OEDIPUS:

Is the mountain
coming to life?

CREON:

That is Thebes, which rises
like a flood to bring her King
down from the cliff.

OEDIPUS:

runs back to the edge of the rock, motions for Creon to come. They both look down.

There,
that tremendous crowd?

CREON:

The people, the priests,
the sacred vessels!

OEDIPUS:

There, what is that dull flash,
sparkling out of the night, lit by no ray of day? [408]

CREON:

That is the royal sword. That is the sword
of Cadmos.

OEDIPUS:

in his tremendous excitement he cannot bear to stand back and wait. He dashes forward, dragging Creon along

Stay with me and be my brother!
No soul can bear the storm that breaks in me
without a brother!

back again with Creon to the edge of the cliff

There,
What is that wrapped in dark veils
drawn in a chariot by six horses, Creon;
is it the statue of a god?

CREON:

That is Jocasta!

OEDIPUS:

away from the edge, suddenly throwing himself forward

Enveloped by a dull glow, like a star
in a cloud! They are veils: my—
ah! my hands will raise them—then flame
will merge into flame!

Elated, he rushes back to the edge, bends over, calls down, regally impatient

Faster, faster!

Then he again steps back from the edge.

CREON:

still looking down, hastens now to Oedipus

They have seen you! They greet you
as a god; they raise holy branches

to you! Ha, do you see the ruby
of the royal headband? It has drunk
the blood of giants. Oedipus, [409]
it will glow upon your forehead!

Suddenly overcome by the feeling of his own fate he throws himself on the ground, beats the rocks with his hands, full of anger and pain.

OEDIPUS:

so absorbed he does not notice what Creon is feeling, pulls him up violently

You Prince,
my brother Creon, how you stand there before me!
how fair you are! Why are you so pale and somber
like olive leaves in the wind! Creon, we want to live
like a blessed race! This Thebes
shall bloom like a flower of fire! Cadmos,
your blood must bloom in a breed of eagles
born of fire!

CREON:

bent again over the edge

Oedipus, she descends
from the chariot!

OEDIPUS:

standing in front, jubilant, while Creon stands at a distance, on the edge of the rock

Creon, if I rule Thebes a hundred years
I shall not forget that you
were the messenger who told me of it!

CREON:

from the edge

King,
she ascends alone.

Creon steps back, toward the left.
Oedipus stands in front staring in expectation. [410]
Jocasta steps up, a crown on her head.
The people, not visible, are approaching the summit. The restlessness of the crowd trying to be quiet surges up now and then.

JOCASTA:

Why are you here, Creon,
when a queen approaches a king?
Step back.

Creon steps farther back.

JOCASTA:

sees Oedipus. She stands with her back near the edge. Calling back over her shoulder she commands

Get back, even you, Creon; let no one approach!
She approaches Oedipus, remains standing ten paces from him.
You are a god. Only the gods re-create
what they touch. I am your creature:
you cast me into a sleep as into a fire
and there renewed
my soul and limbs. Speak: shall your
creature kneel between your hands?

Oedipus is silent.

JOCASTA:

I never before spoke to a god:
tell me yourself how I should greet you.

OEDIPUS:

I am human like you, Jocasta!

JOCASTA:

Blessed be
she who bore you. Tell me the name
of the mother who bore you! I want to honor her
more than a goddess. [411]

OEDIPUS:

Nothing more about my mother!
That is all part of the past. I cut myself
free with the sword. The Oedipus
who stands before you is the child of his own deeds;
he was born this night. Won't you come
closer, my Queen?
Jocasta steps up to him. She halts three steps before him. She raises her hands toward him as toward an image of a god.

OEDIPUS:

Is it your heart
which glows through your hands?
Jocasta lets her hands drop.

OEDIPUS:

more softly, bent forward
For you
of whom I never dreamt have I disdained
the virgins of my homeland.

JOCASTA:

softly, gently, all the force of secret longing in her eyes
O youth,
was it for you that I wanted to die when
I was drawn down to my child? No dream
would reveal it to me—was it that
your living presence
should pierce me with such a shaft of light?

OEDIPUS:

You
wanted to die, Jocasta, you?

JOCASTA:

Yes, I. [412]
Not once but a hundred times. My life was
but a shadow. Am I Jocasta?
Have I not borrowed her body and do I not come
as a guest from the dark world below
desiring the blood from your heart? O youth,
beware of me.

OEDIPUS:

Your voice
stirs the night in the abyss and casts
light upon the mountain tops.

JOCASTA:

Turn your eyes
away from my hands. Their veins have
been too close to the self-drawn knife;
the blood you see glowing in them

must stay forever dark. What does
a sad woman want with a youth? Let me go.
He takes her hand, lets it go immediately.

OEDIPUS:

I seem to know things which, spoken,
turn the blood to ice. Yet, Jocasta,
I learned them only that I might forget them
in your arms.

JOCASTA:

crosses her arms over her chest
I cursed all motherhood
and praised aloud
the childless womb.

OEDIPUS:

Jocasta,
with a spiteful soul I cursed
my life to death. [413]

JOCASTA:

smiling away all darkness
Alas, how alike
we are in misfortune.

OEDIPUS:

How alike we are and yet are not!
Jocasta! How everything wavers, changes,
and yields before the fire which breaks
from the depth of sacred blood.
He wants to draw her to him.

JOCASTA:

O I feel,
so weak and light—
She braces herself on the rock.
I feel I should die
in your arms!

OEDIPUS:

near her without embracing her
For the sake of this death
through which you have passed, Jocasta,

I must love you as no man on earth loves
his virgin wife. The secrets of death
are fastened at your belt,
glowing in somber flames: but I—
I tell you: as truly as this naked stone
which was to be my tomb
now mounts as a throne for you and me—knowing
nothing and adorned in splendor
with sacred forgetfulness—as truly
as that which leaps over the cliffs
winged, and raging, swings across— [414]

JOCASTA:
in reverent awe turning toward a sudden glow
The sacred light!

OEDIPUS:
As truly as this is the messenger
of the monstrous gods, so
you and I are but smoke, which
will radiantly bring forth a new, a holy,
a vivid being.

JOCASTA:
overcome by memory whispers
I did belong to a
man.

OEDIPUS:
draws her to himself
Past! Forgetting we shall live!
Jocasta!

JOCASTA:
sinks in his arm like a bent flower
Ah, what are we doing?

OEDIPUS:
The blind deed of the gods.

PEOPLE:
Hail to our King!
Hail to the unknown King!

CREON:

steps forward

Hail, King Oedipus!

JOCASTA:

with a transfigured look, wresting herself gently away

The man over there knows your name—
and I—who cleave to you, I do not know it. [415]

She utters a short, indescribably light, fleeting laugh.

You—I—not blind!—What were you saying—no, not blind!
We can both see! You are not a god and I,
my boy, not a goddess! My boy, my boy,
they are poor compared to us, these gods who
cannot die, poor they are! But you—and I:
you standing there on this sacred mountain,
your blood that has driven you, the suffering
which has pursued you—my days and nights,
my blood that could not live or die:
and today, this very day, you and I!
The days now before us, days upon days,
the unknown before us and
already here, days and nights, nights and days,
the darkness we know, and still we laugh—
you blessing me, I blessing you, your
face beside mine and my face by yours!
Where are the gods, then, where is this death
with which they always crush our hearts?
Death was forever around me,
before my eyes, in my hair, clinging
to me like smoke; where has it gone?
It has entered into my body,
and become a nameless desire, an immense
promise: O you, my King:
we are more than the gods, we;
we are priest and sacrifice; our hands
sanctify all: we alone
are the world!

She leans against him.

OEDIPUS:

Jocasta, never die and leave me! [416]

JOCASTA:

weakly

Carry me below; I believe there is a house
wherein to rest.

OEDIPUS:

My Queen!

The people, unseen, call out the same exclamation, roaring powerfully like breaking waves.

JOCASTA:

as both of them turn ready to step down, he leading her, almost pulling her, she frees herself from him, and now holding his hand in hers

Yes, my People!
You cry for your King. It is he
whom I have chosen.

PEOPLE:

with force

King Oedipus!

Creon jumps ahead, throws off his cloak and spreads it before the feet of Oedipus and Jocasta. He himself, regally dressed in a purple garment, kneels before them as they pass him to descend.

Curtain.

Literary Criticism

Poetics

Aristotle

Although Aristotle (384–322 B.C.) was born about twenty years after the death of Sophocles, he was well qualified to understand his plays as their author intended them to be understood. Much of his theory of drama is based on *Oedipus the King,* a play he knew and admired.

The *Poetics,* by Aristotle, the famous Greek philosopher, is probably a summary by another person or a body of notes compiled from lectures by some auditor. This would explain its crisp, dry style—its mechanical, authoritarian tone. It provides the basis for formal and structural criticism of imaginative literature, what Aristotle has called "imitation" or "poetry." As it shows how the techniques of literature may be analyzed and evaluated, it marks the true beginning of criticism.

Only tragedy is discussed in any detail. Here may be found the source of our basic ideas on such familiar problems as unity of plot action, characterization and the tragic flaw, probability (plausibility and poetic truth) in plot and character, the nature and definition of tragedy, the tragic emotions and their catharsis, and the universality of art. That Aristotle's penetrating remarks on these issues must be reckoned with, critics of the past and present

From S. H. Butcher, *Aristotle's Theory of Poetry and Fine Art* (4th ed., New York: Dover Publications, Inc. 1951), pp. 11–107. Reprinted through the permission of the publisher.

demonstrate in their own practice. Thus it is no exaggeration to assert that Aristotle's *Poetics* is the most influential work in the entire history of criticism. No critic, ancient or modern, compares with Aristotle in authority.

Butcher's authoritative translation, completed in 1894, was the first critical text of the *Poetics* to appear since Thomas Tyrwhitt's in 1794. It contains a collated Greek text as well as elaborate commentary.

The excerpts that follow include, generally, only those sections of the *Poetics* that are directly concerned with the practice of Sophocles, particularly in his *Oedipus*. These comments make clear the impression that Aristotle regarded Sophocles' play as the type of all Greek tragedy.

Since the objects of imitation are men in action, and these men must be either of a higher or a lower type (for moral character mainly answers to these divisions, goodness and badness being the distinguishing marks of moral differences), it follows that we must represent men either as better than in real life, or as worse, or as they are. It is the same in painting. Polygnotus depicted men as nobler than they are, Pauson as less noble, Dionysius drew them true to life. . . . So again in language, whether prose or verse unaccompanied by music. Homer, for example, makes men better than they are; Cleophon as they are; Hegemon the Thasian, the inventor of parodies, and Nicochares, the author of the Deiliad, worse than they are. . . . [11] The same distinction marks off Tragedy from Comedy; for Comedy aims at representing men as worse, Tragedy as better than in actual life.

There is still a third difference—the manner in which each of these objects may be imitated. For the medium being the same, and the objects the same, the poet may imitate by narration—in which case he can either take another personality as Homer does, or speak in his own person, unchanged—or he may present all his characters as living and moving before us.

These, then, as we said at the beginning, are the three differences which distinguish artistic imitation,—the medium, the objects, and the manner. So that from one point of view, Sophocles is an imitator of the same kind as Homer—for both imitate higher types of character; from another point of view, of the same kind as Aristophanes—for both imitate persons acting and doing. Hence, some say, the name of 'drama' is given to such poems, as representing action. . . . [13]

. . . Tragedy—as also Comedy—was at first mere improvisation The one originated with the authors of the Dithyramb, the other with those of the phallic songs, which are still in use in many of our cities. Tragedy advanced by slow degrees; each new element that showed itself was in turn developed. Having passed through many changes, it found its natural form, and there it stopped.

Aeschylus first introduced a second actor; he diminished the importance of the Chorus, and assigned the leading part to the dialogue. Sophocles raised the number of actors to three, and added scene-painting. Moreover, it was not till late that the short plot was discarded for one of greater compass, and the grotesque diction of the earlier satyric form for the stately manner of Tragedy. The iambic measure then replaced the trochaic tetrameter, which was originally employed when the poetry was of the satyric order, and had greater affinities with dancing. Once dialogue had come in, Nature herself discovered the appropriate measure. For the iambic is, of all measures, the most colloquial: we see it in the fact that conversational speech runs into iambic lines more frequently than into any other kind of verse; rarely into hexameters, and only when we drop the colloquial intonation. The additions to the number of 'episodes' or acts, and the other accessories of which tradition [19] tells, must be taken as already described; for to discuss them in detail would, doubtless, be a large undertaking.

Comedy is, as we have said, an imitation of characters of a lower type,—not, however, in the full sense of the word bad, the Ludicrous being merely a subdivision of the ugly. It consists in some defect or ugliness which is not painful or destructive. To take an obvious example, the comic mask is ugly and distorted, but does not imply pain. . . .

Epic poetry agrees with Tragedy in so far as it is an imitation in verse of characters of a higher type. They differ, in that Epic poetry admits but one kind of metre, and is narrative in form.

They differ, again, [21] in their length: for Tragedy endeavours, as far as possible, to confine itself to a single revolution of the sun, or but slightly to exceed this limit; whereas the Epic action has no limits of time. This, then, is a second point of difference; though at first the same freedom was admitted in Tragedy as in Epic poetry. . . .

. . . Let us now discuss Tragedy, resuming its formal definition, as resulting from what has been already said.

Tragedy, then, is an imitation of an action that is serious, complete, and of a certain magnitude; in language embellished with each kind of artistic ornament, the several kinds being found in separate parts of the play; in the form of action, not of narrative; through pity and fear effecting the proper purgation of these emotions. By 'language embellished,' I mean language into which rhythm, 'harmony,' and song enter. By 'the several kinds in separate parts,' I mean, that some parts are rendered through the medium of verse alone, others again with the aid of song.

Now as tragic imitation implies persons acting, it necessarily follows, in the first place, that Spectacular equipment will be a part of Tragedy. Next, Song and Diction, for these are the medium of imitation. By 'Diction' [23] I mean the mere metrical arrangement of the words: as for 'Song,' it is a term whose sense every one understands.

Again, Tragedy is the imitation of an action; and an action implies personal agents, who necessarily possess certain distinctive qualities both of character and thought; for it is by these that we qualify actions themselves, and these—thought and character—are the two natural causes from which actions spring, and on actions again all success or failure depends. Hence, the Plot is the imitation of the action:—for by plot I here mean the arrangement of the incidents. By Character I mean that in virtue of which we ascribe certain qualities to the agents. Thought is required wherever a statement is proved, or, it may be, a general truth enunciated. Every Tragedy, therefore, must have six parts, which parts determine its quality—namely, Plot, Character, Diction, Thought, Spectacle, Song. Two of the parts constitute the medium of imitation, one the manner, and three the objects of imitation. And these complete the list. . . .

But most important of all is the structure of the [25] incidents. For Tragedy is an imitation, not of men, but of an action and of life, and life consists in action, and its end is a mode of action, not a quality. Now character determines men's qualities, but it is by their actions that they are happy or the reverse. Dramatic action, therefore, is not with a view to the representation of character: character comes in as subsidiary to the actions. Hence the incidents and the plot are the end of a tragedy; and the end is the chief thing of all. Again, without action there cannot be a tragedy; there may be without character. The tragedies of most of our modern poets fail in the rendering of character; and of poets in general this is often true. It is the same in painting; and here lies the difference between Zeuxis and Polygnotus. Polygnotus delineates character well: the style of Zeuxis is devoid of ethical quality. Again, if you string together a set of speeches expressive of character, and well finished in point of diction and thought, you will not produce the essential tragic effect nearly so well as with a play which, however deficient in these respects, yet has a plot and artistically constructed incidents. Besides which, the most powerful elements of emotional interest in Tragedy—Peripeteia or Reversal of the Situation, and Recognition scenes—are parts of the plot. A further proof is, that novices in the art attain to finish of diction and precision of portraiture before they can construct the plot. It is the same with almost all the early poets.

The Plot, then, is the first principle, and, as it were, [27] the soul of a tragedy: Character holds the second place. A similar fact is seen in painting. The most beautiful colours, laid on confusedly, will not give as much pleasure as the chalk outline of a portrait. Thus Tragedy is the imitation of an action, and of the agents mainly with a view to the action.

Third in order is Thought,—that is, the faculty of saying what is possible and pertinent in given circumstances. In the case of oratory, this is the function of the political art and of the art of rhetoric: and so indeed the older poets make their characters speak the language of civic life; the poets of our time, the language of the rhetoricians. Character is that which reveals moral purpose, showing what kind of things a man chooses or avoids. Speeches, therefore, which do not make this manifest, or in which the speaker does not choose or avoid anything whatever, are not expressive of character. Thought, on the other hand, is found where something is proved to be or not to be, or a general maxim is enunciated. . . .

The Spectacle has, indeed, an emotional attraction of its own, but, of all the parts, it is the least artistic, and connected least with the art of poetry. For the power of Tragedy, we may be sure, is felt even apart from representation and actors. Besides, the production of [29] spectacular effects depends more on the art of the stage machinist than on that of the poet.

These principles being established, let us now discuss the proper structure of the Plot, since this is the first and most important thing in Tragedy.

Now, according to our definition, Tragedy is an imitation of an action that is complete, and whole, and of a certain magnitude; for there may be a whole that is wanting in magnitude. A whole is that which has a beginning, a middle, and an end. A beginning is that which does not itself follow anything by causal necessity, but after which something naturally is or comes to be. An end, on the contrary, is that which itself naturally follows some other thing, either by necessity, or as a rule, but has nothing following it. A middle is that which follows something as some other thing follows it. A well constructed plot, therefore, must neither begin nor end at haphazard, but conform to these principles. . . . [31]

. . . And to define the matter roughly, we may say that the proper magnitude is comprised within such limits, that the sequence of events, according to the law of probability or necessity, will admit of a change from bad fortune to good, or from good fortune to bad.

Unity of plot does not, as some persons think, consist in the unity of the hero. For infinitely various are the incidents in one man's life which cannot be reduced to unity; and so, too, there are many actions of one man out of which we cannot make one action. Hence the error, as it appears, of all poets who have composed a Heracleid, a Theseid, or other poems of the kind. They imagine that as Heracles was one man, the story of Heracles must also be a unity. But Homer, as in all else he is of surpassing merit, here too—whether from art or natural genius—seems to have happily discerned the truth. In composing the Odyssey he did not include all the adventures of Odysseus—such as his wound on Parnassus, or his feigned madness at the mustering of [33] the host—incidents between which there was no necessary or probable connexion: but he made the Odyssey, and likewise the Iliad, to centre round an action that in our sense of the word is one. As therefore, in the other imitative arts, the imitation is one when the object imitated is one, so the plot, being an imitation of an action, must imitate one action and that a whole, the structural union of the parts being such that, if any one of them is displaced or removed, the whole will be disjointed and disturbed. For a thing whose presence or absence makes no visible difference, is not an organic part of the whole.

It is, moreover, evident from what has been said, that it is not the function of the poet to relate what has happened, but what may happen,—what is possible according to the law of probability or necessity. The poet and the historian differ not by writing in verse or in prose. The work of Herodotus might be put into verse, and it would still be a species of history, with metre no less than without it. The true difference is that one relates what has happened, the other what may happen. Poetry, therefore, is a more philosophical and a higher thing than history: for poetry tends to express the universal, history the particular. By the universal I mean how a person of a certain type will on occasion speak or act, according to the law of probability or necessity; and it is this universality at which poetry aims in the names she attaches to the personages. The particular is—for example—what Alcibiades did or suffered. . . . [35]

Of all plots and actions the epeisodic are the worst. [37] I call a plot 'epeisodic' in which the episodes or acts succeed one another without probable or necessary sequence. Bad poets compose such pieces by their own fault, good poets, to please the players; for, as they write show pieces for competition, they stretch the plot beyond its capacity, and are often forced to break the natural continuity.

But again, Tragedy is an imitation not only of a complete action, but of events inspiring fear or pity. Such an effect is best produced when the events come on us by surprise; and the effect is heightened when, at the same time, they follow as cause and effect. The tragic wonder will then be greater than if they happened of themselves or by accident; for even coincidences are most striking when they have an air of design. We may instance the statue of Mitys at Argos, which fell upon his murderer while he was a spectator at a festival, and killed him. Such events seem not to be due to mere chance. Plots, therefore, constructed on these principles are necessarily the best. . . . [39]

Reversal of the Situation is a change by which the action veers round to its opposite, subject always to our rule of probability or necessity. Thus in the Oedipus, the messenger comes to cheer Oedipus and free him from his alarms about his mother, but by revealing who he is, he produces the opposite effect. Again in the Lynceus, Lynceus is being led away to his death, and Danaus goes with him, meaning to slay him; but the outcome of the preceding incidents is that Danaus is killed and Lynceus saved.

Recognition, as the name indicates, is a change from ignorance to knowledge, producing love or hate between the persons destined by the poet for good or bad fortune. The best form of recognition is coincident with a Reversal of the Situation, as in the Oedipus. There are indeed other forms. Even inanimate things of the most trivial kind may in a sense be objects of recognition. Again, we may recognise or discover whether a person has done a thing or not. But the recognition which is most intimately connected with the plot and action is, as we have said, the recognition of persons. This recognition, combined with Reversal, will produce either pity or fear; and actions producing these effects are those which, by our definition, Tragedy represents. Moreover, it is upon such situations that the issues of good or bad fortune will depend. [41] Recognition, then, being between persons, it may happen that one person only is recognised by the other—when the latter is already known—or it may be necessary that the recognition should be on both sides. Thus Iphigenia is revealed to Orestes by the sending of the letter; but another act of recognition is required to make Orestes known to Iphigenia.

Two parts, then, of the Plot—Reversal of the Situation and Recognition—turn upon surprises. A third part is the Scene of Suffering. The Scene of Suffering is a destructive or painful action, such as death on the stage, bodily agony, wounds and the like. [43]

. . . we must proceed to consider what the poet should aim at, and what he should avoid, in constructing his plots; and by what means the specific effect of Tragedy will be produced.

A perfect tragedy should, as we have seen, be arranged not on the simple but on the complex plan. It should, moreover, imitate actions which excite pity and fear, this being the distinctive mark of tragic imitation. It follows plainly, in the first place, that the change of fortune presented must not be the spectacle of a virtuous man brought from prosperity to adversity: for this moves neither pity nor fear; it merely shocks us. Nor, again, that of a bad man passing from adversity to prosperity: for nothing can be more alien to the spirit of Tragedy; it possesses no single tragic quality; it neither satisfies the moral sense nor calls forth pity or fear. Nor, again, should the downfall of the utter villain be exhibited. A plot of this kind would, doubtless, satisfy the moral sense, but it would inspire neither pity nor fear; for pity is aroused by unmerited misfortune, fear by the misfortune of a man like ourselves. Such an event, therefore, will be neither pitiful nor terrible. There remains, then, the character between these two extremes,—that of a man who is not eminently good and just, yet whose misfortune is brought about not by vice or depravity, but by some error or frailty. He must be one who is highly renowned and prosperous.—a [45] personage like Oedipus, Thyestes, or other illustrious men of such families.

A well constructed plot should, therefore, be single in its issue, rather than double as some maintain. The change of fortune should be not from bad to good, but, reversely, from good to bad. It should come about as the result not of vice, but of some great error or frailty, in a character either such as we have described, or better rather than worse. The practice of the stage bears out our view. At first the poets recounted any legend that came in their way. Now, the best tragedies are founded on the story of a few houses,—on the fortunes of Alcmaeon, Oedipus, Orestes, Meleager, Thyestes, Telephus, and those others who have done or suffered something terrible. A tragedy, then, to be perfect according to the rules of art should be of this construction. Hence they are in error who censure Euripides just because he follows this principle in his plays, many of which end unhappily. It is, as we have said, the right ending. The best proof is that on the stage and in dramatic competition, such plays, if well worked out, are the most tragic in effect; and Euripides, faulty though he may be in the general management of his subject, yet is felt to be the most tragic of the poets.

In the second rank comes the kind of tragedy which some place first. Like the Odyssey, it has a double thread of plot, and also an opposite catastrophe for the good and for the bad. It is accounted the best because of the weakness of the spectators; for the poet is guided in what he writes by the wishes of his audience. The pleasure, however, thence derived is not the true tragic [47] pleasure. It is proper rather to Comedy, where those who, in the piece, are the deadliest enemies—like Orestes and Aegisthus—quit the stage as friends at the close, and no one slays or is slain.

Fear and pity may be aroused by spectacular means; but they may also result from the inner structure of the piece, which is the better way, and indicates a superior poet. For the plot ought to be so constructed that, even without the aid of the eye, he who hears the tale told will thrill with horror and melt to pity at what takes place. This is the impression we should receive from hearing the story of the Oedipus. But to produce this effect by the mere spectacle is a less artistic method, and dependent on extraneous aids. Those who employ spectacular means to create a sense not of the terrible but only of the monstrous, are strangers to the purpose of Tragedy; for we must not demand of Tragedy any and every kind of pleasure, but only that which is proper to it. And since the pleasure which the poet should afford is that which comes from pity and fear through imitation, it is evident that this quality must be impressed upon the incidents.

Let us then determine what are the circumstances which strike us as terrible or pitiful.

Actions capable of this effect must happen between persons who are either friends or enemies or indifferent to one another. If an enemy kills an enemy, there is nothing to excite pity either in the act or the intention,—except so far as the suffering in itself is pitiful. So again with indifferent persons. But when the tragic incident occurs between those who are near or dear to [49] one another—if, for example, a brother kills, or intends to kill, a brother, a son his father, a mother her son, a son his mother, or any other deed of the kind is done—these are the situations to be looked for by the poet. He may not indeed destroy the framework of the received legends . . . but he ought to show invention of his own, and skilfully handle the traditional material. Let us explain more clearly what is meant by skilful handling.

The action may be done consciously and with knowledge of the persons, in the manner of the older poets. It is thus too that Euripides makes Medea slay her children. Or, again, the deed of horror may be done, but done in ignorance, and the tie of kinship or friendship be discovered afterwards. The Oedipus of Sophocles is an example. Here, indeed, the incident is outside the drama proper; but cases occur where it falls within the action of the play: one may cite the Alcmaeon of Astydamas, or Telegonus in the Wounded Odysseus. Again, there is a third case,—to be about to act with knowledge of the persons and then not to act. The fourth case is when some one is about to do an irreparable deed through ignorance, and makes the discovery before it is done. These are the only possible ways. For the deed must either be done or not done,—and that wittingly or unwittingly. But of all these ways, to be about to act knowing the persons, and then not to act, is the worst. It is shocking without being tragic, for no disaster follows. It is, therefore, never, or very rarely, found in poetry. One instance, however, is in the Antigone, where Haemon threatens to kill Creon. The next and better way is that the deed [51] should be perpetrated. Still better, that it should be perpetrated in ignorance, and the discovery made afterwards. There is then nothing to shock us, while the discovery produces a startling effect. The last case is the best, as when in the Cresphontes Merope is about to slay her son, but, recognising who he is, spares his life. . . . This, then, is why a few families only, as has been already observed, furnish the subjects of tragedy. It was not art, but happy chance, that led the poets in search of subjects to impress the tragic quality upon their plots. They are compelled, therefore, to have recourse to those houses whose history contains moving incidents like these.

Enough has now been said concerning the structure of the incidents, and the right kind of plot.

In respect of Character there are four things to be aimed at. First, and most important, it must be good. Now any speech or action that manifests moral purpose of any kind will be expressive of character: the character will be good if the purpose is good. This rule is relative to each class. Even a woman may be good, and also a slave; though the woman may be said to be an inferior being, and the slave quite worthless. The second thing to aim at is propriety. There is a type of manly valour; but valour in a woman, or unscrupulous cleverness, is inappropriate. Thirdly, character must be true to life: for [53] this is a distinct thing from goodness and propriety, as here described. The fourth point is consistency: for though the subject of the imitation, who suggested the type, be inconsistent, still he must be consistently inconsistent.

As in the structure of the plot, so too in the portraiture of character, the poet should always aim either at the necessary or the probable. Thus a person of a given character should speak or act in a given way, by the rule either of necessity or of probability; just as this event should follow that by necessary or probable sequence. It is therefore evident that the unravelling of the plot, no less than the complication, must arise out of the plot itself, it must not be brought about by the *Deus ex Machina*—as in the Medea, or in the Return of the Greeks in the Iliad. The *Deus ex*

Machina should be employed only for events external to the drama,—for antecedent or subsequent events, which lie beyond the range of human knowledge, and which require to be [55] reported or foretold; for to the gods we ascribe the power of seeing all things. Within the action there must be nothing irrational. If the irrational cannot be excluded, it should be outside the scope of the tragedy. Such is the irrational element in the Oedipus of Sophocles.

Again, since Tragedy is an imitation of persons who are above the common level, the example of good portrait-painters should be followed. They, while reproducing the distinctive form of the original, make a likeness which is true to life and yet more beautiful. So too the poet, in representing men who are irascible or indolent, or have other defects of character, should preserve the type and yet ennoble it. In this way Achilles is portrayed by Agathon and Homer.

These then are rules the poet should observe. Nor should he neglect those appeals to the senses, which, though not among the essentials, are the concomitants of poetry; for here too there is much room for error. . . . [57]

The Chorus too should be regarded as one of the actors; it should be an integral part of the whole, and share in the action, in the manner not of Euripides but of Sophocles. As for the later poets, their choral songs pertain as little to the subject of the piece as to that of any other tragedy. They are, therefore, sung as mere interludes,—a practice first begun by Agathon. Yet what difference is there between introducing such choral interludes, and transferring a speech, or even a whole act, from one play to another?. . . [69]

The element of the wonderful is required in Tragedy. The irrational, on which the wonderful depends for its chief effects, has wider scope in Epic poetry, because there the person acting is not seen. Thus, the pursuit of Hector would be ludicrous if placed upon the stage—the Greeks standing still and not joining in the pursuit, and Achilles waving them back. But in the Epic poem the absurdity passes unnoticed. Now the wonderful is pleasing: as may be inferred from the fact that every one tells a story with some addition of his own, knowing that his hearers like it. It is Homer who has chiefly taught other poets the art of telling lies skilfully. . . .

. . . the poet should prefer probable impossibilities to improbable possibilities. The tragic plot must not be composed of irrational parts. Everything [95] irrational should, if possible, be excluded; or, at all events, it should lie outside the action of the play (as, in the Oedipus, the hero's ignorance as to the manner of Laius' death); not within the drama. . . . The plea that otherwise the plot would have been ruined, is ridiculous; such a plot should not in the first instance be constructed. But once the irrational has been introduced and an air of likelihood imparted to it, we must accept it in spite of the absurdity. Take even the irrational incidents in the Odyssey, where Odysseus is left upon the shore of Ithaca. How intolerable even these might have been would be apparent if an inferior poet were to treat the subject. As it is, the absurdity is veiled by the poetic charm with which the poet invests it. . . . [97]

In general, the impossible must be justified by reference to artistic requirements, or to the higher [105] reality, or to received opinion. With respect to the requirements of art, a probable impossibility is to be preferred to a thing improbable and yet possible. Again, it may be impossible that there should be men such as Zeuxis painted. 'Yes,' we say, 'but the impossible is the higher thing; for the ideal type must surpass the reality.' To justify the irrational, we appeal to what is commonly said to be. In addition to which, we urge that the irrational sometimes does not violate reason; just as 'it is probable that a thing may happen contrary to probability.'

Things that sound contradictory should be examined by the same rules as in dialectical refutation—whether the same thing is meant, in the same relation, and in the same sense. We should therefore solve the question by reference to what the poet says himself, or to what is tacitly assumed by a person of intelligence.

. . . there are five sources from which critical objections are drawn. Things are censured either as impossible, or irrational, or morally hurtful, or contradictory, or contrary to artistic correctness. [107]

The Literature of Ancient Greece

Gilbert Murray

Professor Murray, dean of Hellenic scholars in the English-speaking world, notes that Sophocles, unlike his fellow dramatist Euripides, does not carefully analyze characters, ideas, or situations. Sophocles, according to Murray, is not a sceptical thinker; he presents the traditional conception of the heroes of the ancient legends.

The following comments are extracted from the chapter on "Sophocles, Son of Sophillos, From Colonus."

Another typical difference between the two poets [Euripides and Sophocles] is in their treatment of the incest of Oedipus. Sophocles is always harping on it and ringing the changes on the hero's relationships, but never thinks it out. Contrast with his horrified rhetoric, the treatment of the same subject at the end of Euripides's *Phoenissoe,* the beautiful affection retained by the blind man for Iocasta, his confidence that she at any rate would have gone into exile at his side uncomplaining, his tender farewell to her dead body. What was the respectable burgher to say to such a thing? It was defrauding him of his right to condemn and abomi-

From Gilbert Murray, *The Literature of Ancient Greece* (Chicago: The University of Chicago Press, 1956), pp. 239–242.

nate Iocasta. No wonder Sophocles won four times as many prizes as Euripides! A natural concomitant of this lack of speculative freedom is a certain bluntness of moral imagination which leads, for instance, to one structural defect in the *Oedipus Tyrannus*. That piece is a marvel of construction: every detail follows naturally, and yet every detail depends on the [239] characters being exactly what they were, and makes us understand them. The one flaw, perhaps, is in Teiresias. That aged prophet comes to the king absolutely determined not to tell the secret which he has kept for sixteen years, and then tells it—why? From uncontrollable anger, because the king insults him. An aged prophet who does that is a disgrace to his profession; but Sophocles does not seem to feel it.

Sophocles is thus subject to a certain conventional idealism. He lacks the elemental fire of Aeschylus, the speculative courage and subtle sympathy of Euripides. All else that can be said of him must be unmixed admiration. Plot, characters, atmosphere are all dignified and 'Homeric'; his analysis, as far as it goes, is wonderfully sure and true; his language is a marvel of subtle power; the music he gets from the iambic trimeter by his weak endings and varied pauses is incomparable; his lyrics are uniformly skilful and fine, though they sometimes leave an impression of laboured workmanship; if they have not the irresistible songfulness of Aeschylus and Euripides, they are safe from the rhodomontade of the one, and the inapposite garrulity of the other. And it is true that Sophocles shows at times one high power which but few of the world's poets share with him. He feels, as Wordsworth does, the majesty of order and well-being; sees the greatness of God, as it were, in the untroubled things of life. Few hands but his could have shaped the great ode in the *Antigone* upon the Rise of Man, or the description in the *Ajax* of the 'Give and Take' in nature. And even in the [240] famous verdict of despair which he pronounces upon Life in the second *Oedipus* [*Oedipus at Colonus*] there is a certain depth of calm feeling, unfretted by any movement of mere intellect, which at times makes the subtlest and boldest work of Euripides seem 'young man's poetry' by comparison.

Utterly dissimilar as the two dramatists are, the construction of the *Oedipus Tyrannus* reminds one strongly of Ibsen's later plays. From the very first scene the action moves straight and undistracted towards the catastrophe. The interest turns, not on what the characters do, but on their finding out what they have done. And one of the strongest scenes is made by the husband and wife deliberately and painfully confessing to one another certain dark passages of their lives, which they had hitherto kept concealed. The plot has the immense advantage of providing a deed in the past—the involuntary parricide and incest—which explains the hero's self-horror without making him lose our sympathies. And, as a matter of fact, the character of Oedipus, his determination to have truth at any cost, his utter disregard of his own sufferings, is heroic in itself, and comes naturally from the plot. Iocasta was difficult to treat: the mere fact of her being twice as old as her husband was an awkwardness; but there is a stately sadness, a power of quiet authority, and a certain stern grey outlook on life, which seem to belong to a woman of hard experiences. Of course there are gross improbabilities about the original saga, but, as Aristotle observes, they fall outside the action of the play. In the action everything is natural except the very end. Why did Oedipus put out his eyes? Iocasta realised [241] that she must die, and hanged herself. Oedipus himself meant to slay her if she had not anticipated him. Why did he not follow her? Any free composition would have made him do so; but Sophocles was bound to the saga, and the saga was perfectly certain that Oedipus was alive and blind a long time afterwards. Euripides avoided the awkwardness in an ingenious way. In his *Oedipus* the hero is overpowered and blinded by the retainers when he has murdered Iocasta and is seeking to murder his children and himself. As a mere piece of technique, the *Oedipus* of Sophocles deserves the position given to it by Aristotle, as the typical example of the highest Greek tragedy. There is deep truth of emotion and high thought; there is wonderful power of language, grasp of character, and imagination; and for pure dramatic strength and skill, there are few things in any drama so inexpressibly tragic as the silent exit of Iocasta, when she alone sees the end that is coming. [242]

Sophoclean Tragedy

C. Maurice Bowra

The following excerpt is from Professor Bowra's learned and elaborate discussion of Sophocles' *King Oedipus.* Bowra places the details of the play, such as Oedipus' pollution as a result of parricide and incest, in the context of contemporary Greek social customs and religious beliefs. Sophocles' "explanation for the fall of Oedipus," he asserts, "had its roots in Greek thought."[1] Bowra first presents several of the usual reasons that have been proposed as explanations of the causes of Oedipus' fall—hereditary guilt or the sin of the father visited upon the son, punishment for wanton pride, presumptuous insolence or *hybris,* faulty judgment and tyranny for which he must pay in suffering. But he rejects them all for the view that Oedipus is simply the tragic victim of a conflict with the gods.[2] Voluntarily or not, Oedipus had committed abominable crimes against the laws of the gods, to which they demand obedience. Defiled and polluted, impious and unholy, he was responsible for plagues, blighted crops, barren women, and general disaster. Therefore he had to be humbled and exiled before he could be purified. Moreover, Bowra also states, Oedipus

From C. Maurice Bowra, *Sophoclean Tragedy* (Oxford: The Clarendon Press, 1944), pp. 174–211. By permission of the Clarendon Press, Oxford.

[1] *Sophoclean Tragedy,* p. 163.

[2] *Ibid.,* pp. 167, 202.

> had formally "cursed" himself, and this curse must be fulfilled. Thus "the might and knowledge of the gods are vindicated, and a lesson is given to all men not to be too confident of any prosperity or happiness in this world."[3]

He [the murderer of Laius] must be shut out from human life and perish miserably. Since Oedipus is himself the murderer, we should conclude that he will end in such a way. But does he? Is the curse really fulfilled on him? When he first begins to suspect that he has killed Laius, he certainly believes that it will be. But all depends on the end of the play. It is easy to lay stress on Creon's kind feelings for Oedipus, to show that the Chorus pity him. All that is true. But human behaviour does not alter what has to be, and the gods demand that Oedipus shall carry out the curse which he has so solemnly pronounced in their name. We may be sure that at the end of the play his woes are not finished. His departure from the stage is the prelude to his departure to a life of wandering. In *Oedipus at Colonus* Sophocles was to tell more about Oedipus, and differently. But we cannot look to it for enlightenment on *King Oedipus*. Here the future of Oedipus is forecast by Teiresias. Just as the seer is right in his knowledge of the hidden past, so he must be right about the future:

> A beggar, once so rich, in a foreign land
> A wanderer, with a staff groping his way.

Teiresias has already said that Oedipus will be driven out by the united curse of his father and mother, and this curse is now strengthened by Oedipus' own curse. He becomes the instrument for its fulfilment. It means that he will be turned out of Thebes and sent, blind and helpless, into the wild places of the mountains. Such is the fate in store for him, and though the play closes without emphatically proclaiming it, we must assume [174] that it awaits Oedipus. If Oedipus had not cursed himself, he would surely have suffered less heavily.

Throughout the gods' will is done, and in the usual way. Pollution follows a violent death and must be removed; a curse pronounced with full authority is amply fulfilled; oracles which

[3] *Ibid.*, p. 202.

seemed unlikely to be true are proved all too true; human pity is stirred but can do nothing against the irrefragable decrees of the gods. That Sophocles intended to show the gods at work is seen not only by the part which they take in events but by the dramatic effects which the poet secures by displaying the futility of Jocasta's and Oedipus' scepticism. It is Jocasta's disbelief which leads to Oedipus' discovery that he may be the slayer of Laius, his own dismissal of the oracles which precedes the revelation of his true origin, his wild hope that he is the son of Luck which comes just before the final shattering truth. The play shows the power of the gods at every important turn in its development and leaves no doubt about the poet's theological intention.

King Oedipus shows the humbling of a great and prosperous man by the gods. This humbling is not deserved; it is not a punishment for insolence, nor in the last resort is it due to any fault of judgement or character in the man. The gods display their power because they will. But since they display it, man may draw a salutary lesson. This is kept till the end of the play when the Chorus, or perhaps Oedipus himself, point to the extent of his fall, and comment:

> And, being mortal, think on that last day of death,
> Which all must see, and speak of no man's happiness
> Till, without sorrow, he hath passed the goal of life.

That this moral was thought suitable is clear from its close imitation at the end of Euripides' *Phoenician Women,* though it may not be from his hand. After the hideous and harrowing events this finale of *King Oedipus* may seem a little tame. Yet it provides a quiet end, such as the Greeks liked, and it is Sophocles' conclusion on what has taken place. The old lesson of Solon which it repeats accounts, simply enough, for undeserved suffering and may be used of Oedipus as Herodotus used it of Croesus. That it meant something to Sophocles may also be seen from a fragment of his *Tyndareos:* [175]

> We should not, when a man is fortunate,
> Call his luck good, until his whole life's course
> Is finished and has reached its final end.

For in the shortest, smallest space of time
Fate's evil gift destroys his wealth and bliss,
Just when it changes and the gods decide.

The context of this and its application are not known, but its fullness shows that Sophocles understood the idea and made use of it. Its lesson is that men must be modest in prosperity and remember that at any moment the gods may destroy it. It is a warning not so much against pride as against any confidence or sense of security. To drive this warning home the gods have made an example of Oedipus. From the very beginning he has been chosen to show by his misfortunes the need for modesty in times of success.

Such, reduced to its most abstract and impersonal form, is the theological scheme in *King Oedipus*. In it there is nothing new. It would be accepted by men so different as Herodotus, Pindar, and Euripides. What counts in it is the opportunity which it gives of presenting human greatness in disaster and evoking tragic emotions from such a spectacle. It is much more tragic than the scheme which informs the *Antigone*. But its chief interest is the particular form which it takes. It shows the fortunes of an individual man in an intensely dramatic form. And in doing this it naturally raises questions about the justice of the gods, who treat Oedipus simply as a means to enforce a lesson on others. It is not like this that we expect the gods to act. Sophocles, perhaps, might not have felt our qualms, but he sees the difficulties of his theological scheme and does something to answer possible critics. When the gods humiliate Oedipus they create a situation of great complexity in which much is concerned beside the general main lesson. There is above all the individual problem of Oedipus himself. If they force him to break their own laws, as he does when he kills his father and marries his mother, they should provide means of reconciliation by which he, polluted as he is, can make his peace with them and restore the breach in the divine order which he has made. Sophocles was conscious of this need and took steps to meet it. [176] The play shows not only the crisis which humbles Oedipus and reveals to him that he is polluted but also the first steps by which he begins to overcome the gulf between himself and the gods, to find again a place in the ordered system of things. In this the gods help him.

This reconciliation is the meaning of Oedipus' action in blinding himself. Hard enough to hear of from the Messenger, it is almost unendurable when the king comes out of the palace with his bleeding sightless eyes. The moment is of such tragic import that it is easy to assess its meaning wrongly and to miss what Sophocles intends to show by it. Both ancient and modern critics have thought that Oedipus' action is wrong and should be condemned. There is something to be said for their view, and it must be considered seriously. It goes back to Aelian, who condemns Oedipus because he tries 'to heal by an incurable evil evils that have already occurred.' Aelian appeals to a common rule of Greek morality that it was wrong to try to cure one evil by another, to try to make a right out of two wrongs. Sophocles himself was familiar with the notion and makes the Chorus of his *Ajax* use it when his hero calls on them to kill him. In a fragment of his *Aleadae* the doctrine is stated in plain gnomic words:

> All men's affairs are sick in such a case,
> When they would do a wrong to heal a wrong.

The maxim rings authoritatively, even if it does not express the poet's own opinion. Aelian appeals to a firm body of support. Yet in *King Oedipus* no character condemns Oedipus on this ground, and we have no reason to think that Sophocles did. Like all maxims, it had its exceptions, and when Oedipus blinded himself, it may have been one of them. Modern critics have followed another line, and contend that in blinding himself Oedipus sins against the doctrine that men should accept what the gods decide. The doctrine is well established even for Sophocles, in whose *Tereus* someone said:

> Manifest, Procne, is its pain, and yet
> Since the gods send it, men must not complain. [177]

Resignation before the gods' will is familiar. It follows that if Oedipus resists the doom which they have sent, he is wrong. The argument looks irreproachable, but it is not. There is no real evidence that in blinding himself Oedipus resists the will of the gods or refuses to accept his lot. If he had so chosen, Sophocles could have pointed this lesson. But he gives a different explanation and invites a different judgement.

The chief witness against the innocence of Oedipus is the Messenger who reports the death of Jocasta and the blinding of Oedipus. Before he tells his story, he says with noble emphasis:

> Can Ister or can Phasis wash this house—
> I trow not—with their waters, from the guilt
> It hides . . . Yet soon shall publish to the light
> Fresh, not unpurposed evil. 'Tis the woe
> That we ourselves have compassed, hurts the most.

The Messenger makes a distinction between the old and the new pollution in the House of Laius. The new, which will soon be revealed, is 'not unpurposed'; there seems to be a distinction between the old incest and parricide, which were committed unwittingly, and the new violence of Jocasta's suicide and Oedipus' blinding. The distinction follows that of Attic law and suggests that the new evils are blameworthy. In fact the Messenger is thought to condemn Oedipus for blinding himself as he does not condemn him for his other acts. Yet this view, convincing as it may seem, is open to objection. First, it is extremely dangerous to assume that the messenger is the voice of Sophocles. Sophocles has a way of suggesting that his characters have acted wrongly and then proceeding to show that they are right, as he does with the Chorus and Antigone. Secondly, the Messenger refers in general to what has taken place in the palace. It has incurred a new pollution, and so far as pollution is concerned, only Jocasta can be in question. Oedipus' violence against himself creates no new pollution. Thirdly, and most important, the Messenger speaks not about the rights and wrongs of what has happened but about the miseries Oedipus and Jocasta have brought on themselves. What moves him is not the wickedness of what has been done but its horror, and a special element in this is that the sufferers have inflicted the [178] injuries on themselves. The Messenger does not condemn Oedipus for blinding himself, nor does the poet through him.

Sophocles gives his own opinion and explanation in a more indirect but more impressive way. He tells us what happens and then makes his characters comment upon it. It is that when Oedipus blinds himself, he is prompted and guided by a daimon, a divine spirit which rules his actions for him. The word has no exact equivalent in English and is variously translated 'fate', 'destiny', 'god', and 'spirit'. It has something of all these in it. It is a supernatural power which is inferior to a true god and is closely concerned with an individual man's fortunes. [179] . . . The *daimon* bridges the gulf between Apollo who decides and dictates and the human agent Oedipus who carries out the decision. Apollo ordains; Oedipus fulfils. The *daimon* connects the first cause and the final agent.

Oedipus, then, acts under the influence and pressure of a supernatural power which is in its turn determined by the gods, Zeus or Apollo. If the gods decide to treat a man like this, they have their reasons for it, though these vary with circumstances and persons. It would, for instance, be possible to keep the main lines of the scheme and to assume that the gods make Oedipus mad before destroying him. In that case his blindness is inflicted in a madness sent by the gods. This would be quite familiar to Greek minds. Men who destroyed themselves were thought to be all but mad. Herodotus gives two examples, Cambyses who died from a self-inflicted wound and Cleomenes who killed himself in a peculiarly horrible way. Both were more or less mad, and in both this madness was in some quarters believed to be a punishment for impious acts, to Cambyses for killing the Bull of Apis and to Cleomenes for blasphemous behaviour at Argos. So some might think that Oedipus too is punished for impious acts by a mad fury which impels him to blind himself. This would be consonant with the belief that the gods make mad those whom they wish to destroy. An anonymous tragic fragment states the position:

> When anger of the gods assails a man,
> It does this first,—it empties from his heart
> All noble sense, and turns it to worse thoughts
> That he may choose the wrong in ignorance.

Such seems to have been Aeschylus' explanation of Oedipus' action. His Oedipus acts in 'madness of heart'. Sophocles might have adopted this view, and he was conscious that it was tenable. For when the Chorus first see Oedipus after he has blinded himself, they suggest that he has acted in madness:

> Alas, unhappy one,
> What madness came on thee? [182]

But Sophocles soon shows that Oedipus was not mad, that he knew what he was doing and had his reasons for it. These must be taken seriously. Oedipus is not the victim who does not know what he is doing. His good sense is not destroyed.

The Chorus, naturally enough, do not at first applaud Oedipus' action. But their words do not really condemn it:

> In this I know not how to call thee wise,
> For better wert thou dead than living—blind.

They mean no more than that his life of blindness will be even more miserable than death. They do not understand that he cannot and will not die because in death he would have to face his parents, and that he cannot do. The real explanation of his decision to blind himself is in his own words. When he does it, he cries out that his eyes shall no longer see such horrors as he has been doing and suffering and henceforth must look on the dark. This is not a momentary fancy. Oedipus returns to it and almost argues his case:

> Nay, give me no more counsel. Bid me not
> Believe my deed, thus done, is not well done,

and says that he could not look on his parents, his children, his city and its temples from which he has excluded himself by his own curse. He develops this thought and advances to a new stage. He wishes to be shut off altogether from the converse of the living. If he could have choked the fount of hearing, he would have done this too,

> Sweet for the mind
> To dwell withdrawn, where troubles never come.

He asks to be thrown out of the city, that he may live alone on the mountains; for there Cithaeron will be a living tomb to him.

He has blinded himself because he wishes to be cut off from the living and from the dead.

Oedipus' explanation suggests that he sees himself as a kind of scapegoat, . . . a polluted being whose expulsion from the city will purify it. When grave impiety had been committed, it was right to send out such a scapegoat who might well be the defiling or guilty person himself. In his fierce attack on [183] Andocides for impiety, 'Lysias' demands that Athens should expel the criminal and so purify the city. The expulsion is called 'sending out a scapegoat'. So Oedipus wishes to be treated. He feels that such a punishment is right for him because of the curse which he has laid upon himself. Nor is expulsion enough for him. His blindness too is necessary to complete his severance from the light of day and the company of men. Only by this can he really cut himself off and carry out the penalty which he has called down on the murderers of Laius. He must not live like other men. He must have a special, separate life such as he can have if he is blind and an outcast. He will rid the city of pollution; he will carry out to the full the curse which he has laid on himself.

Neither the Chorus nor Creon says that Oedipus has acted wrongly. The Chorus feel pity and horror, but that is different. They even accept this view that Apollo is the real power behind what he has done:

> 'Twas even as thou sayest.

When Creon tells Oedipus that he must not pollute the sun by staying out of doors, he does not refer to his blindness. What pollutes the sun is the presence of the parricide. It is this that is so foul

> that neither Earth
> Nor Light nor Heaven's rain may welcome it.

Euripides' Heracles, bowed with guilt on killing his children, hides his head from the sun. And this was right. The sun was a 'pure god' and must not be defiled by the sight of any polluted thing. Such a thought seems to have been present to Oedipus' own mind when he found out the truth and cried:

Light, let me look on thee for the last time.

The sun may not look on those who are defiled, and they may not look on it. Therefore Oedipus must hide himself. When Creon demands that he should go inside, the demand is right and proper. But it contains no condemnation of Oedipus for blinding himself.

Oedipus blinds himself because of his curse. He does it both deliberately and by divine prompting. The Greeks would make no real distinction between the two and would certainly praise [184] Oedipus for acting as the gods desire and see that the *daimon's* pressure on him was part of their scheme. As a parricide and incestuous he will exile himself from Thebes which he pollutes and from human society with which he can have no normal relations. To carry out his curse he inflicts a fearful injury on himself. The curse has still to finish its course. Oedipus knows this, makes no attempt to resist it, rather does his best to help it. There is no question of guilt and its punishment, but once pollution has been incurred, once the powers of heaven have been invoked with such solemnity, they cannot be countermanded. There is much to pity when Oedipus blinds himself, but much also to admire. His willingness to shoulder the burden of his pollution, his desire to do at all costs what is right, show that even in the worst crisis of his fortunes he keeps his essential nobility. In his angry scenes with Teiresias and Creon he has lost some of our sympathy and revealed dangerous tendencies in his character, but once he knows who he really is, he throws aside his faults and acts with inspired resolution in his fearful sacrifice. He is not to be condemned for resisting his destiny, but to be admired for accepting it in all its horror and for being ready to work with the god to see that he makes his full amends. He who has been the victim and the sufferer regains the initiative and takes his destiny into his own hands.

The gods have chosen Oedipus for this fate. In so far as he is to be an example to others it is enough that he is a great king. But the lesson that he himself has to learn must be suited to his own nature. The man who is to be taught his own utter insignificance must be endowed with special gifts of character and intellect; for only in such conditions is the lesson worth learning. Such Oedipus undeniably is. But in presenting him Sophocles has boldly faced certain difficulties inherent in the legend and turned them to good account. His Oedipus must be a man who has killed his father, solved the riddle of the Sphinx, married his mother, and became king of Thebes, and at the same time he must be convincing enough to win sympathy in his fate and fall. Sophocles shirks none of these difficulties. The past events of Oedipus' life are worked into the play in the most natural way possible. Through the greater part of it Oedipus shows himself as the sort of man to defend himself when attacked, to answer riddles and assume great responsibilities. But the same characteristics which brought him to success make his downfall more tragic and are almost instruments to it. It is because he is such a superior being, angry when attacked, capable of brief and brilliant action, self-confident and [185] rapid in decision, that his discovery of the truth takes so tragic a turn. His fated life is his own life. It is his character, his typical actions, that make his mistakes so intelligible and fit so naturally into the gods' plan to humble him. . . .

[Professor Bowra concludes his chapter on *Oedipus* with the following observations on the moral meaning of the play:]

By modern standards the gods who decide on Oedipus' fate before he is born and then inflict it on him without mercy treat him cruelly. But this is not a view that Sophocles would have held or admitted. He would more probably hold that men cannot judge the gods and might even agree with Heraclitus that 'For God all things are beautiful and good and just, but men think some things unjust and others just.' For he states emphatically that the gods must be honoured, and shows that their word must be believed. Nor is it legitimate to argue that their word is sometimes hard to understand. That, too, arises from the ignorance and blindness in which man lives. He can only do his best to understand the gods by what means he possesses, to recognize that his own judgment may be wrong. The gods, who know everything, are right. Nor may man complain of them. He must humble himself before them and admit that he is nothing and that he knows nothing. This is the lesson of *King Oedipus*. The last words draw attention to it. Oedipus is [209]

> that mighty King, who knew the riddle's mystery.

But his knowledge is of no avail in dealing with the mysteries of the gods. On this note of ignorance and humiliation the play ends. It is hardly a quiet end. Oedipus is still an abhorred and defiled creature who may not remain in the daylight and is fated to suffer more. Creon, who does correctly what the gods require, insists on his going indoors. His manner may seem rigorous, but he does his religious duty. He cannot do otherwise, and Oedipus, now fully conscious of his nothingness before the gods, knows that Creon is right. He asks to be sent out of the land; he knows that the gods abhor him. What will happen next must, as Creon sees, wait on the gods' decision. We know that Teiresias has prophesied more miseries for Oedipus and that they will infallibly come. The play ends in the anguish of humiliation and the anticipation of more to come. But at last the truth is out, and the gods have had their way.

The gods humble Oedipus as a lesson to men not to trust in their happiness or their knowledge. The horror of his fate and his fall is fore-ordained that others may learn from it. But though this plan determines all that happens, the actual events follow a pattern which is tragic and Sophoclean. When Oedipus kills his father and marries his mother the inviolable laws of the gods are broken and the divine order of things sustains a grievous wound. The wound must be healed, the order restored. Before this can be done, the evil that has been, albeit unconsciously, committed, must show its full force. This it does in the growth of Oedipus' illusions when the plague forces a crisis on him. From illusions he moves to dangerous acts. His fits of fury, his moments of scepticism, his certainty that he is right, are the natural products of his state. Such a condition cannot last, and it is broken by the events which follow the death of Polybus. As Oedipus comes to see the truth and to punish himself for his past actions, he makes his peace with the gods. He does what is right, accepts his position, knows the truth. Through resignation and suffering the rightful harmony of things is restored. By divine standards Oedipus at the end of the play is a better man than at the beginning. His humiliation is a lesson both to others and to him. Democritus' words, 'the foolish learn modesty in misfortune,' may be applied to Oedipus, who has indeed been foolish in his mistakes and illusions and has been [210] taught modesty through suffering. The lesson which the gods convey through his fall is all the more impressive because he is the great king and the great man that he is. In the eyes of the gods what matters is that he should know who and what he really is. To secure this end his power and his glory must be sacrificed. In his acceptance of his fall, his readiness to take part in it, Oedipus shows a greatness nobler than when he read the riddle of the Sphinx and became king of Thebes. [211]

Greek Tragedy

H. D. F. Kitto

Kitto is Professor of Greek Literature at the University of Bristol, England. His critical point of view, as he has explained it in the preface to his recent book *Form and Meaning in Drama,* is that form and content are ultimately identical, and so the play's "real meaning is the total impact which it makes on the senses and the spirit and the mind of the audience." Thus he interprets drama in terms of an implied world-view, which, he believes, gives it religious meaning. Elsewhere in this book on ancient

From H. D. F. Kitto, *Greek Tragedy: A Literary Study* (London: Methuen, 1950), pp. 135–141.

Greek religious drama, Kitto declares that "its Catharsis arises from this, that when we have seen terrible things happening in the play, we understand, as we cannot always do in life, *why* they have happened; or, if not so much as that, at least we see that they have not happened by chance, without any significance. We are given the feeling that the Universe is coherent, even though we may not understand it completely. In this lies the true greatness of the *Tyrannus.* This is a play which Aristotle treats as tragedy of character, and as such it is splendid enough; but how much more splendid is it when we see what Sophocles really meant: that although Life has been so cruel to Oedipus, nevertheless it is not a chaos; and that in his story there is no warrant for our abandoning allegiance to moral law and such prudent foresight as we may have. Pity and Fear are present in abundance, but even so they are overtopped by Awe and Understanding."[1]

Besides his two literary studies, Professor Kitto has also written *The Greeks* (1951), a survey of ancient Greek culture aimed at the general reader. The footnotes in the excerpt that follows are in the original text.

THE OEDIPUS TYRANNUS

The story of the *Tyrannus* is of a common Greek type; something unpleasant is predicted, the persons concerned try to avert it and think themselves safe, but in some natural though surprising fashion the prediction is fulfilled. Next to the *Tyrannus* itself, the most elaborate example is the story of Astyages and the infant Cyrus in Herodotus. What does Sophocles make of this ancient motif?

At the beginning of the play Oedipus is the great King who has saved Thebes in the past and is their only hope now; no one can compare with Oedipus in reading dark secrets. At the end, he is the polluted outcast, himself the cause of the city's distress,

[1] (London: Methuen, 1956), p. 235.

through crimes predicted by Apollo before he was born. Is this grim determinism? Is Sophocles telling us that Man is only the plaything of Fate? Or does he mean, as Dr. Bowra has recently suggested,[2] that the gods have contrived this awful [135] fate for Oedipus in order to display their power to man and to teach him a salutary lesson? Or is Sophocles simply making exciting drama, leaving the philosophical implications unexplored? There is only one way of finding out. Whatever Sophocles meant, he put his meaning into the play, and to get it out again we must contemplate the play—all of it, in all its aspects; not bits of it, and some of its aspects.

As in the *Electra,* the action shows a certain duality. In the foreground are autonomous human actors, drawn vividly and complete. Oedipus himself, Tiresias, Creon, Iocasta, and the two shepherds, are all as lifelike as characters in a play can be; and so, in their degree, are the remoter characters who do not appear—the hot-tempered Laius at the cross-road, and the unknown Corinthian who insulted Oedipus when he was half-drunk. The circumstances too are natural, even inevitable, granted these characters. Oedipus, as we see him time after time, is intelligent, determined, self-reliant, but hot-tempered and too sure of himself; and an apparently malignant chain of circumstances combines now with the strong, now with the weak side of his character to produce the catastrophe. A man of poor spirit would have swallowed the insult and remained safe in Corinth, but Oedipus was resolute; not content with Polybus' assurance he went to Delphi and asked the god about it, and when the god, not answering his question, repeated the warning given originally to Laius, Oedipus, being a man of determination, never went back to Corinth. It was a coincidence, but not an unnatural one, that Laius was on his way from Thebes to Delphi. They met at the cross-road, and as father and son were of similar temper the disaster occurred. Even so, he could have arrived at Thebes safely, had he not been a man of high intelligence; for then he could not have read the riddle of the Sphinx. But again, though intelligent, he

[2] *Sophoclean Tragedy,* p. 175.

was blind enough to marry a woman old enough to be his mother, certain that his mother was in Corinth. The story is not moralized. Sophocles could have put Oedipus in the wrong at the cross-road; he could have suggested that blind ambition made him accept the crown and Queen of Thebes. He does neither of these things; Oedipus is not being given his deserts by an offended Heaven. What happens is the natural result of the weaknesses and the virtues of his character, in combination [136] with other people's. It is a tragic chapter from life, complete in itself, except for the original oracle and its repetition. Sophocles is not trying to make us feel that an inexorable destiny or a malignant god is guiding the events.

But we are made to feel, as in the *Electra,* that the action is moving, at the same time, on a parallel and higher plane.

The presence of some power or some design in the background is already suggested by the continuous dramatic irony—which seems overdone, if it is regarded as only a dramatic effect. In the matter of the Plague this hidden power is definitely stated; and its presence is most imaginatively revealed, as in the *Electra,* in the scene containing Iocasta's sacrifice. She who has been so sceptical of oracles surprises us by coming out with sacrificial offerings. She lays them on Apollo's altar, puts fire to the incense, and prays for deliverance from fear. There is a moment of reverent silence, and this is broken by the arrival of the cheerful messenger from Corinth: Polybus is dead; fear is at an end; the prayer has been heard. But within the hour Iocasta has hanged herself.—And what of her offerings? Still there, on the altar, in full view of the audience; the incense, it may be, still carrying to the god a petition that he has so terribly answered.

This is no theatrical trick, but a revelation of the dramatist's thought. It is the action of the unseen god made manifest. But how does the god answer the pitiful prayer of Iocasta, the impious prayer of Clytemnestra? Not by any direct interposition. The Apollo of Sophocles is nothing like the Zeus of Aeschylus, who works his will by freezing the Strymon or by blasting a fleet. It was not Apollo who incited the Corinthian to come, but his own eagerness to be the first with the good news, and his own hopes (as Sophocles is careful to tell us) of standing well with the new King; for besides the news of his succession to the crown he has another and a much more exciting tale to tell—in his own good time. He . . . is completely autonomous, yet in the coming of each the hand of the god is seen. The action moves on two planes at once.

Nevertheless, the whole texture of the play is so vividly naturalistic that we must be reluctant to interpret it as a bleak Determinism. These people are not puppets of higher powers; [137] they act in their own right. Nor, I think, does this texture encourage us to accept Bowra's explanation.

In the first place, if Sophocles meant that the gods are displaying their power because they will, that they have ordained this life for Oedipus in order to read men a lesson, it was so easy for him to say so—to write an ode on the power and the mysterious ways of the gods. He conspicuously does not do this. Indeed, in the ode that immediately follows the catastrophe the chorus says not that the fate of Oedipus is a special display of divine power, but on the contrary that it is typical of human life and fortunes.

In the second place, although Oedipus is by far the greatest sufferer in the play he is not the only one. There are others who suffer, not by any means in the same degree, but in the same way; and we must take account of them too, not dismiss them as being parts of the dramatic economy but not of the thought. If we contemplate, as we should, the whole play and all its aspects, we see that Oedipus is not a special case, except in the degree to which he suffers; he is, as the chorus says, typical; what has happened to him is part of the whole web of human life. Why for example does Sophocles introduce the children in the last act? Not simply because it is 'natural'; a good play isn't 'nature,' but art. One reason must be that Oedipus may say to them what he does say: 'What a life must yours be! Who will admit you to the festivals? Who will marry you—born as you were born?' Such is life, such are the gods. The innocent suffer with the guilty.

We must contemplate also two other characters who form no inconsiderable part of the play—the two shepherds. It was not merely to liven up his play, or to indulge his talents, that Sophocles drew them like this, with their motives, hopes, fears, so sharply presented. The Corinthian . . . makes no bones about expecting a tip; not for the reason . . . that it was the oriental custom to reward messengers (as if dramatists were only photographers), but because the point bears on the drama. The news that this man brings is great news indeed, but he has something much more astonishing in reserve and the moment for producing it soon comes. 'Polybus? He was no more your father than I [138] am. . . . Why, I gave you to him with my own hands. . . . A hired shepherd? Yes, my son; but that day I saved your life.' A hired shepherd—but this is a great day for him; he began by addressing Oedipus as 'My Lord,' but now he can say 'My son.' 'No, *that* I cannot tell you. . . . You must find the Theban who gave you to me. . . .' Iocasta's last despairing shriek does not disturb him, for, as Oedipus says, probably she is dismayed to find that her husband is of low birth. The chorus is happy and excited; and when the reluctant Theban is brought in, our friend becomes even more bland and helpful, as he works up to his climax:

> Here is the man, my friend, who was that baby!

And this is his last speech. No reward for him; no glory in Corinth—only bewilderment and utter dismay; for in a moment he hears, from his old companion,

> I pitied it, my lord. I thought to send
> The child abroad, whence this man came. And he
> Saved it, for utter doom. For if you are
> The man he says, then you were born for ruin.

He sees his new King rush into the palace; and then—the final ode? Not yet. These two actors have to make their exit, by the long side-passages, in full view of the audience; some forty yards of exit. And as we watch them stumbling out we have time to reflect that this is the outcome, for them, of their merciful interest in an abandoned baby.

Is not this too the work of Apollo? Here, as in the greater case of Oedipus, is that conjunction of well-meant action with a situation which makes it lead to disaster. An act of mercy, tinged with a perfectly honest shrewdness, leads the Corinthian to the verge of what is, for him, greatness; as he stretches out his hand, eagerly and with confidence, it turns into horror.

The other shepherd too is one who refused to kill a baby. Part of his reward comes years later, when he sees the man who killed Laius ascend his victim's throne and marry his Queen—an event which sends him, for his own safety, into half-exile; the rest of his reward comes now, when a sudden command brings him back at last to the city, to learn what he learns here. [139]

These minor tragedies, of the children and the shepherds, are all of a piece with the major one. This is Apollo; this is life. An awful sin is committed in all innocence; children are born to a life of shame; virtuous intentions go awry. What are we to think of it? Of course, moral and prudential lessons can be drawn from it—though Sophocles draws very few—but what do we think of it? Where is the explanation? What, in other words, is the catharsis? That Oedipus accepts his fate? But when you are knocked flat, you must accept it; and if you cannot get up again, you must be resigned. There is little illumination in this.

The catharsis that we are looking for is the ultimate illumination which shall turn a painful story into a profound and moving experience. It has been suggested by Professor Ellis-Fermor[3] that the catharsis of plays like the *Tyrannus* and *Macbeth* lies in the perfection of their form, which, by implication, represents the forces of righteousness and beneficence, of which Aeschylus speaks directly, in his choric odes. This is manifestly true of the *Tyrannus*.

Let us go back to Iocasta's sacrifice, and Apollo's swift and devastating answer. In the corresponding passage of the *Electra* the point was clear. Clytemnestra prayed that injustice, *adikia,* might triumph, and she got the answer she deserved. What of Iocasta? She has been denying the truth of oracles. Was Sophocles then so fiercely orthodox that he could equate Iocasta's scepticism with Clytemnestra's wickedness? Of course not; this was not the size of Sophocles' mind. He means much more than this. Iocasta has said 'Why should we fear oracles, when there is no such thing as fore-

[3] *Frontiers of Drama,* p. 133.

sight? Best live at random, as one may'—a doctrine which would deny the very basis of all serious Greek thought; for while Greek life was still healthy and stable, the Greek believed, as if by instinct, that the universe was not chaotic and 'irrational', but was based on a *logos,* obeyed Law. . . .

The tragic poets too think in this way—as Whitehead saw, when he said that they, rather than the Ionians, were the first scientific thinkers. In the *Oresteia* we find moral laws which have the same sort of validity as physical and mathematical [140] laws. The doer must suffer; *hybris* leads to *Atê* [doom and death]; the problem there—a problem for gods as well as for men—is to find a system of Justice that will fit into this framework without disastrously contravening these laws. To the mind of Sophocles this Law shows itself . . . as a balance, rhythm, or pattern in human affairs. 'Call no man happy until he is dead,' for the chances of life are incalculable. But this does not mean that they are chaotic; if so they seem to us, it is because we are unable to see the whole pattern. But sometimes, when life for a moment becomes dramatic, we can see enough pattern to give us faith that there is a meaning in the whole. In the *Antigone,* when Creon is overwhelmed, it is by the natural recoil of his own acts, working themselves out through the minds and passions of Antigone and Haemon, and we can see in this a natural justice. In the *Electra,* the vengeance that at last falls on the assassins is linked to their crime by natural chains of cause and effect. In the *Tyrannus* we have a much more complex picture. The same Justice is at work, though this time the injustice which it avenges was involuntary and indeed innocent. Oedipus—to repeat our image—is blasted as a man may be who inadvertently interferes with the natural flow of electricity. *Dikê* [justice] here works through many apparently casual and unrelated actions—of the shepherds, of the charioteer who tried to push Oedipus off the road, of the man at the banquet. . . . Things fall out contrary to all expectation; life seems cruel and chaotic. Cruel, perhaps; chaotic, no—for if it were chaotic no god could predict, and Iocasta would be right. 'If these oracles are not manifestly fulfilled, why should I join in the sacred dance?' Piety and purity are not the whole of the mysterious pattern of life, as the fate of Oedipus shows, but they are an important part of it, and the doctrine of chaos would deny them even this. The pattern may harshly cut across the life of the individual, but at least we know that it exists, and we may feel assured that piety and purity are a large part of it.

Every detail in the *Tyrannus* is contrived in order to enforce Sophocles' faith in this underlying *logos;* that is the reason why it is true to say that the perfection of its form implies a world-order. Whether or not it is beneficent, Sophocles does not say. [141]

The Grounds of Criticism in Tragedy

John Dryden

John Dryden (1631–1700), poet, playwright, and critic, dominated the English literary scene during the latter part of the seventeenth century. In the following excerpts, he presents his theory of tragedy, which may help explain his practice in his version of *Oedipus*. Explanatory footnotes have been added to the text.

Dryden begins this section of his preface entitled "The Grounds of Criticism in Tragedy" with a discussion of Aristotle's definition of action in tragedy. Whereas Aristotle states that action "must be one or single," Dryden writes about his own plays that:

From "Preface to Troilus and Cressida" (1679), *Essays of John Dryden,* edited by W. P. Ker (Oxford: Clarendon Press, 1926). 2 volumes. Volume I, pp. 208–221. By permission of the Clarendon Press, Oxford.

I will make bold with my own *Marriage à la Mode,* where there are manifestly two actions, not depending on one another; but in *Oedipus* there cannot properly be said to be two actions, because the love of Adrastus and Eurydice has a necessary dependence on the principal design into which it is woven. The natural reason for this rule is plain; for two different independent actions distract the attention and concernment of the audience, and consequently destroy the intention of the poet; if his business be to move terror and pity, and one of his actions be comical, the other tragical, the former will divert the people, and utterly make void his greater purpose. Therefore, as in perspective, so in Tragedy, there must be a point of sight in which all the lines terminate; otherwise the eye wanders, and the work is false. . . . [208]

The following properties of the action are so easy, that they need not my explaining. It ought to be great, and to consist of great persons, to distinguish it from Comedy, where the action is trivial, and the persons of inferior rank. The last quality of the action is, that it ought to be probable, as well as admirable and great. 'Tis not necessary that there should be historical truth in it; but always necessary that there should be a likeness of truth, something that is more than barely possible; *probable* being that which succeeds, or happens, oftener than it misses. To invent therefore a probability, and to make it wonderful, is the most difficult undertaking in the art of Poetry; for that which is not wonderful is not great; and that which is not probable will not delight a reasonable audience. This action, thus described, must be represented and not told, to distinguish Dramatic Poetry from Epic: but I hasten to the end or scope of Tragedy, which is, to rectify or purge our passions, fear and pity.

To instruct delightfully is the general end of all poetry. Philosophy instructs, but it performs its work by precept; which is not delightful, or not so delightful as example. To purge the passions by example, is therefore the particular instruction which belongs to [209] Tragedy. Rapin,[1] a judicious critic, has observed from

[1] René Rapin (1621–1687), French Jesuit, humanist, and Latin poet. He upheld the authority of Aristotle and the principle of the imitation of the classics. Dryden refers to his *Réflexions sur la Poétique d'Aristote.*

Aristotle, that pride and want of commiseration are the most predominant vices in mankind; therefore, to cure us of these two, the inventors of Tragedy have chosen to work upon two other passions, which are fear and pity. We are wrought to fear by their setting before our eyes some terrible example of misfortune, which happened to persons of the highest quality; for such an action demonstrates to us that no condition is privileged from the turns of fortune; this must of necessity cause terror in us, and consequently abate our pride. But when we see that the most virtuous, as well as the greatest, are not exempt from such misfortunes, that consideration moves pity in us, and insensibly works us to be helpful to, and tender over, the distressed; which is the noblest and most god-like of moral virtues. Here it is observable, that it is absolutely necessary to make a man virtuous, if we desire he should be pitied: we lament not, but detest, a wicked man; we are glad when we behold his crimes are punished, and that poetical justice is done upon him. Euripides was censured by the critics of his time for making his chief characters too wicked; for example, Phaedra, though she loved her son-in-law with reluctancy, and that it was a curse upon her family for offending Venus, yet was thought too ill a pattern for the stage. Shall we therefore banish all characters of villany? I confess I am not of that opinion; but it is necessary that the hero of the play be not a villain; that is, the characters, which should move our pity, ought to have virtuous inclinations, and degrees of moral goodness in them. As for a perfect character of virtue, it never was in Nature, and therefore there can be no imitation of it; but these are alloys of frailty to be allowed for the chief persons, yet so that the [210] good which is in them shall outweigh the bad, and consequently leave room for punishment on the one side, and pity on the other.

After all, if any one will ask me, whether a tragedy cannot be made upon any other grounds than those of exciting pity and terror in us;—Bossu,[2] the best of modern critics, answers thus in general: That all excellent arts, and particularly that of poetry, have

[2] René Le Bossu (1631–1680), French critic, author of the *Traité du poème épique* (*Treatise on the Epic Poem*).

been invented and brought to perfection by men of a transcendent genius; and that, therefore, they, who practise afterwards the same arts, are obliged to tread in their footsteps, and to search in their writings the foundation of them; for it is not just that new rules should destroy the authority of the old. But Rapin writes more particularly thus, that no passions in a story are so proper to move our concernment as fear and pity; and that it is from our concernment we receive our pleasure, is undoubted; when the soul becomes agitated with fear for one character, or hope for another, then it is that we are pleased in Tragedy, by the interest which we take in their adventures. [211] . . .

After the plot, which is the foundation of the play, the next thing to which we ought to apply our judgment, is the manners; for now the poet comes to work above ground. The groundwork, indeed, is that which is most necessary, as that upon which depends the firmness of the whole fabric; yet it strikes not the eye so much, as the beauties or imperfections of the manners, the thoughts, and the expressions.

The first rule which Bossu prescribes to the writer of an Heroic Poem, and which holds too by the same reason in all Dramatic Poetry, is to make the moral of the work; that is, to lay down to yourself what that precept of morality shall be, which you would insinuate into the people; as, namely, Homer's (which I have copied in my *Conquest of Granada*), was, that union preserves a commonwealth, and discord destroys it; Sophocles, in his *Oedipus,* that no man is to be accounted happy before his death. 'Tis the moral that directs the whole action of the play to one centre; and that action or fable is the example built upon the moral, which confirms the truth of it to our experience: when the fable is designed, then, and not before, the persons are to be introduced, with their manners, characters, and passions.

The manners, in a poem, are understood to be those inclinations, whether natural or acquired, which move and carry us to actions, good, bad, or indifferent, in a play; or which incline the persons to such or such actions. I have anticipated part of this discourse already, in declaring that a poet ought not to make the manners [213] perfectly good in his best persons; but neither are they to be more wicked in any of his characters than necessity requires. To produce a villain, without other reason than a natural inclination to villany, is, in Poetry, to produce an effect without a cause; and to make him more a villain than he has just reason to be, is to make an effect which is stronger than the cause.

The manners arise from many causes; and are either distinguished by complexion, as choleric and phlegmatic, or by the differences of age or sex, of climates, or quality of the persons, or their present condition. They are likewise to be gathered from the several virtues, vices, or passions, and many other commonplaces, which a poet must be supposed to have learned from natural Philosophy, Ethics, and History; of all which, whosoever is ignorant, does not deserve the name of poet.

But as the manners are useful in this art, they may be all comprised under these general heads: first, they must be apparent; that is, in every character of the play, some inclinations of the person must appear; and these are shown in the actions and discourse. Secondly, the manners must be suitable, or agreeing to the persons; that is, to the age, sex, dignity, and the other general heads of manners: thus, when a poet has given the dignity of a king to one of his persons, in all his actions and speeches, that person must discover majesty, magnanimity, and jealousy of power, because these are suitable to the general manners of a king. The third property of manners is resemblance; and this is founded upon the particular characters of men, as we have them delivered to us by relation or history; that is, when a poet has the known character of this or that man before him, he is bound to represent him such, at least not contrary to that which fame has reported him to have been. Thus, it is not a poet's choice to make [214] Ulysses choleric, or Achilles patient, because Homer has described 'em quite otherwise. Yet this is a rock on which ignorant writers daily split; and the absurdity is as monstrous as if a painter should draw a coward running from a battle, and tell us it was the picture of Alexander the Great.

The last property of manners is, that they be constant and equal, that is, maintained the same through the whole design: thus, when Virgil had once given the name of *pious* to Aeneas, he was bound to show him such, in all his words and actions, through the whole poem. . . .

From the manners, the characters of persons are derived; for, indeed, the characters are no other than the inclinations, as they appear in the several persons of the poem; a character being thus defined,—that which distinguishes one man from another. Not to repeat the same things over again, which have been said of the manners, I will only add what is necessary here. A character, or that which distinguishes one man from all others, cannot be supposed to consist of one particular virtue, or vice, or passion only; but 'tis a composition of qualities which are not contrary to one another in the same person; thus, the same man may be liberal and valiant, but not liberal and covetous. [215] . . .

The chief character or hero in a tragedy, as I have already shown, ought in prudence to be such a man who has so much more of virtue in him than of vice, that he may be left amiable to the audience, which otherwise cannot have any concernment for his sufferings; and it is on this one character, that the pity and terror must be principally, if not wholly, founded: a rule which is extremely necessary, and which none of the critics, that I know, have fully enough discovered to us. For terror and compassion work but weakly when they are divided into many persons. If Creon had been the chief character in *Oedipus,* there had neither been terror nor compassion moved; but only detestation of the man, and joy for his punishment; if Adrastus and Eurydice had been made more appearing characters, then the pity had been divided, and lessened on the part of Oedipus: but making Oedipus the best and bravest person, and even Jocasta but an underpart to him, his virtues, and the punishment of his fatal crime, drew both the pity and the terror to himself.

By what has been said of the manners, it will be easy for a reasonable man to judge whether the characters be truly or falsely drawn in a tragedy; for if there be no manners appearing in the characters, no concernment for the persons can be raised; no pity or horror can be moved, but by vice or virtue; therefore, without them, no person can have any business in the play. If the inclinations be obscure, it is a sign the poet is in the dark, and knows not what manner of man he presents to you; and consequently you can have no idea, or very imperfect, of that man; nor can you judge what resolutions he ought to take; or what words or actions are proper for him. Most comedies made up of accidents [216] or adventures are liable to fall into this error; and tragedies with many turns are subject to it; for the manners can never be evident, where the surprises of fortune take up all the business of the stage; and where the poet is more in pain to tell you what happened to such a man, than what he was. [217] . . .

By considering the second quality of manners, which is, that they be suitable to the age, quality, country, dignity, etc., of the character, we may likewise judge whether a poet has followed Nature. In this kind, Sophocles and Euripides have more excelled among the Greeks than Aeschylus; and Terence more than Plautus, among the Romans. Thus, Sophocles gives to Oedipus the true qualities of a king, in both those plays which bear his name; but in the latter, which is the *Oedipus Colonaeus,* he lets fall on purpose his tragic style; his hero speaks not in the arbitrary tone; but remembers, in the softness of his complaints, that he is an unfortunate blind old man; that he is banished from his country, and persecuted by his next relations. [218] . . .

Under this general head of manners, the passions are naturally included as belonging to the characters. I speak not of pity and of terror, which are to be moved in the audience by the plot; but of anger, hatred, love, ambition, jealousy, revenge, etc., as they are shown in this or that person of the play. To describe these naturally, and to move them artfully, is one of the greatest commendations which can be given to a poet: to write pathetically, says Longinus,[3] cannot proceed but from a lofty genius. A poet must be born with this quality: yet, unless he help himself by an acquired knowledge of the passions, what they are in their own nature, and by what springs they are to be moved, he will be subject either to raise them where they ought not to be raised, or not to raise them by the just degrees of nature, or to amplify them beyond the natural bounds, or not to observe the crisis and turns of

[3] Cassius Longinus (d. 273), Greek scholar, the reputed author of the treatise *On the Sublime,* to which Dryden refers.

them, in their cooling and decay; all which errors proceed from want of judgment in the poet, and from being unskilled in the principles of Moral Philosophy. Nothing is more frequent in a fanciful writer, than to foil himself by not managing his strength; therefore, as in a wrestler, there is first required some measure of force, a well-knit [220] body and active limbs, without which all instruction would be vain; yet, these being granted, if he want the skill which is necessary to a wrestler, he shall make but small advantage of his natural robustuousness: so, in a poet, his inborn vehemence and force of spirit will only run him out of breath the sooner, if it be not supported by the help of Art. The roar of passion, indeed, may please an audience, three parts of which are ignorant enough to think all is moving which is noise, and it may stretch the lungs of an ambitious actor, who will die upon the spot for a thundering clap; but it will move no other passion than indignation and contempt from judicious men. Longinus, whom I have hitherto followed, continues thus: If the passions be artfully employed, the discourse becomes vehement and lofty: *if otherwise, there is nothing more ridiculous than a great passion out of season.* . . . He who would raise the passion of a judicious audience, says a learned critic, must be sure to take his hearers along with him; if they be in a calm, 'tis in vain for him to be in a huff; he must move them by degrees, and kindle with 'em; otherwise he will be in danger of setting his own heap of stubble on fire, and of burning out by himself, without warming the company that stand about him. [221] . . .

The English Dramatic Poets

Gerard Langbaine

As a result of his review of the drama, Langbaine (1656–1692) is considered one of the standard contemporary authorities on information concerning the playwrights of the Restoration period. A footnote has been added to the original text by the present editors.

Oedipus, a Tragedy acted at his Royal Highness the Duke's Theatre, written by Mr. Dryden and Mr. Lee, printed in quarto Lond. 1679. This Play is certainly one of the best Tragedies we have extant; the Authors having borrow'd many Ornaments not only from Sophocles, but also from Seneca; though in requital Mr. Dryden has been pleas'd to arraign the Memory of the latter by taxing him of 'Running after Philosophical notions more proper for the study than the stage.' As for Corneille he has scouted him for failing in the Character of his Hero, which he calls an Error in the first Concoction: tho' possibly 'twas so in him to fall upon two such Great Men, without any provocation, and to whom he has been more than once oblig'd for beautiful Thoughts. As to the Plot, 'tis founded on the Tragedies of Sophocles and Seneca. [167]

From Gerard Langbaine, *An Account of the English Dramatic Poets* (Oxford: George West and Henry Clements, 1691), pp. 167, 320–321.

[Lee is] One whose Muse deserv'd a better Fate than Bedlam. How truly he has verified the Saying of the Philosopher, *Nullum* [320] *fit Magnum Ingenium sine mixturâ dementiae;*[1] even to the Regret and Pity of all that knew him, is manifest: I heartily wish his Madness had not exceeded that Divine Fury which Ovid mentions and which usually accompanies the best Poet . . . there being several of his Tragedies . . . which have forc'd Tears from the fairest Eyes in the World: his Muse indeed seem'd destin'd for the Diversion of the Fair Sex; so soft and passionately moving, are his Scenes of Love written. [321] . . .

The Impartial Critick

John Dennis

At the time he wrote *The Impartial Critick,* John Dennis (1657–1734), perhaps the most important English critic in the generation after John Dryden's death in 1700, was an ambitious member of the group of wits that frequented Will's, a famous London coffee house. Here he was an associate of Dryden, who presided for many years over the informal gatherings of these London critics. *The Impartial Critick* is a series of five dialogues on problems

From John Dennis, *The Impartial Critick: Or, Some Observations Upon A Late Book, Entituled, A Short View of Tragedy, Written by Mr. Rymer* (1693), ed. Joel E. Spingarn, *Critical Essays of the Seventeenth Century* (Oxford: Clarendon Press, 1908). Three volumes. Vol. III, pp. 151–166. By permission of the Clarendon Press, Oxford.

[1] Seneca slightly misquoted: "There has not been any great mind without an admixture of folly."

of the theatre. In a prefatory letter that accompanied the dialogues, Dennis makes clear his view that it is improper for the English stage to adopt ancient Greek practices because of differences in religion, polity, climate, and customs (including attitudes towards romantic love). He asserted that to attempt to put into practice the dogmatic opinions of Thomas Rymer "instead of reforming would ruine the English drama." The ideas and methods of literary work must be consistent, he believed, with those prevalent when the work was written and in the country where the work was performed.

The Impartial Critick has also been reprinted with an elaborate annotation in the first volume of *The Critical Works of John Dennis,* edited by E. N. Hooker (Baltimore: Johns Hopkins Press, 1939).

The first excerpt is from the prefatory "Letter to a Friend," the second from "Dialogue II" between Beaumont and Freeman. All the footnotes have been added by the editors of this text.

I shall now give you some account of a thing which is very well receiv'd upon our Stage, but would have succeeded but ill with the Ancient Grecians, by reason of the same difference of Climate and Customs.

The thing that I mean is Love, which could but rarely be brought upon the Grecian Stage without the violation of probability, considering that their Scene lay generally in their own, or a warmer Country: For two People in a Tragedy cannot make Love without being together, and being alone. Now when Lovers came together in Greece, they found something else to do than to talk. Their Women, under so warm a Sun, melted much sooner than ours. Nor were they so fantastick as long to refuse what they eternally desire[d], or to pretend a mortal displeasure for being offer'd to be oblig'd in the most sensible part of them. Therefore most of the Love that appear'd upon the Athenian Stage was between such People as their own Customs oblig'd to cohabit, as Admetus and Alcestis,[1] who were Man and Wife, Hippolitus and Phedra,[2] who were Son and Mother-in-Law, and with which last the only Obstacle to Enjoyment was the Horrour

[1] Characters in the *Alcestis* of Euripides (480–406 B.C.).
[2] Characters in Euripides' *Hippolytus.*

which so Criminal a Passion inspir'd. Had the Athenian Poets introduc'd upon their Stage two passionate Lovers who had not been related, and engag'd them in a Conversation both tender and delicate, an Audience would have been apt to ask, with the Spanish Lady mentioned by Monsieur St. Euremont:[3] *Que d'esprit mal employé! A quoy bon tous ces beaux discours quand ils sont ensemble?*[4] You know, Sir, that this Lady made this Reflection, which St. Euremont commends so much, upon the Reading a Conversation in *Cleopatra*[5] between two passionate Lovers. Upon which that ingenious Gentleman, with his usual good Sence, takes occasion to condemn Calprenede for making no distinction betwixt the Love of a Southern Climate and that of England or France. [151]

By what I have said, Sir, it may be easily guess'd that it is in vain to think of setting up a Chorus upon the English Stage because it succeeded at Athens, or to think of expelling Love from our Theatres because it was rarely in Grecian Tragedies. [152] . . .

BEAUMONT: I thank you; and now to our business: but before we proceed to this Book again, I desire you to give me some satisfaction in relation to a passage in the Dedication. For Mr. Rymer, mentioning the Greek *Oedipus,* says afterwards of the French and the English, *Quantum mutatus.*[6] Now I have always taken our English *Oedipus* to be an admirable Play.

FREEMAN: You have had a great deal of reason to do so; and it

[3] Charles St.-Évremond (1616–1703) was a French critic in exile in England who influenced Dryden's opinions about the effect of climate on manners.

[4] "What wit badly employed! To what good are all these beautiful speeches when they [the lovers] are together?"

[5] A play, written in 1646, by the French author Gauthier de La Calprenède (1610–1663). It was translated into English and was very popular in the seventeenth century.

[6] A hit at the *Oedipus* of Dryden and Lee. Dennis takes up this accusation which is first made in Thomas Rymer's Dedication to his *Short View of Tragedy* (1693): "Three, indeed, of the Epick (the two by Homer and Virgil's *Aeneids*) are reckon'd in the degree of Perfection: But amongst the Tragedies only the *Oedipus* of Sophocles. That, by Corneille, and by others, of a Modern Cut, *quantum Mutatus*!" While admiring the English *Oedipus,* Dennis is inclined to agree with Rymer. Dryden responded to this sneer in his Dedication to *Examen Poetiucum* (1693). The Latin is from *Aeneid,* II, 274: "How terribly changed from that, Hector."

would certainly have been much better, if Mr. Dryden had had the sole management of it. If Mr. Rymer, by his *Quantum mutatus,* designs to fix any mark of disesteem upon Mr. Dryden's Tragedy, he is doubtless to blame; but if he only means that Mr. Dryden has alter'd the Character of Oedipus, and made it less suitable to the design of Tragedy, according to Aristotle's Rules, then Mr. Rymer is in the right of it.

BEAUMONT: Pray shew me that.

FREEMAN: I shall do it as succinctly as I can. The Design of Tragedy, according to Aristotle, is to excite compassion and terrour; from whence it necessarily follows that we [161] are not to make choice of a very vertuous Man to involve him in misery, nor yet, on the other side, of one who is very vicious.

BEAUMONT: I desire to know how you draw that Consequence.

FREEMAN: The Consequence is just: For the making a very good Man miserable can never move compassion nor terror; no, that must rather occasion horrour, and be detested by all the World. On the other side, by representing a very bad Man miserable, a Poet may please an Audience, but can neither move terrour nor pity in them; for terrour is caused in us by a view of the Calamities of our Equals, that is, of those who, resembling us in their faults, make us, by seeing their Sufferings, apprehensive of the like Misfortune. Now, if at any time an Audience sees a very wicked Man punished, each Man who knows himself less guilty is out of all fear of danger, and so there can be no terrour; nor can the calamity of a very wicked Man raise compassion, because he has his desert.

BEAUMONT: What sort of Person must be made choice of then?

FREEMAN: Why, one who is neither vertuous in a sovereign degree nor excessively vicious, but who, keeping the middle between these extreams, is afflicted with some terrible calamity for some involuntary fault.

BEAUMONT: Well, and just such a Man is Mr. Dryden's Oedipus, who cannot be said to be perfectly vertuous, when he is both Parricide and Incestuous, nor yet on the other side excessively vicious, when neither his Parricide nor Incest are voluntary, but caused by a fatal ignorance.

FREEMAN: Aye, but says Dacier,[7] to punish a man for Crimes that are caused by invincible ignorance is in some measure unjust, especially if that Man has other ways extraordinary Vertues. Now Mr. Dryden makes his Oedipus just, generous, sincere, and brave, and indeed a Heroe, without any Vices [162] but the foremention'd two, which were unavoidable both. Now Sophocles represents Oedipus after another manner: the distinguishing Qualities which he gives him are only Courage, Wit, and Success, Qualities which make a Man neither good nor vitious. The extraordinary things that he pretends to have done, in Sophocles, are only to have kill'd four Men in his Rage, and to have explain'd the Riddle of Sphinx, which the worst Man in the World that had Wit might have done as well as Oedipus.

BEAUMONT: Well, but does not Sophocles punish Oedipus for the very same Crimes that Mr. Dryden does, *vid.* for his Incest and Parricide? If not, for what involuntary faults does the Sophoclean Oedipus suffer?

FREEMAN: Aristotle, by those Offences which his Interpreter Dacier calls involuntary, does not mean only such faults as are caus'd by invincible ignorance, but such to which we are strongly inclin'd either by the bent of our Constitutions or by the force of prevailing Passions. The faults for which Oedipus suffers in Sophocles are his vain Curiosity in consulting the Oracle about his Birth, his Pride in refusing to yield the way in his return from that Oracle, and his Fury and Violence in attacking four Men on the Road the very day after he had been fore-warn'd by the Oracle that he should kill his Father.

BEAUMONT: But, pray, how were those involuntary faults?

FREEMAN: Dacier means here by involuntary faults, faults that have more of human frailty in them than any thing of design or of black malice. The Curiosity of Oedipus proceeded from a Vanity from which no Man is wholly exempt; and his Pride, and the Slaughter that it caused him to commit on the Road, were partly caused by his Constitution and an unhappy and violent Temper. These are faults that both Aristotle and

[7] André Dacier, a highly influential contemporary French critic, had just published (in 1692) a commentary on Aristotle's *Poetics.*

Dacier suppose that he might have prevented, if he would have used all his diligence; but being guilty of them thro' his neglect, they afterwards plunged [163] him in those horrible Crimes which were follow'd by his final Ruine. Thus you see the Character of the Athenean Oedipus is according to these Rules of Aristotle, the fittest that can be imagin'd to give Compassion and Terrour to an Audience. For how can an Audience choose but tremble, when it sees a Man involv'd in the most deplorable Miseries only for indulging those Passions and Frailties which they are but too conscious that they neglect in themselves? And how can they choose but melt with compassion, when they see a Man afflicted by the avenging Gods with utmost severity for Faults that were without malice, and which, being in some measure to be found in themselves, may make them apprehensive of like Catastrophes? For all our Passions, as Dacier observes, are grounded upon the Love of ourselves, and that Pity which seems to espouse our Neighbor's Interest is founded still on our own.

BEAUMONT: Why, will you perswade me that because an Audience finds in itself the same vain Curiosity and the same ungovern'd Passions that drew Oedipus to Murder and Incest, that therefore each Spectator should be afraid of killing his Father and committing Incest with his Mother?

FREEMAN: No, you cannot mistake me so far; but they may very well be afraid of being drawn in by the like neglected Passions to deplorable Crimes and horrid Mischiefs which they never design'd.

BEAUMONT: Well, then, now I begin to see the reason why, according to the Sence of Aristotle, the Character of Mr. Dryden's Oedipus is alter'd for the worse: For he, you'll say, being represented by Mr. Dryden Soveraignly Vertuous, and guilty of Parricide only by a fatal invincible Ignorance, must, by the severity of his Sufferings, instead of compassion create horrour in us, and a murmuring, as it were, at Providence. Nor can those Sufferings raise terrour in us for his Crimes of fatal invincible Igno- [164] rance, not being prepar'd, as they are in Sophocles, by some less faults, which led him to those Crimes, as it were, by so many degrees. I do not conceive how we can be concern'd at this; for

Terrour, you say, arises from the Sufferings of others, upon the account of Faults which are common to us with them. Now what Man can be afraid, because he sees Oedipus come down at two Leaps from the height of Vertue to Parricide and to Incest, that therefore this may happen to him? For a man who is himself in Security cannot be terrified with the Sufferings of others, if he is not conscious to himself of the Faults that caus'd them; but every Man who is disturb'd by unruly Passions, when he sees how the giving way to the same Passions drew Sophocles' Oedipus into Tragical Crimes which were never design'd, must by reflection necessarily be struck with Terrour and the apprehension of dire Calamities. This, I suppose, is your Sence.

FREEMAN: Exactly.

BEAUMONT: Well, but the Authority of Aristotle avails little with me against irrefutable Experience. I have seen our English *Oedipus* several times, and have constantly found that it hath caus'd both Terrour and Pity in me.

FREEMAN: I will not tell you that possibly you may have mistaken Horrour for Terrour and Pity; for perhaps it is not absolutely true that the Sufferings of those who are Sovereignly Vertuous cannot excite Compassion. But this is indubitable, that they cannot so effectually do it as the Misfortunes of those who, having some Faults, do the more resemble ourselves. And I think that I may venture to affirm two things: First, That if any one but so great a Master as Mr. Dryden had had the management of that Character, and had made the same mistake with it, his Play would have been hiss'd off the Stage. And Secondly—

BEAUMONT: I must beg leave to interrupt you. Why should you believe that another Man's Play upon the same subject [165] would have miscarried upon that mistake, when I never heard it yet taken Notice of?

FREEMAN: It would have miscarried, tho' the mistake had ne're been found out: For a common Author, proceeding upon such wrong Principles, could never have touch'd the Passions truly. But Mr. Dryden having done it by his extraordinary Address, the Minds of his Audience have been still troubled, and so the less able to find his Error.

BEAUMONT: But what was that second thing which you were going to observe?

FREEMAN: It was this: That if Mr. Dryden had not alter'd the Character of Sophocles, the Terrour and Compassion had been yet much stronger.

BEAUMONT: But how could so great a Man as Mr. Dryden make such a mistake in his own Art?

FREEMAN: How did Corneille do it before him, who was certainly a great Man too? And if you'll believe Dacier, *C'etoit le plus grand genie pour le Theatre qu'on avoit jamais veu.*[8] Great Men have their Errors, or else they would not be Men. Nay, they are mistaken in several things in which Men of a lower Order may be in the right. This has been wisely order'd by Providence that they may not be exalted too much; for if it were not for this, they would look down upon the rest of Mankind as upon Creatures of a lower Species.

BEAUMONT: Do you believe, then, that Aristotle, if he could rise again, would condemn our English *Oedipus?*

FREEMAN: He would condemn it, or he would be forc'd to recede from his own Principles; but at the same time that he passed Sentence on it, he would find it so beautiful that he could not choose but love the Criminal; and he would certainly crown the Poet before he would damn the Play. [166]

[8] "This was the greatest genius for the Theatre that one had ever seen."

Biographies Dramatica

David E. Baker

Baker's work contains a mine of information about dramatists and the drama of the long-gone past. Two entries are excerpted here, the first on Nathaniel Lee, Dryden's collaborator, and the second on the play *Oedipus* by Dryden and Lee.

In 1675, his [Nathaniel Lee's] first play appeared; and he wrote nine plays, besides two in which he joined with Dryden, between that period and the year 1684, on the 11th of November of which he was taken into Bedlam [a mental institution], where he continued four years. All his tragedies contain a very great portion of true poetic enthusiasm. None ever felt the passion of love more truly; nor could any one describe it with more tenderness. Addison commends his genius highly; observing that none of our English poets had a happier turn for tragedy, although his natural fire and unbridled impetuosity hurried him beyond all bounds of probability, and sometimes were quite out of nature. The truth is, the poet's imagination ran away with his reason. While in Bedlam, he made that famous witty reply to

From David Erskine Baker, *Biographia Dramatica; or A Companion to the Playhouse: Containing Historical and Critical Memoirs and Original Anecdotes of British and Irish Dramatic Writers* (London: Longman, Hurst, Rees, Orme, & Brown, 1812). 3 volumes. Vol. I, pp. 448–449, Vol. III, p. 93.

a coxcomb scribbler who had the cruelty to jeer him with his misfortune, by observing that it was an easy thing to write like a madman: "No (said Lee) it is [448] not an easy thing to write like a madman; but it is very easy to write like a fool." [449] [Lee was discharged from the mental hospital, but died soon after, in 1691 or 1692, "aged about thirty-five years," probably of complications due to alcoholism.]

This is a very excellent tragedy, being one of the best executed pieces that either of those two celebrated authors were concerned in; yet the critics have justly found fault with the impropriety of Oedipus's relishing an embrace from Jocasta, after he had quitted his crown, and was gone to such extremity of distraction, as to have pulled out his own eyes. The plot is from history; and the authors have happily availed themselves of several beauties both in Sophocles and Seneca. . . . The tragedy was performed about fifty years since [1679], and never failed to affect the audience very strongly. Nor can we in this place avoid relating an anecdote in regard to the power it has shown of this kind; which is, that some years ago, at a representation of it in Dublin, where Elrington acted the part of Oedipus, one of the instrument performers, who was sitting in the orchestra to see the piece, was affected in so violent a manner with the feigned distraction of that monarch, that he was immediately seized with a real madness, which, if we are not mistaken, never left him but with life. [III, 93]

Account of the English Stage

John Genest

The English Stage by John Genest (1764–1834) is very important in the history of the English theatre because it is a source for facts dealing with dates and places of production, cast, and number of performances. For example, Genest lists seven performances of *Oedipus:* at Dorset Garden in 1679; at Drury Lane on October 23, 1708, November 19, 1740, and April 2, 1744; at Lincoln's Inn Fields on November 8, 1722; and at Covent Garden on March 25, 1738, and January 10, 1755.

This book is a mixture of pungent critical comment by the author himself and information (as he notes on the title page) "from all quarters." Genest bases his study, in the main, on John Downes' *Roscius Anglicanus,* Langbaine's *Historia Histrionica,* and the work of the great eighteenth-century antiquarian and editor Edmond Malone, the famous *Diary* of Samuel Pepys, the writings of Dr. Samuel Johnson and his biographer James Boswell, and accounts by the actor Colley Cibber as well as materials found in newspapers, magazines, and playbills of actual performances.

The first selection presents Genest's reactions to the English *Oedipus;* the second concerns an anecdote about

From John Genest, *Some Account of the English Stage, from the Restoration in 1660 to 1830* (Bath: no pub., 1832). 10 volumes. Vol I, pp. 260–265, Vol. IV, p. 420.

an eighteenth-century performance of the play by Dryden and Lee.

Œdipus—Œdipus = Betterton: Adrastus = Smith: Creon = Sandford: Tiresias = Harris: Ghost of Laius = Williams: Phorbas = Gillow: Jocasta = Mrs. Betterton: Eurydice = Mrs. Lee: Manto = Mrs. Evans:—Malone could not find any notice of this play in the Stationers' Register—it was published in 1679—the time at which it came out might be nearly ascertained by the time in which the Act for burying in woollen was passed—the Prologue concludes thus—

"Record it, in memorial of the fact,
The first play buried since the Woollen Act."

Œdipus Tyrannus was the most celebrated play of all antiquity, it was the master-piece, not only of the 7 plays of Sophocles which still remain, but also of the greater number that are lost—the other Tragedies written on the same subject are miserably inferiour to it—Seneca has some few good lines, but his play on the whole is a very bad one, both as to the management of the plot, and as to the language—Dryden says that Corneille fills up a great part of his piece with the Episode of Theseus and Dirce, and that he totally fails in the character of Œdipus.

Of the English play Dryden is said to have formed [260] the general scheme, and to have written the 1st and 3d acts—the remainder was Lee's—there are some good speeches in it, but on the whole it is a poor production.

Act 1st. Eurydice is absurdly said to be the daughter of Laius—whereas he never had but one child—Creon is made a very different character from what he is represented in the Greek Tragedies.

Act 3d—the scene lies in the Grove of the Furies—Tiresias and the Priests perform certain rites—the Ghost of Laius rises—he says that Œdipus had killed him, and committed incest with Jocasta—this is borrowed from Seneca—a tolerable scene ensues between Œdipus and Jocasta.

Act 4th—the two shepherds of Sophocles are foolishly transformed into persons of some rank—all that they say in Sophocles is natural to the last degree—in this play the scene is very bad in comparison with what it might have been made with the greatest ease.

Act 5th—Œdipus enters after having pulled out his eyes—a wretched and disgusting scene ensues between him and Jocasta—

> JOCASTA: "O my lov'd lord—for you are still my husband.
> OEDIPUS: "Swear I am,
> And I'll believe thee, steal into thy arms,
> Renew endearments, think 'em no pollutions."

The Ghost of Laius ascends, and calls on Œdipus and Jocasta—Dryden and Lee have no where shown their want of judgment so much as in this scene—whereas in Sophocles, as soon as Jocasta finds out [261] that Œdipus is her son, she leaves the stage without acquainting him with the circumstance, and puts an end to her life—after Œdipus and Jocasta have gone off severally, Creon kills Eurydice—Adrastus kills Creon—and is killed by Creon's soldiers—Jocasta kills herself and her children—Œdipus is destroyed by throwing himself purposely from a window—here we have a gross perversion of the original story—of the 33 Greek Tragedies which still remain, one relates to Œdipus in his banishment—two to the contention between his sons—Eteocles and Polynices—and a fourth to his daughters—Antigone and Ismene—the love Episode between Adrastus and Eurydice is bad—people are not very amorous in the time of a plague—Eurydice, in the 1st act, after describing the dreadful state in which Thebes was, asks very properly—"if these be hours of courtship?"—the moral which Dryden and Lee deduce from the story of Laius is—

> —— "How sacred ought
> Kings' lives be held, when but the death of one
> Demands an empire's blood for expiation."

Dryden in the preface says—"Sophocles is admirable every where, and therefore we have followed him as close as possibly we could"—this is so far from being true, that one is astonished they could write so bad a play with the Œdipus Tyrannus before them.

Lord Lansdown, in his preface to Heroick Love, censures the audiences for suffering the noble and sublime thoughts and expressions of Dryden to pass [262] unnoticed; and for applauding the rants and fustian of Lee.

His Lordship is so far right, as Lee has some things only fit for Tom Thumb—thus in the 2d act

——————"Fate has torn
The lock of Time off, and his head is now
The ghastly ball of round eternity!
..... The tapers of the Gods,
The Sun and Moon, run down like waxen globes,
And shooting stars end all in purple jellies."

Tiresias says—

"Each trembling Ghost shall rise,
And leave their grisly king without a waiter."

At the close of the 4th act, Œdipus wishes for everlasting night—

"May there not be a glimpse, one starry spark,
But Gods meet Gods, and justle in the dark."

He had just before said—

"O that, as oft I have at Athens seen
The stage arise, and the big clouds descend."

There was no stage at Athens till about 700 years after the death of Œdipus.

Addison facetiously finishes the 1st act of the Drummer with the tag of the 2d act of this play.

But tho' Lee is worse than Dryden, yet Dryden at times is bad enough—in the 1st act he says—

"The Sun's sick too; shortly he'll be an earth."

—— again ——

"This Creon shook for fear,
The blood of Laius curdled in his veins." [263]

Creon had not a drop of the blood of Laius—he was only brother to the wife of Laius—Laius was lineally descended from

Cadmus—Creon was descended from one of those who sprang from the Dragon's teeth.
In act 3d—

> MANTO: "O what laments are those?
> TIRESIAS: "The groans of Ghosts that cleave the earth with pain;
> And heave it up: they pant and stick half way."

Œdipus says—

> "Did I kill Laius?
> Then I walk'd sleeping in some frightful dream,
> My soul then stole my body out by night;
> And brought me back to bed e're morning wake."

In the Epilogue the Authors intimate that they had rather consulted the taste of the town, than their own judgment.

> "Their treat is what your palates relish most,
> Charm! Song! and Show! a Murder and a Ghost."

. . .

Œdipus by Voltaire came out in 1718—some parts of this T. [version of *Œdipus Tyrannus*] are very well written, but on the whole it is very far from a good play—Voltaire has omitted the character of Creon, and turned Tiresias into the High Priest—this is a manifest absurdity, as Tiresias had the gift of prophecy, but the High Priest had not—the two Shepherds of Sophocles are, with much impropriety, turned—one of them into the counsellor of Laius, and the other into the counsellor of Polybus [264] —Œdipus in some few words explains to Jocasta that the Oracle is fulfilled in all its parts, and then makes his final exit—this is judiciously managed—Jocasta stabs herself—Philoctetes occupies a considerable portion of this play—his character is a most vile botch.

If any person in future should be inclined to dramatize the story of Œdipus, his best plan would be, to adhere pretty closely to Sophocles, and to write his play in 3 acts. [265]

[The following concerns a performance of *Oedipus* at the Covent Garden theatre, January 10, 1755.]

10. Not acted 12 years, Œdipus = Sheridan: Creon = Sparks: Adrastus = Smith: Phorbas = Ryan: Jocasta = Mrs. Woffington: Eurydice = Mrs. Bellamy:–she says, that tho' so long used to the stage and its feigned terrors, she was so overcome by the horror of the piece that she was carried off in a state of insensibility–if she had been well sluiced with a bucket of cold water, she would never have fainted at a stage Ghost again–her name is in the bill on the 11th, but on the 15th the manager had provided for the part an actress with less delicate nerves–it is however to be hoped, that he did not do this without saying to Mrs. Bellamy–

"Nay if you faint–'tis monstrous affectation."

11. Œdipus. Eurydice = Mrs. Bellamy. . . .
15. Œdipus. Eurydice = Mrs. Vincent. [IV, 420]

Restoration Tragedy

Bonamy Dobrée

In this brief survey, Professor Dobrée (b. 1891) of Oxford University has written a discerning critical commentary on English drama of the Restoration period.

According to Addison: 'Among our English poets, there was none who was better turned for tragedy than Lee, if instead of favouring the impetuosity of his genius, he had restrained it, and kept it

From Bonamy Dobrée, *Restoration Tragedy 1660–1720* (Oxford: Clarendon Press, 1929), pp. 115–117. By permission of Clarendon Press, Oxford.

within its proper bounds. His thoughts are wonderfully suited to tragedy, but frequently lost in such a cloud of words, that it is hard to see the beauty of them: there is an infinite fire in his works, but so involved in smoke that it does not appear in half its lustre.'[1] Addison had a better chance of judging than we have, since he must often have seen Lee upon the stage; but we may venture to doubt whether, had the clouds of words been absent, the thoughts would have seemed so wonderfully suited to tragedy. For the clouds themselves are the thoughts. Certainly Lee did not much dally with poetic justice. He could write verse; he was prolific of imagery; and he could recognize the things which ought to be tragic. But take away the plethora of words, leave him only such psychological handling as he was capable of, such subtlety of emotion as he could portray, and his tragedies would be lamentable indeed. Feeling the force of words, he built out of them: it is no mere accident that he twice collaborated with Dryden, in *Oedipus* and in *The Duke of Guise*.

But if both relied upon words as their chief instrument, where of course they differ is in what they tried to make words do: they were not really fitting duettists. Dryden's voice, though virile, is sweet; Lee's is a terrific 'hollow,' to use a favourite word of his. Thus the atmospheres of *Oedipus* are strikingly incongruous.

[1] The source of Dobrée's quotation is Joseph Addison's *Spectator* essay No. 39, April 14, 1711. This essay can be found in *The Spectator,* ed. G. Gregory Smith (London: J. M. Dent, 1907), I, 145–146. The conclusion to Addison's comment on Lee's diction, which Dobrée omits, is as follows: "He frequently succeeds in the passionate Parts of the Tragedy, but more particularly where he slackens his Efforts, and eases the Stile of those Epithets and Metaphors, in which he so much abounds. What can be more natural, more soft, or more passionate, than that Line in *Statira's* Speech, where she describes the Charms of *Alexander's* Conversation?

Then he would talk: Good Gods! how he would talk!

That unexpected Break in the Line, and turning the Description of his manner of Talking into an Admiration of it, is inexpressibly beautiful, and wonderfully suited to the fond Character of the Person that speaks it. There is a Simplicity in the Words, that outshines the utmost Pride of Expression." (*Ibid.*, I, 146) Elsewhere in the same essay (I, 144) Addison asserts, "For my own part, I prefer a noble Sentiment that is depressed with homely Language, infinitely before a vulgar one that is blown up with all the Sound and Energy of Expression."

Acts I and III have all Dryden's mellowness, the remainder the harsh, grinding tones of Lee—the tones of a man who, if not mad (his confinement in Bedlam may have been due to *delirium tremens*), [115] would try to exacerbate his audience to madness. Let us compare the two in the play, merely for the words, and not for the grace which distinguishes Dryden, or the welter of blood, the concentration of Grand Guignol horror which marks the ending by Lee: [At this point, Professor Dobrée quotes two passages from *Oedipus:* Act III, Tiresias's speech on p. 388, "The gods are just"; and the opening of Act II, p. 370.] Lee is always at the extremity of passion; there is no measure in him; his fancy is ever at full gallop, and there is no judgment to lay hold upon the reins. His people are all madmen in fact, even if they are not, like Britannicus in *Nero* and Nero himself, 'distracted.' They hurtle and bang across the stage, and when they meet are immediately fast locked in love or friendship, or rush upon each other with swords and daggers. But we expect it of them. Their words and actions have all the infernal consistency of madness, a logic which ignores the checks of actual life. The frequent imprecation, slightly varied, 'Night, horror, [116] death, confusion, hell and furies,' is a kind of *leit-motiv* running through all Lee's work. . . . The atmosphere he produces is that of a stage hothouse; the tension is so great that if anything were at any moment to relax, the whole structure would collapse to the ground. That it does not collapse is evidence of some queer driving power in the man—a power in many ways admirable.

It is likely that he himself sometimes felt that the pace was too hot to last, for he often introduces portentous shows, or pieces of ritual, which, while they do not relax the tension, at least vary it, and slow down the tumultuous action. . . . [117]

Spirit and Blood in Hofmannsthal's *Oedipus und die Sphinx*

William H. Rey

William H. Rey (b. 1911) is head of the Department of Germanic Languages at the University of Washington. Some of his critical writings on Hofmannsthal are contained in a book, *Weltentzweiung und Weltversöhnung, in Hofmannsthals Griechischen Dramen,* (Philadelphia, 1962), in papers, and in scholarly journals. In the following selection, Professor Rey examines Hofmannsthal's use of ancient Greek tragedies in relation to his problems and assumptions in writing *Oedipus and the Sphinx.*

. . . We want to try to free H. v. Hofmannsthal from many prejudices (caused by inadequate criticism over the past fifty years) and to recognize the real Hofmannsthal, who remains true to himself even in the gloomy world of Greek myth, and who actually has put himself to test right here. To begin with we will,

From William H. Rey, "Geist und Blut in Hofmannsthals *Oedipus und die Sphinx*," *The German Quarterly,* Vol. XXI (March, 1958), pp. 84–93. Translated by Gertrude Schoenbohm.

therefore, put all critical pretexts in the background and attempt to understand the situation and intention of the author. Our question is, what is Hofmannsthal's concern? In what form and under what assumptions does he seek a solution? The crisis Hofmannsthal underwent after the year 1900, as reflected in the Chandos Letter[1] has been mentioned often enough: his belief in the magical power of the poetic word, which inspired his early work, was shaken. The fascinating and frightening force of life broke out of the intellectually controlled world of the young poet and rose up before him as an anti-intellectual, elemental and chaotic threat. For Hofmannsthal's concept of life is actually confirmed through the philosophy of Schopenhauer and Nietzsche. His attitude toward the problems of life, however, cannot be identified with any of the preceding philosophical positions. He is neither concerned with ascetic denial, nor barbarian glorification nor intellectualization. We know what admiration the late Hofmannsthal had for the genius of Goethe. We know also that his Greek dramas, marking his transition to poetic maturity, have been written because of his classical need for synthesis and for the reconciliation of our contradictory existence. They also reflect the demand which Hofmannsthal set down in his great speech in 1927, *Literature as the Spiritual Domain of the Nation:* "may spirit become life, and life become spirit." Just as Thomas Mann, who also struggled with the life-mind problem, Hofmannsthal strives for a new humanism which will overcome the provocation of the irrational by confronting it with the image of the *whole* man uniting in himself instinct, spirit and intellect. The mission of the *whole,* divine man in his Greek dramas consists of the redemption of natural existence from the state of fragmentation and contradiction. Divine man represents the concerns of the poet. [85] In the harmony of ideal humanity, based on sacrifice and love, the Dionysian event takes place. In *this* sense (in Hofmannsthal's, not in Nietzsche's sense) the Greek dramas may be characterized as Dionysian tragedies. Even as a young man, Hofmannsthal notes: "the basic tragic myth: the world par-

[1] Hugo von Hofmannsthal, *Gesammelte Werke in Einzelausgaben,* edited by Herbert Steiner, Prosa IV, 1955, p. 412.

celled out to individuals longs for unity; Dionysus Zagreus wants to be reborn."[2]

We have already said that Hofmannsthal's turning to Greek myth necessitates neither an imitation of the ancient tragedy nor a reinterpretation of Greek culture. Rather it involves a creative meeting in which traditional subject matter and form-elements are used and fused together with original concepts. Thus Hofmannsthal accepts and transforms the basic dramatic structure: he turns to *those* ancient tragedies which are based upon the basic triangular configuration of life: father-mother-child. But the conflict, resolved in *Electra* by the violence of the mother, and in *Oedipus and the Sphinx* by the violence of the father, does not appear to Hofmannsthal in the traditional moral sense of transgression against the eternal justice of the Apollonian gods; for under the influence of Nietzsche's apocalyptic insight God is dead. Our modern author, rather, renounces the doubtful transcendence of the intellect but finds the Divine, the Eternal and Oneness in the immanence of life. Nietzsche interprets life from the one-sided aspect of becoming; Hofmannsthal sees immanence in the light of the true polarity of being and becoming. This poses a decisive metaphysical assumption in Greek drama which, until now, only a few critics have recognized. Blood, which in *Electra* and *Oedipus* appears to be the unconditional, primordial basis of existence, is certainly, on the one hand, the bearer of the unrestrainable instinct for life, pressing through the dynamics of birth and death toward an ever renewing embodiment and pursuing the *principium individuationis*. It casts its creations into the life struggle of all against all. On the other hand, blood represents, at the same time, the supra-individual and extra-temporal wholeness of life which rests self-contained in the heart of the world and the [86] all-embracing unity not inspired by the spirit of discord, but by reconciling love. In the overall structure of *Oedipus and the Sphinx,* these polar aspects of the blood appear in the representative figures of Antiope, the mother of Laios, and Teiresias, the soothsayer. Antiope glorifies

[2] "Aus Hugo von Hofmannsthals Aufzeichnungen 1890–95," *Corona,* 9, p. 679.

the golden blood as the symbol of fertility, and Teiresias immerses himself by means of the inner sight of the blind into the core of the world and there, removed from woe and delusion, observes the harmony of "holy blood." The reconciliation of the polar opposites between golden and holy blood, that is, between being and becoming, life and death, is represented at the end of the drama in "blessed blood."

After this short sketch of the metaphysical background, we are now ready to clarify the basic concept of Greek drama. We now understand that the guilt of the mother in *Electra,* and of the father in *Oedipus,* is not brought about by a transgression against the mores anchored in transcendence, but rather against the unity of life symbolized in family structure. The doers of violence, Clytemnestra and Laios, however, are not to be looked upon as individual characters in Greek drama; they are individualized representatives of the elemental forces of reality. In them the egocentric drive turns against the mystical unity of being.

. . . [W]ith Hofmannsthal the polar tension of existence itself as a tragic conflict in the process of life becomes acute. The will of the shattered world cries loudly for reconciliation through the voice of fate. Fate, therefore, may not in any way be identified with elemental instinct. It is identified much more with the Dionysian mysterium which seeks to regain the lost unity of existence. Hero and fate are, therefore, linked together by a secret, pre-established harmony. Here also . . . the tragic dissension between the human and the divine is comparable to the "lovers quarrel" ending in reconciliation.[3] For Hofmannsthal, who tires to express his concept of Dionysian poetic existence, the tasks of self-integration become identical. *Oedipus* [87] *and the Sphinx* can therefore be considered as a poetic self-portrait and at the same time as world theatre.

We have often used the expression "Dionysian." It may be well to point out once more that Hofmannsthal's concept is neither identical with Nietzsche's nor with that of the mythological legend. Dionysian elevation for him is more than elemental intoxi-

[3] Friedrich Hölderlin, *Sämtliche Werke, Historical-Critical Edition* (Berlin: 1923). Vol. II, p. 291.

cation of the senses because it is based on the morality of self-sacrifice and on the mysterium of ideal love. The motive of sacrifice is of central importance in Greek drama: Alcestis sacrifices herself for Admet[4] and Electra for Agamemnon.[5] In *Oedipus and the Sphinx* mutual self-sacrifice, as it unfolds from the beginning, is raised, thereby, to the level of allomatic love, which leaves its imprint on the mature work of Hofmannsthal. Through this attitude of sacrifice, the voluntary giving of oneself to another, man transcends the egocentricity of natural drives. Moral principle, as the counter principle of elemental nature, becomes an event. In the immanent world of Greek drama, the sanction "from above" is, however, denied him. But in its place stands the divine unity of existence. For Hofmannsthal, the *principium individuationis* is overcome through sacrifice. In his *Discussion of Poetry* (1903), he showed that the sacrificial act consists of a magic identity between the one who sacrifices and the one who is sacrificed. Not only the split between I and Thou, but also the gap between life and death has thus been bridged by the sacrifice of love. For, the one who sacrifices, and who at the same time is ready to give up his own life out of love, submits himself to death; he does not find in it, however, complete nothingness, but finds, instead, the undivided fullness of the universe. Dionysian death is identical with the unity of life.

After explaining the assumptions, means, and aims of the dramatist Hofmannsthal, we now turn to the figure of Oedipus himself. We understand why Hofmannsthal must have felt attracted to it: in the legend of Oedipus, interpreted in modern times as the basic myth of psychoanalysis, the demands of drives found their strongest expression. By choosing Oedipus as his hero, the poet accepted a challenge. What he wanted to express in his drama was the self-affirmation of the high-minded individual in the chaos of life, and at the same time, the redemption of chaotic drives in the harmony of the whole. But how was this redemptive act to be accomplished? There was only one possibili-[88]ty: Oedipus, while alive, had to suffer his destiny, including guilt, and

[4] In Euripides' *Alcestis* (438 B.C.).

[5] In the *Electra* plays by Sophocles and Euripides.

at the same time transform it. He had to follow the natural law of titanic drives of power and lust without becoming their slave. He had to comply with necessity and yet prove his freedom by this very compliance. Here the paradoxical concept of freedom in the form of self-resignation, the basis of his mature work, becomes visible. . . . [T]he life-role of Oedipus is determined, but the manner in which he plays it is up to him. Thus he accomplished the titanic act of patricide, but without titanic spirit. For in contrast to the hero of Sophocles, he is ready to humble himself before his father and become his servant only to avoid a violent act. The readiness for self-denial does not stem from the titanic blood of his ancestors. His father, Laios, was filled with titanic self-esteem and sacrificed his own child to save himself. In the son Oedipus, marked by the characteristics of high-mindedness and readiness for self-sacrifice, two basically different attitudes toward life face each other. The transformation of elemental drives can be pursued even more clearly in the meeting of the son with his equally unknowing mother. She, who according to the law of instinctive life, would be the goal of his unbridled sexual desire, becomes for him the ideal of regal womanhood, the embodiment of the sensual and meta-sensual ideal womanhood. Womanhood is raised, therefore, far above the level of basic eroticism. Here the act of sublimation is decisive, based upon the polarity of the "golden" and "holy" blood, that is, the polarity of instinct and soul. Instinct is not subjected to consciousness, but to the transforming power of the soul. The soul mediates in the conflict between the exalted and the base which the high-minded man bears within himself. The soul initiates thereby the process of self-integration where also guilt, although transformed guilt, is present.

The willingness to sacrifice, which is at the root of Oedipus' attitude toward Laios, is even heightened in his meeting with Jocasta. He is immediately ready to give his life for her and for the city devastated by the Sphinx. But in spite of his will to sacrifice, he has not yet accomplished the deciding sacrificial deed, which is to overcome self-will [89] and surrender to his *Fate*. Since he has heard the oracle at Delphi, and since he has decided not to return to his supposed parents, he is fleeing from his fate, that is, his true self. He lives under the illusion that he has been called to heroism through great deeds, and he wants to strengthen his calling with a victory over the Sphinx. Instead, he experiences the inescapability of fate in the encounter with the Sphinx. This scene is the core of the drama and deserves therefore special attention. Here Hofmannsthal deviates in decisive points from the ancient fable. He drops the riddle motif and makes the Sphinx proclaim Oedipus' fate which he had already heard at Delphi. After calling him by his name and reminding him of the oracle, the Sphinx shows him that all his attempts to escape are fruitless. She then thrusts herself into the abyss with an agonized cry of triumph.

Throughout the years the prize question has been raised again and again about the interpretation of this drama: who is the victor? Most have placed themselves on the side of the Sphinx. It is important, however, to understand that this line of questioning cannot be applied here at all. What is being decided is rather that the encounter means both fulfillment and destruction for the Sphinx as well as Oedipus. In this, particularly, is expressed the unresolvable entanglement of the human and the divine. Certainly the pride of the great "man of action" comes to naught before the voice of fate. However, the messenger of fate sacrifices himself for the one chosen for self-sacrifice. Just as the I and Thou of lovers, here the human and divine are also linked in mutual surrender. For the divine needs idealistic man in order to realize itself in the world. And the idealistic man can only reach his true self through sacrifice in the service of the divine. These relationships, of course, are hidden to the hero. He sees himself much more as being thrust into the horrifying abyss of life by the cruel, mocking gods than as a helpless plaything of his own instinctive forces. Out of the desperation of his spirit comes the will to die. The low-point of the action is reached: idealistic man experiences his deepest humiliation and comes close to suicide. However, the low-point is at the same time the turning point. In his death wish Oedipus overcomes the creaturely dependence on
[90] life. The moral importance of his freedom to die is even heightened in the following scene: Oedipus wants to let himself

be sacrificed by his rival Creon, the brother of Jocasta. Led into the mountains by Creon who is disguised as a torchbearer, Oedipus wants to protect the revered queen from defilement and himself from greed, illusion, and guilt of life. He now realizes he cannot escape from all this as a living being. Here the leitmotif of sacrifice develops to its full meaning. In the same moment that Creon extols Oedipus as victor over the Sphinx and as King of Thebes, and as all of Oedipus' desires lie like assured possessions before him, Oedipus overcomes the drive to possess. He overcomes selfishness through his willingness for total self-surrender in sacrificial death. This extreme will for self-denial is, of course, also renunciation of fate. It is, nevertheless, the necessary supposition for the fulfillment of fate because only he who has conquered life in face of death can return to life without becoming its slave. This is why lightning strikes as the sign of divine sanction only *after* the sacrificial offer of the hero.

At this point we must add that Jocasta, too, undergoes an experience like that of Oedipus, one leading her from negation of life and will to sacrifice to the overcoming of life. Guiltless-guilty, seeing-blind, they are both ready to surrender to their fate which will lead them by the miracle of love out of the shadow of death and grant their happiness to be elevated to divine unity of existence. After they absorbed the contradictions of the world, the Dionysian paradox of necessity and freedom, life and death, instinct and morality, being and becoming, can manifest itself in their union. With the wedding of mother and son who face each other in the twilight of knowing and not-knowing, the wound which the titanic father has inflicted upon the world is healed. Dionysus is re-born. Therein lies the true significance of the incest motif. With the secularization of god and the deification of the world, the highest deed of the Dionysian man—and the poet—is accomplished.

In order not to interrupt the continuity of the motif, we have shown up till now only the positive aspect of the Dionysian mysterium, in which the catastrophe of the disunited immanence is taken up. Now, in conclusion, we want to mention that the Dionysian task [91] of the hero is in itself of tragic nature, not only because he is of necessity bound to be transformed though not expiated of guilt, but rather because he allots to *man* the task of self and world redemption. In *Oedipus and the Sphinx* existence appears as immanence and the human being as a fulfiller of divine fate, that is, as a demigod. However, the claim of the Dionysian man to godliness reveals itself as sacrilege as soon as he is elevated into the sphere of Apollonian transcendence. This happens in the Sophoclean tragedy of *King Oedipus,* which Hofmannsthal translated in order to add it to his own drama. Under the merciless light of eternal truth, the glittering happiness of the self-centered life is scattered. In the face of the powerful Apollonian gods, the Dionysian man is undone. The demigod must recognize himself as a sinner, the creator, as a creature. With the presentation of the irrevocable counterpart of man, Hofmannsthal draws away from the concept of the Dionysian poet which forms the basis of *Alcestis* and *Electra.* He is approaching his transition to "Everyman." The polarity between "pagan" and "Christian," the basis of his later work, becomes visible. If, however, Hofmannsthal proposes his *Oedipus and the Sphinx* as a prelude to the tragedy of Sophocles, then the following question arises. Is not fate, after all, aimed at crushing the great man? Is the oracle not, after all, to be understood as the plan of destruction? And is not the Dionysian joy of the united Oedipus and Jocasta, with which *Oedipus and the Sphinx* closes, to be interpreted as the cry of damnation? . . . It is clear that we cannot follow this interpretation. It becomes evident from the letters of Hofmannsthal that he planned an Oedipus trilogy which was to be concluded with his version of the aged Oedipus.[7] . . . [92]

From these plans, which were not published until now, Edgar Hederer has revealed a series of notes (p. 157–160) in his recently published book *Hugo von Hofmannsthal* (1960). They show that Hofmannsthal's Oedipus trilogy was to end with the uplifting of the hero to the gods. Even more strongly than in the Sophoclean piece, everything is set aside for the transformation and redemption of the severely tried sufferer. The aged Oedipus is "wonder-

[7] Hugo von Hofmannsthal, *Briefe 1900–1909* (Wien, 1937), pp. 166, 217 f.

fully illumined"; his voice is "freed as never before." In "unnamable misery" he has experienced the dialectic of human fate, which encompasses blessing and curse, elevation and downfall, and is now ready for the highest insight into the purport of his fate and for the highest devotion of *amor fati:* "our misfortune is great, in that it carries something of happiness in it. We now understand the whole world."

The last message, based upon affirmation of fate and of the world, which the homeless, isolated and blinded man announces is: "I bless the sun, which I do not see." His love of existence finds an answer in nature, which opens itself lovingly to the "child of grief." Nature is, in Hofmannsthal's words, "full of compassionate arms, full of healing power, a loving womb and grave." What seemed to be a curse of fate to the young Oedipus reveals itself to the aged man as divine grace. His religious confidence receives one last confirmation. Guilt, delusion, hybris, and suffering are justified as phases of a divine plan of redemption. "For this reason," notes Hofmannsthal, "the tragedy is able to pass on to the idyll." The humanly tragic is absorbed into the divine mysterium. The Oedipus trilogy was therefore chosen for the purpose of representing the tragic conflict between man and fate as a "lovers' quarrel," in the sense of Hölderlin, which ends in reconciliation. Here it becomes clear that the "pagan" dreamplay and the "Christian" world-theater are not in contradiction, but rather that they announce the same message under different assumptions and in different forms. [93]

Zeitgenossen

Josef Hofmiller

Josef Hofmiller (1872–1933) was a teacher, critic, and editor, a professor of literature at Freising and Munich. He wrote critical essays about music and the theatre as well as about Nietzsche, Emerson, Thoreau, and Maeterlinck, among others. He was, at the time of his death, editor of a scholarly journal, *Süddeutsche Monatschrift.*[1] In this selection, Hofmiller presents his view on Hofmannsthal's Dionysian mythology and contrasts Sophocles' and Hofmannsthal's concept of Oedipus.

"We need not develop the contrast between this drama and modern drama. . . . Sophocles' plot unfolds through human, psychological forces and has therefore a lasting effect and value. The characters and situations are expanded in as many directions as possible with greatest psychological import. . . . Sophocles' treatment of the myth has, however, one disadvantage: it gives way to universal human elements, expressed by inner truths, resulting in a conflict with the static motifs of the myth. . . . Oedipus follows the oracles irrevocably and literally as the old myth demands it and ends up in the depth of misery."—JACOB BURCKHARDT.

From Josef Hofmiller, *Zeitgenossen* (München, 1930), pp. 284–288. Translated by Gertrude Schoenbohm.

[1] *Southern German Monthly.*

Hofmannsthal leads us into a totally different world from the one of Sophocles. The world of Sophocles is bright in spite of all the fright and horror, evenly illuminated, calm, dignified, and clear; it unfolds fate with certain subtlety; it is a human, conservative, and reverent world of noble attitude and restraint even when at its worst. Hofmannsthal has turned this humanized myth into a Dionysian [284] one, thus placing it in early antiquity. Its people still believe in the magic of heroic time, e.g., Creon: "I do not call upon my ancestor who roars below to rise enraged from his bed and drag the adventurer down for me."[2] With all its terror, the belief in the gods who are envious of human happiness and human greatness is still alive. Even mightier than the gods, fate, the Moira,[3] hovers with merciless threat, over human existence. Voices of ancestors penetrate the air. The body and soul of the Seer are separated for hours; the visionary dream in the temple seals the fate of the dreaming Oedipus for it reveals to him his future. The condition of the soul of these people is most uncertain, fearful, unrestrained, and restless. Dreams, oracles, magicians, and visionaries come between them and life as messengers and foretellers of fate. Passions are without bounds, turbulent and degenerate. The background consists of the rigid and merciless myth, for psychological causes are nonexistent, and all depends on the mechanism of fate. The drama in this work does not arise from the conflicts experienced by one who wills and fights, who braces himself against the course of the world, who wrestles and dies. Man here does not "will," and he has hardly any self-awareness; he, driven by the force of unseen powers, only stumbles down a descending path. Unaware, he ultimately falls like a rock into the abyss. [285]

The work of Sophocles is like a marble statue of noble grain. It stands there, magnificent and still, and gently sad. There is nothing of the superhuman about it but only the serene and the simple, illuminated by a soft light so that each line and fold, each curve of the body is gently clarified and transfigured. Hof-

[2] Hugo von Hofmannsthal, "Oedipus and the Sphinx," Act III.

[3] In Greek mythology, the goddesses of Fate who spin out the thread of a man's life.

mannsthal's work is like a statue with face, arms, legs, and chest of ivory, draped in purple marble, plentifully adorned by precious stones and sparkling gold, with jewels set in place of eyes. Its movements and poses are of extreme expressiveness; each detail is carried out with the finely chiselled artistry of a Cellini, although as a whole it is somewhat without style when seen in the artificially lit temple hall; before it stand three-legged golden stools; from sacrificial bowls smoke of aromatic resin and spices rises and spreads like a sultry veil. Wrapped in semi-darkness, everything is secretive and threatening. As in the epic, each important person of the tragedy has a special problem of his own. Laios, who had already condemned the scarcely-born infant to death, is unhappy in his marriage because he is aware of Jocasta being consumed by the longing for a child,—all life is poisoned for him since that deed. Jocasta cannot bear the knowledge that the fruit of her womb is dead through the command of her husband and her silent consent. [286] Creon, the ambitious coward who, in the final analysis, always lacks courage, is wholly a malefactor with a polite facade. The ancient Antiope looks in anger with burning, yet halfblind eyes upon the fruitless womb of Jocasta. The young swordbearer kills himself because he believes that this sacrifice will force Creon out of his royal dreams and spur him to royal deeds. All details are terribly interesting in Hofmannsthal—almost too interesting. The persons are not characterized by their speech. They all speak with the same lyric preciosities, revel in marvelous verse, but all talk past and not to each other. When a dramatic dialogue is attempted, it has only the purpose of initiating a great narrative, a concert-like outpour of beautiful language. There is no joy in dialetics as in Sophocles' play, no polite intellectuality, no refined spirituality—everything is all at once archaic, more oriental than Hellenic, more Salammbo[4] than Oedipus. Even in Sophocles' *Oedipus,* pure dialectics are felt as something strange, and the myth itself as something foreign. The ancient drama which is essentially religious, barely joins myth and psychology, Moira and the individual. The

[4] A military leader in the Punic Wars between Rome and Carthage about whom Flaubert wrote an exotic novel.

drama of the modern poet shifts consciously and completely to the myth of Moira. It exludes the treatment of characters as individuals.

However, Hofmannsthal writes under different conditions, for different reasons and for another public. [287] He does not write for Athenians, who know the myth by heart, and are a believing audience, and a people to whom what occurs in the drama is vivid. He writes, rather, for a skeptical public, one hardly acquainted with the fable. He is a philologist who knows the myth and is a reader of Burckhardt's *History of Greek Culture*. He is acquainted with all the treasures of world literature. Thus, he presents a cultural-historical study. In his personages of the heroic age there is a suggestion of pathological traits. Throughout the play, myth and psychology jostle—however, it is not a question here of the psychology of the characters but rather the psychological reaction of the listener. What is Hecuba to us? Who is Oedipus? We feel no pious terror in view of their evolving fates. Not religious myth but academic facts bind us to this world. Artistically interested but inwardly cold, we listen to the colorful and exciting play. It is able to move us aesthetically but it is not able to purge us ethically. Why, after all, should this long-forgotten world really concern us? Are these men of our own flesh and blood? We do not understand their fears; we do not believe them. Who called the poet to unbolt the gates of the chthonian[5] world to make mere ghosts drunk with fiery blood?

For no matter how emphatic their gesticulations, no matter how loud their cries, they simply are not alive. [288] . . .

[5] Designating, or relating to, gods or spirits of the underworld.

Hofmannsthal's Drama *Oedipus und die Sphinx*

Eduard Lachmann

Eduard Lachmann (b. 1891) has been teacher, critic, and literary historian. He was in charge of the Department of Germanics at Innsbruck University. He has written literary criticism and text analyses of the works of Hölderlin and Schiller. He holds the Ph.D. and J.D. degrees and was awarded the prize as the best critic of modern poetry by the Bavarian Academy of Fine Arts.

In "The Meaning of the Plot" Lachmann interprets Hofmannsthal's play, the delusion of his characters, their relationship to the gods and the forces of the underworld. He compares, finally, the attitudes of Sophocles and von Hofmannsthal toward the gods.

From Eduard Lachmann, "Hofmannsthal's Drama *Oedipus und die Sphinx*," *Enzinger Festschrift,* Schlern-Schriften-Reihe (Innsbruck, Austria; Universitätsverlag Wagner, 1953), pp. 148–152. Translated by Gertrude Scoenbohm.

THE MEANING OF THE PLOT

In the drama of Sophocles man stands under the inescapable supremacy of the gods. Whomever they choose is struck by them as if by lightning, and stands there ultimately like a mighty, split tree, a worthy sign of divine power. The grave of Oedipus is a holy site. Does man become guilty when he wants to bow out before the will of the gods, or when parents attempt to kill their child, so that the oracle might be avoided?

Hofmannsthal is not concerned with the questions of guilt. What his characters and those of the antique tragedies have in common is their delusion. In reading the Sophoclean drama, we question how the parents can believe that they might be able to lift the curse of the oracle by getting rid of their child; we ask why Jocasta doesn't question the strange man more closely before she gives herself to him. Similar questions might also be directed to Oedipus himself. The answer can only be that the gods strike with blindness he who wants to circumvent their will. This erroneous attitude leads to destruction.

In Hofmannsthal this delusion has an even harsher effect. His characters recognize the truth in a dream. This truth reveals itself so clearly that their action during the day, contrary to the truth manifested in the dream, is like a dream itself. The imminent prevails even more inexorably than in the ancient tragedy. In the latter, a submission to the will of the gods, a struggle against the gods, an unflinching acceptance of fate is conceivable. Perhaps then the gods would decide differently. This, however, is not considered in Hofmannsthal's work. In it a blind power dominates, turning men blind, unconcerned with the question of justice or injustice. It is like the power of blood in *Electra*. If there, as well as here, we speak of the vengeance of blood, it is not so much as if the blood, already shed, were crying for new blood to be shed, but, rather, in the sense that this blood cannot tolerate encroachment on its law and cannot rest until that law is carried out or re-established. Oedipus, the son of the King of Thebes, must become King of Thebes after his father's death. The exile must return and must, as king, perpetuate the royal blood even if it must be of the womb of his own mother. The blood of the race is indifferent to the happiness or unhappiness of its bearer. To it the person is meaningless. Its paths are veins linking the living with the dead. [148] Through these dark paths it sends dreams into the souls of its victims. It creates confusing phantoms as does the Sphinx. It breaks the soul of a man as it does Creon's soul and poisons him.

The poet gives expression to this blood through the voices of the ancestors, through the voices of the dead boy-swordbearer whose voluntary death also—even if in vain—is a witness to the power of blood. Besides these voices from the realm of the dead, it is above all Antiope who is close to the forces of blood. She, for whom a woman's blessing consists only in fruitfulness ("Woe to those who are barren!"), confesses:

> age-old gods nourish
> my blood, the night and others,
> to whom you do not pray enough—I
> have no need for sleep. My eyes see
> the night even in the day, just as one
> who descends
> deep enough into an old well
> can see the stars at high noon.
> I live half in life and half in death.

Jocasta replies:

> Yes, you speak to gods
> as to familiar blood. You wrestle with them
> like a giant torch with a storm.

Jocasta has "no name" for it. When she prays, she prays to "what is dark."

Out of yonder "dark world" the gods have sent the Sphinx as messenger for the child.

The priests who listen to the cawing of birds and inhale the fumes of earth don't know these gods. Queen Antiope feels herself to be their table and bed partner. When she mentions Bacchus, she has in mind the master of life and death who dwells below, the same one whom Rilke calls "the Neptune of the blood."

The speech of the Seer Teiresias is saturated with the word "blood":

> until blood
> meets with blood in dark forests. . . .
>
> O sacred blood!
> They do not know your force;
> they never plunged into your living depths
> where pain and illusions die; where love
> and hate, hunger and thirst,
> age and death do not dwell.
>
> In my blood the world blooms
> and stars rise and fall.[1] [149]

Teiresias sees in his vision "the abyss of torment" and "the final night," "the cave of suffering" and "the crater of horror." This is reminiscent of Nietzsche's abyss of blood.

A radiance breaks out of the abyss as Oedipus approaches his native city. The radiance in the abyss, the jubilant voices of the forefathers, the triumph in the death-cry of the Sphinx, the flame upon the altar when the staff of Oedipus is burned, the tree at the abyss turning into a wedding torch, the sparkling of the ruby in the diadem of him who has drunk the blood of giants, all these are signs by which the dead express their joy concerning the victory of their law. Finally the blood of Oedipus is proclaimed blessed:

> How everything wavers and changes
> and yields before the fire which breaks
> from the depth of *sacred* blood.[2]

At the end of the drama, in the dithyrambic union of Oedipus and Jocasta, Oedipus answers Jocasta's question:

> Ah, what are we doing?

with the words:

> The *blind* deed of the gods.[2]

[1] This is a composite of two speeches in Act II.
[2] Italics by Hofmannsthal.

But Jocasta contradicts:

> No, not blind,
> we can both see!

She speaks of Oedipus' blood, which has driven him to this place, and she speaks of her own blood, "that could neither live nor die."

> O, we are more than the gods, we;
> we are priest and sacrifice; our hands
> sanctify all: we alone are the world!

The play ends with this truly classical hybris.

This ending has often been misunderstood. Even such a sensitive interpreter as Max Kommerell believes that this ending might break the structure and perhaps the soul of the legend. He feels the poet Hofmannsthal may have known this, and may have communicated through Oedipus that great unrequited yearning of his own existence, and the never fully experienced depths of his own drives which were reaching out to all of society. According to Kommerell, to live out of fullness, to live out of world depths might be here the fortune of those of royal blood. This royal blood, which reigned in the drama as an active force, gave the mother (and what a mother) to her son as the only possible woman to love. . . . [150]

The end of the drama does not imply happy providence, but points to destruction. It is not unintentionally that Hofmannsthal calls this work a tragedy. Oedipus and Jocasta seal their own destruction by their hybris and delusion. Not these two people, but the blood of their family triumphs. To the dithyrambic verses of Oedipus and Jocasta, scornful laughter echoes from the abyss. This triumph could not have been portrayed more powerfully than through human delusion which is even more horrifying since dreams, prophecies, and signs should have opened the eyes of these two people.

Hofmannsthal's tragedy, although complete in itself, is a fragment. It is the middle part of a trilogy, of which the first part was not written, of which the third part was supposed to be replaced by Hofmannsthal's rendition of Sophocles' *Oedipus Rex*. But such a combination proves in itself already impossible, due, alone, to the contrasting and different attitude toward the central problem, the gods, which the ancient and the modern poets take. In Sophocles they are the piously revered gods of Olympus, august in their unrecognizable authority. In Hofmannsthal they are the powers of the blood, which dwell in man himself. Each time the gods are spoken of in his poetry, we must distinguish whether they are referred to as it is conventionally done in dramas with ancient subject matter, or whether they are to be believed in and conjured up as genuine powers of an underworld.

Concerning Antiope, there can be no doubt that she explicitly acknowledges the latter. Jocasta can be compared with Electra; for both of them, the concept of the gods is undecided. The men in the tragedy do not recognize the powers of the underworld and sometimes suspect them only darkly. The gods, however, are not honored as helpers, but as envious fiends who drive man into their net with dogs and then gloat over the captured.

OEDIPUS:
I tremble before you, gods;
I won't look upon you any longer, throw
darkness upon me, throw death
upon my face like a mantle, O gods.
stretching out his arms
I want nothing but death.

Similar to Orestes in *Electra,* Oedipus does not respond to the powers of the underworld as the women do. He is not their priest, but their sacrificial victim. Only at the end does he feel how the blood-gods are stirring in him also: [151]

As truly as this is the messenger
of the frightful gods, so
are you and I but smoke, which
radiantly will bring forth a new, a holy,
a vivid being.

There is no connection with Sophocles. Twice it becomes clear, and later on Hofmannsthal indicates implicitly what alone mattered to the disturbed triangle of father, mother, and son.

OEDIPUS:

Nothing was left after the prophecy
but we three: father,
mother, and child with trembling,
eternal chains of fate welded body to body.

OEDIPUS:

—ah, there is but one,
the dream of Delphi, woe, the dream about the father,
the mother and child!

Hofmannsthal recognizes the life-ties between father, mother, and child as being created through blood. This marks all of his Greek plays as works of transition. How this bond can also be formed on the spiritual plane and what ethical consequences result from it are only shown in the works of his mature period. . . .

Modern Anthropological and Psychological Interpretations of the Oedipus Myth

Myths of Greece and Rome

H. A. Guerber

Under the aegis of the famous German philologist Max Müller, the "solar myth" interpretation of classical folklore was adopted by most students during the nineteenth century. The following excerpt is presented as a typical example of solar mythology which present-day anthropologists no longer accept.

In the Theban solar myth, Laius (derived from the same root as "Leto" and "Latmus") is the emblem of darkness, who, after marrying Jocasta (like Iole, a personification of the violet-tinted clouds of dawn), becomes the father of Oedipus, doomed by fate to be the murderer of his father. Early in life Oedipus is exposed on the barren hillside to perish,—an emblem of the horizontal rays of the rising sun, which [392] seem to lie for a while upon the mountain slopes, ere they rise to begin their journey.

He too, like Cadmus, Apollo, Hercules, Perseus, Theseus, and Jason, is forced to wander far from home, and, after a prolonged journey encounters and slays Laius (the darkness), from whom he derived his existence, and kills the dread monster of drought, the Sphinx, whose very name means "one who binds fast,"—a crea-

From H. A. Guerber, *Myths of Greece and Rome* (New York: American Book Company, 1893), pp. 392–393. Copyright 1893 and 1921 by American Book Company.

ture who had imprisoned the rain in the clouds, and thus caused great distress.

Urged on by unrelenting fate, he marries his own mother, Jocasta, now the violet-tinted twilight, and ends his life amid lightning flashes and rolls of thunder, after being accompanied to the end of his course by Antigone ("the pale light which springs up opposite the sun at his setting"). This story—which at first was merely intended to signify that the sun (Oedipus) must slay the darkness (Laius) and linger for a while beside the violet-colored clouds (Jocasta)—having lost its physical meaning, the Thebans added the tragic sequel, for it seemed but poetic justice that the author of such crimes should receive signal punishment.

The Golden Bough

Sir James G. Frazer

Frazer (1854–1941) was a Scottish anthropologist whose best-known work is *The Golden Bough.* First published in 1890, this famous learned essay was revised in 1900 and expanded to twelve volumes in 1915. Frazer's primary purpose in this discussion of the origins of religion is to explain a primitive fertility myth personified in the succession to the priesthood of Diana, at Aricia, Italy,—the so-called King of the Wood. This primitive priest-king is the

From Sir James George Frazer, *The Golden Bough: A Study in Magic and Religion* (New York: The Macmillan Company, 1935). 12 volumes. The following selection comes from *The Magic Art and the Evolution of Kings,* Volume II, pp. 113–117.

keeper of the sacred oak tree on which grew the Golden Bough, a mistletoe, symbol of the divine source of light and life. As he traces the various manifestations of this vegetation myth in widely scattered cultures, in Africa, Asia, Europe, and the Americas, Frazer explains how to our primitive ancestors the worship of deities of vegetation ensured, through their ritual death and resurrection, the fertility of nature and men. Frazer was the author of a number of other books, the best-known being *Folklore in the Old Testament* (1918) and *Man, God, and Immortality* (1927).

These examples suffice to prove that among many savage races breaches of the marriage laws are thought to blast the [113] fruits of the earth through excessive rain or excessive drought. Similar notions of the disastrous effects of sexual crimes may be detected among some of the civilised races of antiquity, who seem not to have limited the supposed sterilising influence of such offences to the fruits of the earth, but to have extended it also to women and cattle. Thus among the Hebrews we read how Job, passionately protesting his innocence before God, declares that he is no adulterer; "For that," says he, "were an heinous crime; yea, it were an iniquity to be punished by the judges: for it is a fire that consumeth unto Destruction, and would root out all mine increase." In this passage the Hebrew word translated "increase" commonly means "the produce of the earth"; and if we give the word its usual sense here, then Job affirms adultery to be destructive of the fruits of the ground, which is just what many savages still believe. This interpretation of his words is strongly confirmed by two narratives in Genesis, where we read how Sarah, Abraham's wife, was taken into his harem by a king who did not know her to be the wife of the patriarch, and how thereafter God visited the king and his household with great plagues, especially by closing up the wombs of the king's wives and his maid-servants, so that they bore no children. It was not till the king had discovered and confessed his sin, and Abraham had prayed God to forgive him, that the king's women again became fruitful. These narratives seem to imply that adultery, even when it is committed in ignorance, is a cause of plague and especially of sterility among women. Again, in Leviticus, after a long list of sexual crimes, we read: "Defile not ye yourselves in any of these things: for in all these the nations are defiled which I cast out from before you: and the land is defiled: therefore I do visit the [114] iniquity thereof upon it, and the land vomiteth out her inhabitants." This passage appears to imply that the land itself was somehow physically tainted by sexual transgressions so that it could no longer support the inhabitants.

It would seem that the ancient Greeks and Romans entertained similar notions as to the wasting effect of incest. According to Sophocles the land of Thebes suffered from blight, from pestilence, and from the sterility both of women and of cattle under the reign of Oedipus, who had unwittingly slain his father and wedded his mother, and the Delphic oracle declared that the only way to restore the prosperity of the country was to banish the sinner from it, as if his mere presence withered plants, animals, and women. No doubt the poet and his hearers set down these public calamities in great part to the guilt of parricide, which rested on Oedipus; but they can hardly have failed to lay much also of the evil at the door of his incest with his mother. Again, in ancient Italy, under the Emperor Claudius, a Roman noble was accused of incest with his sister. He committed suicide, his sister was banished, and the emperor ordered that certain ancient ceremonies traditionally derived from the laws of King Servius Tullius should be performed, and that expiation should be made by the pontiffs at the sacred grove of Diana, probably the famous Arician grove, which has furnished the starting-point of our enquiry. As Diana appears to have been a goddess of fertility in general and of the fruitfulness of women in particular, the atonement made at her sanctuary for incest may perhaps be accepted as evidence that the Romans, like other peoples, attributed to the sexual immorality a tendency to blast the fruits both of the earth and of the womb. This inference is strengthened by a precept laid down by grave Roman writers that bakers, cooks, and butlers ought to be strictly chaste and continent, because it was most important that food and cups should be handled either by persons under the age of puberty, or at all events by persons who indulged very sparingly in sexual intercourse; for which reason if a baker, a cook, or a butler broke this rule of continence it was his bounden duty to wash in a river or other running water [115] before he applied himself again to his professional duties. But for all such duties the services of a boy or of a virgin were preferred. The Celts of ancient Ireland similarly believed that incest blighted the fruits of the earth. According to legend Munster was afflicted in the third century of our era with a failure of the crops and other misfortunes. When the nobles enquired into the matter, they were told that these calamities were the result of an incest which the king had committed with his sister. In order to put an end to the evil they demanded of the king his two sons, the fruit of his unholy union, that they might consume them with fire and cast their ashes into the running stream. However, one of the sons, Corc by name, is said to have been purged of his inherited taint by being sent out of Ireland to an island, where a Druid purified him every morning, by putting him on the back of a white cow with red ears, and pouring water over him, till one day the cow jumped into the sea and became a rock, no doubt taking the sin of Corc's father away with her. After that the boy was brought back to Erin.

Thus the belief that incest or sexual crime in general has power to blast the fruits of the earth is widespread and probably goes back to a very remote antiquity; it may long have preceded the rise of agriculture. We may conjecture that in its origin the belief was magical rather than religious; in other words, that the blight was at first supposed to be a direct consequence of the act itself rather than a punishment inflicted on the criminal by gods or spirits. Conceived as an unnatural union of the sexes, incest might be thought to subvert the regular processes of reproduction, and so to prevent the earth from yielding its fruits and to hinder animals and men from propagating their kinds. At a later time the anger of spiritual beings would naturally be invoked in order to give a religious sanction to the old taboo. If this [116] was so, it is possible that something of the horror which incest has excited among most, though by no means all, races of men, sprang from this ancient superstition and has been transmitted as an instinct in many nations long after the imaginary ground of it had been forgotten. Certainly a course of conduct which was supposed to endanger or destroy the general supply of food and therefore to strike a blow at the very life of the whole people, could not but present itself to the savage imagination as a crime of the blackest dye, fraught with the most fatal consequences to the public weal. How far such a superstition may in the beginning have operated to prevent the union of near kin, in other words, to institute the system of prohibited degrees which still prevails among the great majority of mankind, both savage and civilised, is a question which deserves to be considered by the historians of marriage. [117]

The Interpretation of Dreams

Sigmund Freud

On the basis of his study of dreams, Sigmund Freud (1856–1939) inaugurated the modern psychological interpretation of symbolic language and myth. But Freud tended to see in myth—as in the dream—the expression of irrational, antisocial impulses rather than the wisdom of past ages expressed in a specific language, that of symbols.

The concept of the Oedipus Complex which Freud first

From Sigmund Freud, *The Interpretation of Dreams* (1900), in *The Basic Writings of Sigmund Freud,* translated and edited by A. A. Brill (New York: Random House. The Modern Library, 1938), pp. 306–311. Copyright 1938 by Random House, Inc. Copyright renewed 1965 by Gioia B. Bernheim and Edmund R. Brill. Reprinted by permission.

worked out in his classic *Interpretation of Dreams* became one of the cornerstones of his psychological system.[1] He eventually came to believe that this concept provided the key to an understanding of history and of the evolution of religion and morality. He was convinced that this complex constituted the fundamental mechanism in the development of the child—the cause of psychopathological development and the "kernel of neurosis."

Freud felt that the Oedipus myth confirmed his view that unconscious incestuous drives and the resulting hate of the father-rival are to be found in every male child. Freud's views have been defended, challenged, debated, modified by numerous disbelievers and disciples. The interpretations of Theodor Reik and Erich Fromm may be cited as interesting psychoanalytical adaptations. Fromm, for example, sees no incest in the Oedipus story (the woman came along with the throne); on the contrary, he detects roots of the struggle against paternal authority in the ancient conflict between matriarchal and patriarchal systems of society. He understands the myth as a symbol of the rebellion of the son against the authority of the father in the patriarchal family, and that in the Oedipus cycle "Sophocles intended to convey the idea that the patriarchal world was triumphant, but that it would be defeated unless it adopted the humanistic principles of the older matriarchal order," Oedipus representing the matriarchal world. [*The Forgotten Language* (New York: Rinehart, 1951), p. 229] A selection from Reik's essay on Oedipus and the Sphinx is given in this collection. For further discussion of the various psychoanalytical interpretations of the Oedipus saga, see Patrick Mullahy, *Oedipus: Myth and Complex* (New York: Grove Press, 1955; first edition 1948).

According to my already extensive experience, parents play a leading part in the infantile psychology of all persons who subsequently become psychoneurotics. Falling in love with one parent and hating the other forms part of the permanent stock of the

[1] Actually, Freud announced his discovery of the Oedipus Complex in his famous letter to his friend, Wilhelm Fliess, October 15, 1897, in which he also includes an analysis of *Hamlet*. This letter is summarized by Ernest Jones in *The Life and Work of Sigmund Freud* (New York: Basic Books, 1953), I, 356.

psychic impulses which arise in early childhood, and are of such importance as the material of the subsequent neurosis. But I do not believe that psychoneurotics are to be [306] sharply distinguished in this respect from other persons who remain normal—that is, I do not believe that they are capable of creating something absolutely new and peculiar to themselves. It is far more probable—and this is confirmed by incidental observations of normal children—that in their amorous or hostile attitude toward their parents, psychoneurotics do no more than reveal to us, by magnification, something that occurs less markedly and intensively in the minds of the majority of children. Antiquity has furnished us with legendary matter which corroborates this belief, and the profound and universal validity of the old legends is explicable only by an equally universal validity of the above-mentioned hypothesis of infantile psychology.

I am referring to the legend of King Oedipus and the *Oedipus Rex* of Sophocles. . . .

The *Oedipus Rex* is a tragedy of fate; its tragic effect depends on the conflict between the all-powerful will of the gods and the vain efforts of human beings threatened with disaster; resignation to the divine will, and the perception of one's own impotence is the lesson which the deeply moved spectator is supposed to learn from the tragedy. Modern authors have therefore sought to achieve a similar tragic effect by expressing the [307] same conflict in stories of their own invention. But the playgoers have looked on unmoved at the unavailing efforts of guiltless men to avert the fulfilment of curse or oracle; the modern tragedies of destiny have failed of their effect.

If the *Oedipus Rex* is capable of moving a modern reader or playgoer no less powerfully than it moved the contemporary Greeks, the only possible explanation is that the effect of the Greek tragedy does not depend upon the conflict between fate and human will, but upon the peculiar nature of the material by which this conflict is revealed. There must be a voice within us which is prepared to acknowledge the compelling power of fate in the *Oedipus,* while we are able to condemn the situations occurring in [Franz Grillparges's] *Die Ahnfrau* or other tragedies of fate as arbitrary inventions. And there actually is a motive in the story of King Oedipus which explains the verdict of this inner voice. His fate moves us only because it might have been our own, because the oracle laid upon us before our birth the very curse which rested upon him. It may be that we were all destined to direct our first sexual impulses toward our mothers, and our first impulses of hatred and violence toward our fathers; our dreams convince us that we were. King Oedipus, who slew his father Laius and wedded his mother Jocasta, is nothing more or less than a wish-fulfilment—the fulfilment of the wish of our childhood. But we, more fortunate than he, in so far as we have not become psychoneurotics, have since our childhood succeeded in withdrawing our sexual impulses from our mothers, and in forgetting our jealousy of our fathers. We recoil from the person for whom this primitive wish of our childhood has been fulfilled with all the force of the repression which these wishes have undergone in our minds since childhood. As the poet brings the guilt of Oedipus to light by his investigation, he forces us to become aware of our own inner selves, in which the same impulses are still extant, even though they are suppressed. The antithesis with which the chorus departs:—

> ". . . Behold, this is Oedipus,
> Who unravelled the great riddle, and was first in power,
> Whose fortune all the townsmen praised and envied;
> See in what dread adversity he sank!"

—this admonition touches us and our own pride, us who since the years of our childhood have grown so wise and so powerful in our own estimation. Like Oedipus, we live in ignorance of the desires that offend morality, the desires that nature has forced upon us and after their unveiling we may well prefer to avert our gaze from the scenes of our childhood.[1] [308]

[1] None of the discoveries of psychoanalytical research has evoked such embittered contradiction, such furious opposition, and also such entertaining acrobatics of criticism, as this indicaton of the incestuous impulses of childhood which survive in the unconscious. An attempt has even been made recently, in defiance of all experience, to assign only a "symbolic" significance to incest. Ferenczi has given an ingenious reinterpretation of the Oedipus

In the very text of Sophocles' tragedy there is an unmistakable reference to the fact that the Oedipus legend had its source in dream-material of immemorial antiquity, the content of which was the painful disturbance of the child's relations to its parents caused by the first impulses of sexuality. Jocasta comforts Oedipus—who is not yet enlightened, but is troubled by the recollection of the oracle—by an allusion to a dream which is often dreamed, though it cannot, in her opinion, mean anything:—

> "For many a man hath seen himself in dreams
> His mother's mate, but he who gives no heed
> To suchlike matters bears the easier life."

The dream of having sexual intercourse with one's mother was as common then as it is to-day with many people, who tell it with indignation and astonishment. As may well be imagined, it is the key to the tragedy and the complement to the dream of the death of the father. The Oedipus fable is the reaction of fantasy to these two typical dreams, and just as such a dream, when occurring to an adult, is experienced with feelings of aversion, so the content of the fable must include terror and self-chastisement. The form which it subsequently assumed was the result of an uncomprehending secondary elaboration of the material, which sought to make it serve a theological intention. The attempt to reconcile divine omnipotence with human responsibility must, of course, fail with this material as with any other.

Another of the great poetic tragedies, Shakespeare's *Hamlet,* is rooted in the same soil as *Oedipus Rex.* But the whole difference in the psychic life of the two widely separated periods of civilization, and the progress, during the course of time, of repression in the emotional life of humanity, is manifested in the differing treatment of the same material. In *Oedipus Rex* the basic wish-phantasy of the child is brought to light and realized as it is in

---

myth, based on a passage in one of Schopenhauer's letters, in *Imago,* i, 1912. The "Oedipus complex," which was first alluded to here in *The Interpretation of Dreams,* has through further study of the subject, acquired an unexpected significance for the understanding of human history and the evolution of religion and morality. See *Totem und Taboo* [Note by Brill.]

dreams; in *Hamlet* it remains repressed, and we learn of its existence—as we discover the relevant facts in a neurosis—only through the inhibitory effects which proceed from it. In the more modern drama, the curious fact that it is possible to remain in complete uncertainty as to the character of the hero has proved to be quite consistent with the overpowering effect of the tragedy. The play is based upon Hamlet's hesitation [309] in accomplishing the task of revenge assigned to him; the text does not give the cause or the motive of this hesitation, nor have the manifold attempts at interpretation succeeded in doing so. According to the still prevailing conception, a conception for which Goethe was first responsible, Hamlet represents the type of man whose active energy is paralysed by excessive intellectual activity: "Sicklied o'er with the pale cast of thought." According to another conception, the poet has endeavoured to portray a morbid, irresolute character, on the verge of neurasthenia. The plot of the drama, however, shows us that Hamlet is by no means intended to appear as a character wholly incapable of action. On two separate occasions we see him assert himself: once in a sudden outburst of rage, when he stabs the eavesdropper behind the arras, and on the other occasion when he deliberately, and even craftily, with the complete unscrupulousness of a prince of the Renaissance, sends the two courtiers to the death which was intended for himself. What is it, then, that inhibits him in accomplishing the task which his father's ghost has laid upon him? Here the explanation offers itself that it is the peculiar nature of this task. Hamlet is able to do anything but take vengeance upon the man who did away with his father and has taken his father's place with his mother—the man who shows him in realization the repressed desires of his own childhood. The loathing which should have driven him to revenge is thus replaced by self-reproach, by conscientious scruples, which tell him that he himself is no better than the murderer whom he is required to punish. I have here translated into consciousness what had to remain unconscious in the mind of the hero; if anyone wishes to call Hamlet an hysterical subject I cannot but admit that this is the deduction to be drawn from my interpretation. The sexual aversion which Hamlet expresses in conversation with Ophelia is perfectly consistent with this deduction—the same sexual aversion which during the next few years was increasingly to take possession of the poet's soul, until it found its supreme utterance in *Timon of Athens.* It can, of course, be only the poet's own psychology with which we are confronted in *Hamlet;* and in a work on Shakespeare by Georg Brandes (1896) I find the statement that the drama was composed immediately after the death of Shakespeare's father (1601)—that is to say, when he was still mourning his loss, and during a revival, as we may fairly assume, of his own childish feelings in respect of his father. It is known, too, that Shakespeare's son, who died in childhood, bore the name of Hamnet (identical with Hamlet). Just as *Hamlet* treats of the relation of the son to his parents, so *Macbeth,* which was written about the same period, is based upon the theme of childlessness. Just as all neurotic symptoms, like dreams themselves, are capable of hyper-interpretation, and even require such hyper-interpretation before they become perfectly intelligible, so every genuine poetical creation must have proceeded [310] from more than one motive, more than one impulse in the mind of the poet, and must admit of more than one interpretation. I have here attempted to interpret only the deepest stratum of impulses in the mind of the creative poet. . . . [311]

Psychoanalysis and Religious Origins

Sigmund Freud

It is in attempting to master the Oedipus complex—that is to say, a person's emotional attitude towards his family, or in a narrower sense towards his father and mother—that individual neurotics come to grief, and for this reason that complex habitually forms the nucleus of their neuroses. It does not owe its importance to any unintelligible conjunction; the emphasis laid upon the relation of children to their parents is an expression of the biological facts that the young of the human race pass through a long period of dependence and are slow in reaching maturity, as well as that their capacity for love undergoes a [261] complicated course of development. Consequently, the overcoming of the Oedipus complex coincides with the most efficient way of mastering the archaic, animal heritage of humanity. It is true that that heritage comprises all the forces that are required for the subsequent cultural development of the individual, but they must first be sorted out and worked over. This archaic heirloom is not fit to be used

From Sigmund Freud, "Preface to Reik's *Ritual: Psycho-Analytic Studies*" (1919), in *The Standard Edition of the Complete Psychological Works of Sigmund Freud,* ed. James Strachey (London: The Hogarth Press, 1955), XVII, 261–263.

for the purposes of civilized social life in the form in which it is inherited by the individual.

To find the starting-point for the psycho-analytic views upon religious life we must go a step further. What is to-day the heritage of the individual was once a new acquisition and has been handed on from one to another of a long series of generations. Thus the Oedipus complex too may have had stages of development, and the study of prehistory may enable us to trace them out. Investigation suggests that life in the human family took a quite different form in those remote days from that with which we are now familiar. And this idea is supported by findings based on observations of contemporary primitive races. If the prehistoric and ethnological material on this subject is worked over psycho-analytically, we arrive at an unexpectedly precise result: namely that God the Father once walked upon earth in bodily form and exercised his sovereignty as chieftain of the primal human horde until his sons united to slay him. It emerges further that this crime of liberation and the reactions to it had as their result the appearance of the first social ties, the basic moral restrictions and the oldest form of religion, totemism. But the later religions too have the same content, and on the one hand they are concerned with obliterating the traces of that crime or with expiating it by bringing forward other solutions of the struggle between the father and sons, while on the other hand they cannot avoid repeating once more the elimination of the father. Incidentally, an echo of this monstrous event, which overshadowed the whole course of human development, is also to be found in myths.

This hypothesis, which is founded upon the observations of Robertson Smith [1889] and was developed by me in *Totem and Taboo* [1912–1913] has been taken by Theodor Reik as the basis of his studies upon the problems of the psychology of religion, of which this is the first volume. In accordance with psycho-analytic technique these studies start out from hitherto [262] unexplained details of religious life, and by means of their elucidation gain access to the fundamental postulates and ultimate aims of religions; moreover they keep steadily in view the relation between prehistoric man and contemporary primitive societies as well as the connection between the products of civilization and the substitutive structures of neurotics. [263] . . .

Psycho-analysis

Sigmund Freud

The Corner-stones of Psycho-analytic Theory.—The assumption that there are unconscious mental processes, the recognition of the theory of resistance and repression, the appreciation of the importance of sexuality and of the Oedipus complex—these constitute the principal subject-matter of psycho-analysis and the foundations of its theory. No one who cannot accept them all should count himself a psycho-analyst. [247] . . .

The Non-Medical Applications and Correlations of Psycho-analysis.—Any estimate of psycho-analysis would be incomplete if it failed to make clear that, alone among the medical disciplines, it has the most extensive relations with the mental sciences, and that it is in a position to play a part of the same importance in the studies of religious and cultural history and in the sciences of mythology and literature as it is in psychiatry. This may seem strange when we reflect that originally its only object was the understanding and improvement of neurotic symptoms. But it is easy to indicate the starting-point of the bridge that [252] leads over to the mental sciences. The analysis of dreams gave us an in-

From Sigmund Freud, "Psycho-Analysis" (1923), in *The Standard Edition of the Complete Psychological Works of Sigmund Freud,* ed. James Strachey (London: The Hogarth Press, 1955), XVIII, 247, 252–253.

sight into the unconscious processes of the mind and showed us that the mechanisms which produce pathological symptoms are also operative in the normal mind. Thus psycho-analysis became a *depth-psychology* and capable as such of being applied to the mental sciences, and it was able to answer a good number of questions with which the academic psychology of consciousness was helpless to deal. At quite an early stage problems of human *phylogenesis* arose. It became clear that pathological function was often nothing more than a *regression* to an earlier stage in the development of normal function. C. G. Jung was the first to draw explicit attention to the striking similarity between the disordered phantasies of sufferers from dementia praecox and the myths of primitive peoples; while the present writer pointed out that the two wishes which combine to form the Oedipus complex coincide precisely with the two principal prohibitions imposed by *totemism* (not to kill the tribal ancestor and not to marry any woman belonging to one's own clan) and drew far-reaching conclusions from this fact. The significance of the Oedipus complex began to grow to gigantic proportions and it looked as though social order, morals, justice and religion had arisen together in the primaeval ages of mankind as reaction-formations against the Oedipus complex. Otto Rank threw a brilliant light upon mythology and the history of literature by the application of psycho-analytical views, as did Theodor Reik upon the history of morals and religions, while Dr. Pfister, of Zurich, aroused the interest of religious and secular teachers and demonstrated the importance of the psycho-analytical standpoint for education. Further discussion of these applications of psycho-analysis would be out of place here, and it is enough to say that the limits of their influence are not yet in sight. [253]

Dostoevsky and Parricide

Sigmund Freud

. . . It can scarcely be owing to chance that three of the masterpieces of the literature of all time—the *Oedipus Rex* of Sophocles, Shakespeare's *Hamlet* and Dostoevsky's *The Brothers Karamazov* —should all deal with the same subject, parricide. In all three, moreover, the motive for the deed, sexual rivalry for a woman, is laid bare.

The most straightforward is certainly the representation in the drama derived from the Greek legend. In this it is still the hero himself who commits the crime. But poetic treatment is impossible without softening and disguise. The naked admission of an intention to commit parricide, as we arrive at it in analysis, seems intolerable without analytical preparation. The Greek drama, while retaining the crime, introduces the indispensable toning-down in a masterly fashion by projecting the hero's unconscious motive into reality in the form of a compulsion by a destiny which is alien to him. The hero commits the deed unintentionally and apparently uninfluenced by the woman; this latter element is, however, taken into account in the circumstance that the hero can only obtain possession of the queen mother after he has re-

From Sigmund Freud, "Dostoevsky and Parricide" (1928), in *The Standard Edition of the Complete Psychological Works of Sigmund Freud,* ed. James Strachey (London: The Hogarth Press, 1961), XXI, 188.

peated his deed upon the monster who symbolizes the father. After his guilt has been revealed and made conscious, the hero makes no attempt to exculpate himself by appealing to the artificial expedient of the compulsion of destiny. His crime is acknowledged and punished as though it were fully conscious—which is bound to appear unjust to our reason, but which psychologically is perfectly correct. [188]

Symbols of Transformation

Carl G. Jung

Carl G. Jung (1875–1961) was one of Freud's early disciples, but soon he developed views of his own. Jung refused to accept the exclusive importance which Freud attached to sexuality and the universality of its psychological implications. Some of the results of this difference in point of view can be seen in Jung's interpretations of the Oedipus myth, the meaning of the Sphinx and the incest-taboo, all of which are found in his early work, *Symbols of Transformation.*

Concerning incest, Jung states that it "is the urge to get back to childhood. For the child, of course, this cannot be called incest; it is only for an adult with a fully developed sexuality that this backward striving becomes incest, because he is no longer a child but possesses a sexuality

From *The Collected Works of Carl Gustav Jung,* edited by Herbert Read, Michael Fordham, and Gerhard Adler. Vol. V, *Symbols of Transformation* (New York: Pantheon Books, 1956), pp. 224–225, 328–331, 181–82. First published in German in 1912.

which cannot be allowed a regressive outlet." (p. 235n.) Thus for Jung the basis of "incestuous" desire is not cohabitation but "the strange idea of becoming a child again, of returning to the parental shelter, and of entering into the mother in order to be reborn through her." (pp. 223–224) For Jung the mother is an image or symbol of the unconscious to which an individual wishes to return in order to seek a solution for his psychic conflicts. But, he continues, "the incest prohibition acts as an obstacle and makes the creative fantasy inventive." (p. 224) Jung's discussion follows:

(All the footnotes in this selection have been added by the editors of this textbook.)

. . . The effect of the incest-taboo and of the attempts at canalization is to stimulate the creative imagination, which gradually opens up possible avenues for the self-realization of libido.[1] In this way the libido becomes imperceptibly spiritualized. The power which 'always desires evil' thus creates spiritual life. That is why the religions exalt this procedure into a system. It is instructive to see the pains they take to further the translation into symbols. The New Testa-[224]ment gives us an excellent example of this: in the dialogue about rebirth (John 3:4 ff.), Nicodemus cannot help taking the matter realistically:

How can a man be born when he is old? Can he enter the second time into his mother's womb, and be born?

Jesus tries to purify the sensuous cast of Nicodemus' mind by rousing it from its dense materialistic slumbers, and translates the passage into the same, and yet not the same, words:

Verily, verily, I say unto thee, Except a man be born of water and of the Spirit, he cannot enter into the kingdom of God.

That which is born of flesh is flesh, and that which is born of the Spirit is spirit.

Marvel not that I said unto thee, Ye must be born again.

The wind bloweth where it listeth, and thou hearest the sound thereof, but canst not tell whence it cometh, and whither it goeth: so is every one that is born of the Spirit.

[1] In Freud, this term refers only to sexual energy; in Jung, however, it refers to all psychic energy, including the sexual.

To be born of water simply means to be born of the mother's womb; to be born of the Spirit means to be born of the fructifying breath of the wind, as can be seen from the Greek text of the passages italicized above, where spirit and wind are expressed by the same word. . . . [225]

[Elsewhere in this volume, Jung interprets the symbol of the mother and the theriomorphic god.]

In reality the whole drama takes place in the individual's own psyche, where the 'parents' are not the parents at all but only their imagos: they are representations which have arisen from the conjunction of parental peculiarities with the individual disposition of the child. The imagos are activated and varied in every possible manner by an energy which likewise pertains to the individual; it derives from the sphere of instinct and expresses itself as instinctuality. This dynamism is represented in dreams by theriomorphic symbols. All the lions, bulls, dogs, and snakes that populate our dreams represent an undifferentiated and as yet untamed libido, which at the same time forms part of the human personality and can therefore fittingly be described as the anthropoid psyche. Like energy, the libido never manifests itself as such, but only in the form of a 'force,' that is to say, in the form of something in a definite energic state, be it moving bodies, chemical or electrical tension, etc. Libido is therefore tied to definite forms or states. It appears as the *intensity* of impulses, affects, activities, and so on. But these phenomena are never impersonal; they manifest themselves like parts of the personality. The same is true of complexes: they too behave like parts of the personality. It is this anthropoid psyche which will not fit into the rational [328] pattern of culture—or only very unsatisfactorily and with extreme reluctance—and resists cultural development to the utmost. It is as though its libido were constantly striving back to the original unconscious state of untamed savagery. The road of regression leads back to childhood and finally, in a manner of speaking, into the mother's body. . . .

Scenting the dangers in this situation, religious and conventional morality joins forces with Freudian theory in consistently devaluing the regression and its ostensible goal—reversion to infantilism—as 'infantile sexuality,' 'incest,' 'uterine fantasy,' etc. Reason must here call a halt, for it is hardly possible to go farther back than the maternal uterus. At this point, concretism comes up against a brick wall; what is more, moral condemnation seizes upon the regressive tendency and tries by every trick of devaluation to prevent this sacrilegious return to the mother, surreptitiously aided and abetted by the one-sided 'biological' orientation of the Freudian school. . . .

. . . It must [329] be remembered that the 'mother' is really an imago, a psychic image merely, which has in it a number of different but very important unconscious contents. The 'mother' as the first incarnation of the anima archetype,[2] personifies in fact the whole unconscious. Hence the regression leads back only apparently to the mother; in reality she is the gateway into the unconscious, into the 'realm of the Mother.' Whoever sets foot in this realm submits his conscious ego-personality to the controlling influence of the unconscious, or if he feels that he has got caught by mistake, or that somebody has tricked him into it, he will defend himself desperately, though his resistance will not turn out to his advantage. For regression, if left undisturbed, does not stop short at the 'mother' but goes back beyond her to the prenatal realm of the 'Eternal Feminine,' to the immemorial world of archetypal possibilities where, 'thronged round with images of all creation,' slumbers the 'divine child,' patiently awaiting his conscious realization. This son is the germ of wholeness, and he is characterized as such by his specific symbols.

When Jonah was swallowed by the whale, he was not simply imprisoned in the belly of the monster, but, as Paracelsus tells us, he saw 'mighty mysteries' there. . . .

In the darkness of the unconscious a treasure lies hidden, the same 'treasure hard to attain' [which may be the 'mystery' ac-

[2] Jung thinks of the *anima* as the personification in dreams or fantasies of the contents of the unconscious. It appears to a man in the figure of a woman. But when it appears to a woman in the figure of a man, it is called *animus*. Jung refers to *archetypes* as primordial images that represent remnants of racial memories or the collective unconscious. Examples are such archetypes as rebirth, the fatal woman, God, and the devil.

cording to Paracelsus]. It is these inherent possibilities of 'spiritual' or 'symbolic' life and of progress which form the ultimate, though unconscious, goal of regression. By serving as a means of expression, as bridges and pointers, symbols help to [330] prevent the libido from getting stuck in the material corporeality of the mother. Never has the dilemma been more acutely formulated than in the Nicodemus dialogue: on the one hand the impossibility of entering again into the mother's womb; on the other, the need for rebirth from 'water and spirit.' [331] . . .

[As for the Sphinx, a monster with the face of a maiden and the body of a winged lion, Jung thinks of her as a "semi-theriomorphic representation of the mother-imago, or rather of the Terrible Mother," the devouring mother. (p. 179) It is thus apparent that Jung has a dual image of the mother archetype. This view is explained by the fact that, even though the individual needs to enter his unconscious in order to resolve his internal conflict, he is at the same time afraid of what may confront him there. Jung's interpretation follows:]

The Sphinx is a fear-animal of this kind and still shows clear traces of a mother derivative. In the Oedipus legend the Sphinx was sent by Hera, who hated Thebes on account of the birth of Bacchus.[3] Oedipus, thinking he had overcome the Sphinx sent by the mother-goddess merely because he had solved her childishly simple riddle, fell a victim to matriarchal incest and had to marry Jocasta, his mother, for the throne and the hand of the widowed queen belonged to him who freed the land from the plague of the Sphinx. This had all those tragic consequences which could easily have been avoided if only Oedipus had been sufficiently intimidated by the frightening appearance of the 'terrible' or 'devouring' Mother whom the Sphinx personified. He was far indeed from the philosophical wonderment [181] of Faust: 'The Mothers, the Mothers, it has a wondrous sound!' Little did he know that the riddle of the Sphinx can never be solved merely by the wit of man.

[3] That is, Hera was hostile to Thebes as the city of her rival Semele, daughter of Cadmus (the founder of Thebes) and mother by Zeus of Dionysius (Bacchus). Hera, Queen of Heaven, was the wife and sister of Zeus.

The genealogy of the Sphinx has manifold connections with the problem touched upon here: she was a daughter of Echidna, a monster with the top half of a beautiful maiden, and a hideous serpent below. This double being corresponds to the mother-imago: above, the lovely and attractive human half; below, the horrible animal half, changed into a fear-animal by the incest prohibition. Echidna was born of the All-Mother, Mother Earth, Gaia, who conceived her with Tartarus, the personification of the underworld. Echidna herself was the mother of all terrors, of the Chimera, Scylla, the Gorgon, of frightful Cerberus, of the Nemean lion, and of the eagle that devoured the liver of Prometheus. She also gave birth to a number of dragons. One of her sons was Orthrus, the dog of the monster Geryon, who was slain by Heracles. With this dog, her own son, Echidna incestuously begat the Sphinx. This should be sufficient to characterize the complex whose symbol is the Sphinx. It is evident that a factor of such magnitude cannot be disposed of by solving a childish riddle. The riddle was, in fact, the trap which the Sphinx laid for the unwary wanderer. Overestimating his intellect in a typically masculine way, Oedipus walked right into it, and all unknowingly committed the crime of incest. The riddle of the Sphinx was *herself*—the terrible mother-imago, which Oedipus would not take as a warning. [182]

Dogma and Compulsion

Theodor Reik

Reik (b. 1888) is one of the disciples of Freud in the Viennese school of psychoanalysis. In the following passage, taken from his essay on "Oedipus and the Sphinx" (written 1919), Reik explores the hidden meaning of the Sphinx episode in the Oedipus saga as well as the part which this episode played in the destiny of Oedipus. In examining the Sphinx legend, he attempts to separate those features which are primary (primordial) from those which are subsequent expansions, which elaborate and perhaps obscure the original story with apparently inconsistent details. Reik explains the symbolic relationships of the figures in the ancient legend and their original motivations in the light of Freudian dream theory. The excerpt is not complete; Reik's final elaborate conclusion is omitted because the language is too technical. However, his method and basic interpretation are made clear.[1]

. . . But before we attempt to wrest from the Sphinx of Oedipus the secret of its nature, we must first of all clearly understand which features of our legend are accepted by the mythologists

From Theodor Reik, *Dogma and Compulsion* (New York: International Universities Press, 1951), pp. 319–326.

[1] Jebb has a discussion of the Sphinx in *Sophocles: The Plays and Fragments, Part I: The Oedipus Tyrannus* (Cambridge: University Press, 1893), pp. 226–229.

and philologists as primordial, and which they have regarded as subsequent expansions, embellishments, variants, or what not. No complete reconstruction of the original version is practicable; but the scholars tell us that the legend must once have existed in a much cruder form, and that originally the slaying of the father must have been followed immediately by the violation of the mother, who was present at his murder. [319] . . .

The ancient legend speaks of a mysterious relation between Laios and the Sphinx, and psychoanalysis tells us that such relations have a psychic—that is, a real—motivation. If we do not perceive its nature we must wait patiently until we find it; at all events we must not simply deny its existence. Even the parallelism between the slaying of Laios and the slaying of the Sphinx seems to indicate that the two figures are somehow related.

Perhaps we shall find an explanation of the relationship if we consider the result of one analysis of the Sphinx; the Sphinx, a late development of the divine totemic animal,[2] confronts the young Oedipus. He fights and kills her, and the city is his reward. [321] If we accept the results obtained by the analysis of the origin of totemism we must assume that in the last resort the Sphinx is equivalent to Laios, the father of the young hero, so that her slaying repeats the murder of the king. But through the symbolism of dreams and myths and poetry and wit we have learned that the significance of the city, and of the country, is, in the unconscious, woman. Moreover, we recognize in this disguise a repetition of the great event which constitutes the kernel of the human, all-too-human story of Oedipus: the slaying of the father and the seizure of the mother.

If we accept this interpretation we are again confronted by

[2] According to Freudian theory, the Totem is an animal serving as a symbolic substitute for the father of the primal horde, whose life was to be protected, treated as sacred, and in relation to whom certain taboos were developed. The totemic system is a kind of agreement with the father in which he, through the magic powers of the totem, exercises protection, care, and forebearance in exchange for the pledge to honor his life (by proscribing the killing of the totem animal). Thus according to Reik, Oedipus killed the totemic animal god—hence symbolic of destroying his father or the authority of his father—hence a sacrilegious deed. [Note by the editors.]

difficult questions which have to be answered. Which forms of the legend is the original one, and why is its content repeated in a different form? How did it come about that the earlier, male figure of the Sphinx was translated into a female figure? What psychic motives determined the change, and through what psychic mechanism was the transformation effected?

The Oedipus myth hands down to us in its antique forthrightness and simplicity a theme whose emotional content is so universally human that as psychoanalysts we are accustomed to cite it as typical of the strongest unconscious wishes of childhood. But the very naiveté of the Greek tradition, which develops this theme in historical time, in all its crudity, before the eyes and ears of the auditor, should give us cause for reflection. One should always be distrustful when a myth openly relates crudely sexual themes; almost invariably the myth conceals other significant motives, and the emphasis laid on the one sexual subject often serves to conceal other fragments of sexual or innocuous themes.

If we omit the oracle, the episode of the Sphinx, and other specific mythological features of the Oedipus myth, what is left? The life and the actions of a criminal, a patricide and an incestuous son, for whom we cannot even feel compassion, a man whose destiny strikes no profounder note of tragedy. We should not understand why this particular criminal was chosen by so many of the Greeks to be immortalized as a tragic hero, and why for him especially the tribunal should become the stage. [322]

Reflection, as well as the particularly crude form of the tradition, the obscure connection between the role of the Sphinx and the fate of Laios, and its mythological significance—all these motives justify our assumption that the Sphinx legend is not a later interpolation, as the majority of mythologists believe, but is one of the most essential components of the original myth. But if this be so, the question of the relation of one part of the legend to another, which repeats the same story on another plane, now becomes urgent. We will answer it briefly thus: The Sphinx plays much the same part in the life of Oedipus as the Ghost in the tragedy of Hamlet. The episode of the Sphinx is older than what we may call the human legend of Oedipus in its present form.

There, in the description of the death of the Sphinx, the typical event of the Oedipus legend occurs in its first, elementary, terrible force; in later versions the superhuman crime has become a deed that rids the country of a monster. But the motive—the fact that the action was that of a young hero, and the victim a late representative of the ancient totemic animal, of the inviolable god—reveals it in all its tragic momentousness, and its true significance, which far exceeds the fate of the individual. Here, in the murder of Laios, all happens, so to speak, within the setting of private life, and the ambit of a legal code; but as regards the slaying of the Sphinx, from which the action subsequently received the strongest subterranean repercussion, it is obvious that the exploit of the young saviour Oedipus was a crime against deity, since the god was its victim. The human actions and mundane events of the legend now appear in the light of higher powers. The tragic note is greatly enhanced by the fact that Oedipus has not only offended against the transitory morals and questionable customs of mankind, but that he has violated the sacred and eternal laws decreed by the gods. Oedipus has not only slain his father, but in his father he has struck at the supreme authority, the God himself. [323]

One may indeed say that it was just because the terrible gravity of Oedipus's crime was concealed by the story of the Sphinx that it was possible to represent his action as that of an ordinary human being, and to describe it without disguise. We should then assume that the Oedipus of an earlier form of the legend killed the divine totemic animal and had to pay dearly for his crime. Subsequently the original slaying of the totem was no longer recognized in its momentous real significance by the Greeks, who had progressed to the creation of anthropomorphic deities. The totemic animal, degraded by progress to the status of monster, was retained in the very late transformation of the legend as the Sphinx; and the killing of the totem was likewise retained; but now, by a conversion of affect, it acquired a meritorious character.

The whole event was thus misunderstood owing to the influence of the tendencies of a more highly cultured period. We

[324] must not forget that the gods had already assumed human form, that religious feeling had become more sensitive and refined, and had suppressed, even though unconsciously, any impulse of sympathy with the monstrous act of deicide. But then another crime offered itself as a substitute for this unique act: a crime grievous enough, and resembling the other, but without the character of a violent insurrection against the deity. This crime was parricide.

However, we do not believe that the choice of this substitute was directed by chance. Let us consider what the substitution of the father for the totem meant: The totemic animal itself had been a primeval substitute for the Father, and the slaying of the totem revived memories of the murder of the chieftain of the primeval horde. If the legend now made Oedipus kill his father, what it recorded was a form of the primitive legend not uninfluenced by the anthropomorphization of the gods, and adapted to the later cultural standards of the period. If we consider this process of evolution, which started from a primitive era that had no conscious memory of the actual event, that found a late echo in the Oedipus myth, and which in the slaying of the totemic animal revealed the act in its religious significance, and later on, compelled by the impatience of the repressing forces, allowed it to be replaced by the parricide, we then have the following aspect of the matter: *The myth as we know it does not reflect the primary content of the legend, but already represents a late recurrence of the repressed matter.* An episode broadly resembling the present events of the Oedipus legend may have formed the content of the original nucleus of the legend. [325] . . .

We have realized that in the Oedipus legend, side by side with the more recent form, the older version of the story of the Sphinx persists, erroneously conceived and interpreted; and further, that the chief emphasis, which formerly rested on the story of the Sphinx, is now transferred to the fate of Oedipus, struggling against a human father. Such a displacement of accent is not unknown to us in the psychic field; in dreams also what was once the kernel makes its appearance as the shell. [326] . . .

The Hero: A Study in Tradition, Myth, and Drama

Lord Raglan

Lord Fitzroy R. S. Raglan (1885–1964) was President of the Anthropological Section of the British Association in 1933, and of the Folk-Lore Society from 1945 to 1947. Some of his other publications include *Jocasta's Crime, The Origins of Religion, How Came Civilization?,* and *Death and Rebirth.* The excerpt that follows is from Chapter XVI, wherein striking parallels between Oedipus and several other heroes of Greek, Roman, Hebraic, Germanic, and Welsh myth are drawn: Theseus, Romulus, Perseus, Apollo, Zeus, Joseph, Moses, Elijah, Siegfried, Arthur.

In the earlier chapters of this book I took a succession of well-known heroes of tradition, and attempted to show that there is no justification for believing that any of these heroes were real persons, or that any of the stories of their exploits had any historical foundation. In the course of the discussion I had frequent occasion to suggest that these heroes, if they were genuinely heroes of tradition, were originally not men but gods, and that the stories were accounts not of fact but of ritual, that is, myths. Since

From Lord Raglan, *The Hero: A Study in Tradition, Myth, and Drama* (London: Watts and Co., 1949), pp. 177–185. First published in 1936.

my chief object in those chapters was, however, to show that the heroes had no claim to historicity, I made no attempt to link them, or the beliefs connected with them, to any general ritual scheme. Before so doing it seemed desirable to demonstrate, both theoretically and by examples, the intimate association of myth with ritual, an association which has been recognized by many leading students of these subjects, and upon which depends the validity of the conclusions which I have reached.

Some years ago I had occasion to study the myth of Oedipus, and to try to analyse it, and I was struck by the similarity of many of the incidents in it to incidents in the stories of Theseus and Romulus. I then examined the stories of a number of other traditional heroes of Greece, and found that when these stories were split up into separate incidents, there were certain types of incident which ran through all the stories.

Whether these parallels have any significance, or whether they are merely coincidences, the sort of thing that might happen to or be readily invented about any hero, are questions to which we shall come later. My first task is to show that the parallels exist, and for that [177] purpose it is necessary to tabulate and number them. What I have done is to take a dozen heroes whose stories are narrated in sufficient detail, to tabulate the incidents in their careers, and to regard as typical such incidents as occur in the majority of the stories. By tabulating these typical incidents, I have arrived at what appears to be a pattern, in which I include all incidents, whether they are miraculous or whether they seem insignificant, which occur with sufficient regularity. I have then fitted the pattern back on to my dozen heroes, and finding that it fits, have extended it to a number of heroes from outside the classical area, with what have been to me surprising results.

I should like it to be quite clear that in the . . . biographies which follow there is no intention of giving a complete account of the heroes. Irrelevant incidents and alternative versions are omitted, and no attempt is made to distinguish between genuine mythology, that is, mythology connected with ritual, and the imitation mythology which probably forms a large part of the stories of Arthur and of Romulus. The wearing of an imitation sword may be just as significant as the wearing of a real one, and it is with the uniform of the heroes and not with their outfitters that I am at present concerned.

The pattern, then, is as follows:—

(1) The hero's mother is a royal virgin;
(2) His father is a king, and
(3) Often a near relative of his mother, but
(4) The circumstances of his conception are unusual, and
(5) He is also reputed to be the son of a god.
(6) At birth an attempt is made, usually by his father or his maternal grandfather, to kill him, but
(7) He is spirited away, and
(8) Reared by foster-parents in a far country.
(9) We are told nothing of his childhood, but
(10) On reaching manhood he returns or goes to his future kingdom. [178]
(11) After a victory over the king and/or a giant, dragon, or wild beast,
(12) He marries a princess, often the daughter of his predecessor, and
(13) Becomes king.
(14) For a time he reigns uneventfully, and
(15) Prescribes laws, but
(16) Later he loses favour with the gods and/or his subjects, and
(17) Is driven from the throne and city, after which
(18) He meets with a mysterious death,
(19) Often at the top of a hill.
(20) His children, if any, do not succeed him.
(21) His body is buried, but nevertheless
(22) He has one or more holy sepulchres.

Let us now apply this pattern to our heroes, and we will start with

OEDIPUS

His mother, Jocasta, is (1) a princess, and his father is (2) King Laius, who, like her, is (3) of the line of Cadmus. He has sworn to have no connection with her, but (4) does so when drunk, probably (5) in the character of Dionysus. Laius (6) tries to kill Oedipus at birth, but (7) he is spirited away, and (8) reared by the king of Corinth. (9) We hear nothing of his childhood, but (10) on reaching manhood he returns to Thebes, after (11) gaining victories over his father and the Sphinx. He (12) marries Jocasta, and (13) becomes king. For some years he (14) reigns uneventfully, but (16) later comes to be regarded as the cause of a plague, and (17) is deposed and driven into exile. He meets with (18) a mysterious death at (19) a place near Athens called the Steep Pavement. He is succeeded by (20) Creon, through whom he was deposed, and though (21) the place of his burial is uncertain, he has (22) several holy sepulchres.

He does not seem to have been regarded as a [179] legislator; apart from that we may award him full marks. . . . [180]

MOSES

His parents (1 and 2) were of the principal family of the Levites, and (3) near relatives; he is (5) also reputed to be the son of Pharaoh's daughter. Pharaoh [184] (6) attempts to kill him at birth, but (7) he is wafted away, and (8) reared secretly. We are told (9) nothing of his childhood, but on reaching manhood he (11) kills a man, and (10) goes to Midian, where (12) he marries the ruler's daughter. Returning (10) to Egypt, he (11) gains a series of magical victories over Pharaoh, and (13) becomes a ruler.

His rule lasts a long time, and (15) he prescribes laws, but later he (16) loses the favour of Jehovah, is (17) removed from his leadership, and (18) disappears mysteriously from (19) the top of a mountain. His children (20) do not succeed him. His body (21) is not buried, but (22) he has a holy sepulchre near Jerusalem.

He scores twenty points, several of them twice, or, if we include Josephus's account, even three times. [185]

Recurrent Themes in Myths and Mythmaking

Clyde Kluckhohn

In this essay, Professor Kluckhohn, formerly Chairman of the Department of Anthropology at Harvard University, discusses the results of recent scientific investigations of "certain features of mythology that are apparently universal or that have such wide distribution in space and time that their generality may be presumed to result from recurrent reactions of the human psyche to situations and stimuli of the same general order." (p. 268) He refers to such recurrent themes in myth and folklore as father-seekers, father-slayers, mother-murder, the eternal return, animal stories, slaying of monsters, the Orpheus story, the creation, flood or catastrophe, androgynous deities, witchcraft, brother rivalry, incest, castration (especially the symbolic kind). His point of view regarding the origin of these universal myths is

From Clyde Kluckhohn, "Recurrent Themes in Myths and Mythmaking," *Daedalus,* LXXXVIII (Spring, 1959), pp. 273–278.

indicated in this quotation: "their persistence cannot be understood except on the hypothesis that these images have a special congeniality for the human mind as a consequence of the relations of children to their parents and other childhood experiences which are universal rather than culture-bound." (p. 270)

OEDIPUS-TYPE MYTHS

Let us now turn to a brief examination of two patterns in which themes are combined. The Oedipus story has long haunted European literature and thought, even if in very recent times the myth of Sisyphus may have replaced that of Oedipus in popularity (see Kafka, Camus, and many others). Jones (1954) has tried to show that *Hamlet* is basically an Oedipal plot. Others insist that Great Mother or Mater Dolórosa tales are simply special variants.

At all events, some scholars have regarded the Oedipal tale as prototypical of all human myths. Critical scrutiny of this generalization, and particularly one's conclusions as to the prevalence of Oedipus-type myths outside the areas the story may have reached through historical diffusion, will rest on how much credence one is [273] prepared to give to psychoanalytic interpretations of latent content, on the one hand; and on how many elements of the Greek myth one demands be replicated, on the other. Thus Roheim's (1950, pp. 319–347) contention that certain Navaho myths are Oedipal strikes many as strained....

In a very interesting paper Lessa (1956) has suggested that the Oedipus-type story spread by diffusion from the patriarchal Euro-Asiatic societies to Oceanic peoples with whom the situation is very different. He writes:

> . . . we find such stories limited to a continuous belt extending from Europe to the Near and Middle East and southeastern Asia, and from there into the islands of the Pacific. It seems to be absent from such vast areas as Africa, China, central Asia, northeastern Asia, North America, South America, and Australia.

In an examination of several thousand Oceania narratives Lessa found twenty-three that bore some resemblance to the Oedipus tale. He points out, however, that none meet all three of his major criteria (prophecy, parricide, and incest) nor his minor criteria (succorance from exposure, rearing by another king, fulfillment of prophecy); only a third meet the combination of parricide and incest. [274] . . .

Nevertheless, even if one grants Lessa's inference of diffusion (with culturally appropriate substitutions), I do not think one can at present assent to his main argument without exception. Roheim's (1950) case for Oedipal pattern in the myths of Australian aborigines, Yurok, Navaho, and others does indeed involve too much reliance upon "unconscious ideas" and "real motifs." And yet, in my opinion, something remains that cannot altogether be explained away. Lessa asserts flatly that Oedipal tales are absent from Africa, but they are found among the Shilluk (Bascom, 1957, p. 111); and the Lamba (Central Bantu) have a story of a son killing his father, in which there is a fairly overt motif of sexual rivalry for the mother.

Herskovits and Herskovits (1958, p. 94) make two significant points as regards testing generalizing conclusions about the Oedipus myth in cross-cultural perspective. The first (abundantly confirmed by the present small study) is neglect of rivalry between brothers. Then they say:

> In analyzing the motivating forces underlying the myth clusters that fall into the Oedipus category, we must take into account not only the son's jealousy of the father, but also the father's fear of being displaced by his son. Parent-child hostilities, that is, are not unidirectional. As manifest in myth, and in the situations of everyday experience, they are an expression of the broader phenomenon of intergenerational competition. These tensions, moreover, begin in infancy in the situation of rivalry between children of the same parents for a single goal, the attention of the mother. This rivalry sets up patterns of interaction that throughout life give rise to attitudes held toward the siblings or sibling substitutes with whom the individual was in competition during infancy, and it is our hypothesis that these attitudes are later projected by the father upon his offspring. In myth, if the psychological interpretation is to be granted validity, we must posit that the threat to the father or father-surrogate is to be seen as a projection of the infantile experience

of sibling hostility upon the son. It may be said to be the response to the reactivation of early attitudes toward the mother under the stimulus of anticipated competition for the affection of the wife.

The hypothesis that the main direction of hostility is from father to son received much confirmation from our reading from the following: fourteen North American peoples; four Circum-Mediterranean peoples; five from East Eurasia; three from the Insular Pacific; four from Africa. These were noted incidentally in searching for material [275] on our selected themes. In many cases the myth states as an explicit motif the father's fear of being killed or displaced by his son. In some instances a prophecy is mentioned. Sometimes the son is expelled by the father rather than killed. . . .

THE MYTH OF THE HERO

It strikes me that the Oedipal pattern may best be considered as one form of a far more widespread myth, which has been treated by Rank (1952), Raglan (1956), and Campbell (1956). Rank abstracts the following pattern in thirty-four myths from the Mediterranean basin and western Asia:

> The hero is the child of most distinguished parents; usually the son of a king. His origin is preceded by difficulties, such as continence, or prolonged barrenness . . . of the parents, due to external prohibition or obstacles. During the pregnancy, or antedating the same, there is a prophecy in the form of a dream or oracle, cautioning against his birth, and usually threatening danger to the father, or his representative. As a rule, he is surrendered to the water, in a box. He is then saved by animals, or lowly people (shepherds) and is suckled by a female animal, or by a humble woman. After he is grown up, he finds his distinguished parents in a highly versatile fashion; takes his revenge on his father, on the one hand, and is acknowledged on the other, and finally achieves rank and honors (page 61).

Raglan's first thirteen (of twenty-two) points correspond strikingly to this formula. [276] . . .

Let us . . . take an example from the New World, Spencer's (1957, see esp. pp. 19, 73) analysis of Navaho mythology. The following similarities [with the Oedipus story] may be noted:

1. These are also hero stories: adventures and achievements of extraordinary kind (e.g., slaying monsters, overcoming death, controlling the weather).

2. There is often something special about the birth of the hero (occasionally heroine).

3. Help from animals is a frequent motif.

4. A separation from one or both parents at an early age is involved.

5. There is antagonism and violence toward near kin, though mainly toward siblings or father-in-law. This hostility may be channeled in one or both directions. It may be masked but is more often expressed in violent acts.

6. There is eventual return and recognition with honor. The hero's achievements are realized by his immediate family, and redound in some way to their benefit and that of the larger group to which the family belongs.

Contrasts between the Old World and New World forms are clearly reflected in content and emphasis. The themes of social hierarchy and of triumph over (specifically) the father are absent in the American Indian version, and the Navaho theme of anxiety over subsistence is absent from the Euro-Asian plot. Yet at a broad psychological level the similarities are also impressive. In both cases we have a form of "family romance": the hero is separated but in the end returns in a high status; prohibitions and portents and animals play a role. [277] . . .

In conclusion, it may be said that this incomplete and exploratory study adds a small bit of confirmation to the findings of others and there are detectable trends toward regularities both in myths and in mythmaking. At least some themes and the linking of certain features of them, while differently stylized and incorporating varying detailed content according to culture and culture area, represent recurrent fantasies that have held the imaginations of many, if not most, social groups. [278]

BIBLIOGRAPHICAL REFERENCES

Bascom, William, "The Myth-Ritual Theory," *Journal of American Folklore,* 1957, 70: 103–115.

Campbell, Joseph, *The Hero with a Thousand Faces.* New York: Meridian Books, 1956. (1st edn., New York: Pantheon Books, 1949; Bollingen Series, 17.)

Jones, Ernest, *Hamlet and Oedipus.* New York: Doubleday Anchor Books, 1954. (Published first as an article in the *American Journal of Psychology* in 1910; again in 1923 as Ch. 1 in *Essays in Applied Psycho-Analysis;* revised edn., London: V. Gollancz; New York: W. W. Norton, 1949.)

Lessa, William, "Oedipus-Type Tales in Oceania," *Journal of American Folklore,* 1956, 69: 63–73.

Raglan, Lord Fitzroy R. S., *The Hero: A Study in Tradition, Myth and Drama.* New York: Vintage Books (Alfred A. Knopf), 1956. 1st edn., London: Methuen and Company, 1936.

Rank, Otto, *The Myth of the Birth of the Hero,* trans. F. Robbins and S. E. Jellife. New York: Robert Brunner, 1952. (1st edn., *Der Mythus von der Geburt des Helden,* Leipzig-Wein: F. Deuticke, 1909.)

Roheim, Geza, *Psychoanalysis and Anthropology.* New York: International Universities Press, 1950.

Spencer, Katherine, *Mythology and Values.* Memoir 48, American Folklore Society, Philadelphia, 1957.

Edward

Anonymous

The popular ballad *Edward,* which flourished in the British Isles as late as the fifteenth century, is characteristic of its type in its concern with domestic tragedy. And the great popularity of the ballad throughout the Middle Ages attests to the fact that the medieval audience was very close to the folklore which originally derived from primitive myth and ritual. As it clearly reflects the link between mother and son, *Edward* further substantiates Kluckhohn's view that some themes, while differently stylized and varying in detail according to the culture in which they appear, represent "recurrent fantasies that have held the imaginations of many . . . social groups."

'Why dois your brand° sae drap wi bluid, *sword*
        Edward, Edward,
Why dois your brand sae drap wi bluid,
    And why sae sad gang yee O?'
'O I hae killed my hauke sae guid,
        Mither, mither,

From Helen Child Sargent and George L. Kittredge, *English and Scottish Popular Ballads* (Boston: Houghton Mifflin Co., 1932), p. 25.

O I hae killed my hauke sae guid,
  And I had nae mair bot hee O.

'Your haukis bluid was nevir sae reid,
      Edward, Edward,
Your haukis bluid was nevir sae reid,
  My deir son I tell thee O.'
O I hae killed my reid-roan steid,
      Mither, mither,
O I hae killed my reid-roan steid,
  That erst was sae fair and frie O.'

'Your steid was auld, and ye hae gat mair,
  Sum other dule° ye drie° O.' *grief; suffer*
'O I hae killed my fadir deir,
      Mither, mither,
O I hae killed my fadir deir,
  Alas, and wae is mee O!'

'And whatten penance wul ye drie for that,
      Edward, Edward?
And whatten penance will ye drie for that?
  My deir son, now tell me O.'
'Ile set my feit in yonder boat,
      Mither, mither,
Ile set my feit in yonder boat,
  And Ile fare ovir the sea O.'

'And what wul ye doe wi your towirs° and your ha,° *castel; hall, manor house*
  That were sae fiar to see O?'
'Ile let thame stand tul they doun fa,
      Mither, mither,
Ile let thame stand tul they doun fa,
  For here nevir mair maun I bee O.'

'And what wul ye leive to your bairns° and your wife, *children*
      Edward, Edward?

And what wul ye leive to your bairns and your wife,
  Whan ye gang ovir the sea O?'
'The warldis room,° late them beg thrae life, *the space of the world*
      Mither, mither,
The warldis room, late them beg thrae life,
  For thame nevir mair wul I see O.'

'And what wul ye leive to your ain mither deir,
      Edward, Edward?
And what wul ye leive to your ain mither deir?
  My deir son, now tell me O.'
'The curse of hell frae me sall ye beir,
      Mither, mither,
The curse of hell frae me sall ye beir,
  Sic counseils° ye gave to me O.' *advices*

SUGGESTIONS FOR PAPERS AND DISCUSSIONS

Depending on the nature of the assignment, short or long research papers may be written. These may be critical, analytical, or comparative in type. Topics may be chosen from among the following: (1) treatment of plot and related problems; (2) development of character; (3) theme and the concept of tragedy.

TREATMENT OF PLOT AND RELATED PROBLEMS

Consider the plan of action and the different adaptations of the ancient myth. Evaluate the treatment of episodes, acts, or scenes. For example, is suspense an important dramatic factor? Is conflict significant? What is the nature of the climax and the resolution of the action? *Hamartia,* the tragic hero, improbabilities, and ambiguities may become topics for discussion.

1. Relate the ancient mythological legend to Sophocles' *Oedipus.* What is meant by the mythological legend as distinct from Sophocles' treatment of the myth in *Oedipus?* (Discussed in the Lachmann, Hofmiller, and Rey criticisms.)

2. In each of the three plays, point out the conflicts which Oedipus faces: those involving external forces, those imposed by Fate, and those having a psychological basis.

3. Seek out dramatic elements in the plays.

4. In Greek theatre "reversal of fortune" (Aristotle's *peripetia*) was a vital part of the tragic technique. (For example, in Sophocles' play, the messenger comes from Corinth to cheer Oedipus and free him from worry concerning his parents, but by revealing who he is produces the opposite result.) Describe the contribution irony makes to the "dramatic effect" of each play.

5. Compare the way in which the three dramatists present the first entrance of Oedipus.

6. Explain the dramatic significance of the episode in *Oedipus the King* dealing with Jocasta's prayer to Apollo. Why does she pray to Apollo? What happens immediately before and after her prayer and her offering as the play proceeds to its climax?

7. What is the function of the Sphinx in the three plays?

8. To what extent is probability important in Sophocles' play? For example, consider the plague—is it improbable that so many years passed after the death of Laius before it reached Thebes? Consider Oedipus' ignorance—is it improbable that he never asked about Laius' death and the time of his murder?

9. What other improbabilities or ambiguities do you detect in each of the three versions of the Oedipus myth? In each play do such considerations make the expositions dramatically ineffective or do they deepen its meaning?

10. Comment on Lachmann's statement that in Hofmannsthal's drama "the imminent prevails even more inexorably than in the ancient tragedy."

DEVELOPMENT OF CHARACTERS

Development of characters involves the treatment of major and minor characters in the dramas. Similarities and differences in their motivation and their relationships may be analyzed. For example, the treatment of Jocasta by Sophocles and by Hofmannsthal might be contrasted, or the personalities of Oedipus and Creon within one play might be compared.

1. Show how Sophocles in the Prologue (the Chorus of Suppliants) succeeds in establishing the character of Oedipus.

2. Describe the young Oedipus as Hofmannsthal sees him.

3. Oedipus' name is significant. It has two meanings: Swollen-foot (his feet were pierced) or Know-foot (he solved the riddle of the feet). Oedipus does not know his own identity. How do the three dramatists treat his "self-discovery" and its repercussions?

4. Does Oedipus in Sophocles' play manifest *hybris*—man considering himself the equal or the superior of the gods—as referred to in the second stasimon of Sophocles' play? How does the *hybris* of Oedipus contribute to our understanding of him?

5. The second motto of the Delphic Oracle refers to the Golden Mean (Measure is Best, or Modest Measure). Does it imply a criticism of the excesses in Oedipus' character?

6. Does Sophocles present Oedipus as a tragic hero in accord with the Aristotelian definition—a man neither very good nor very bad but one of distinction who meets with disaster through some failing of his own?

7. How do the dramatists deal with the problem of Oedipus' guilt or innocence?

8. Comment on Rey's interpretation: "He [Oedipus] had to follow the natural law of titanic drives of power and lust without becoming their slave. He had to comply with necessity and yet prove his freedom by this very compliance."

9. Contrast Sophocles', Hofmannsthal's, and Dryden's concept of Oedipus. Which Oedipus is, in your opinion, the most tragic

and/or heroic figure? Justify your answer by quoting significant passages from the texts.

10. In what way does Hofmannsthal's characterization of Creon present an antithesis to Oedipus?

11. Compare and contrast how each author presents the Oedipus–Creon conflict.

12. What is Jocasta's attitude toward the gods? Is Jocasta sceptical of the oracles? Explain her words and actions concerning her belief. In Sophocles' play is her prayer to Apollo sincere? Estimate the effect of Jocasta's offering at the conclusion of the Sophoclean tragedy.

13. Jocasta commits suicide in two of these plays. Does this act appear to be inevitable?

14. Compare and contrast Hofmannsthal's Jocasta and Antiope.

15. What differences do you find in the three presentations of Jocasta?

16. What is the nature of the relationship between Oedipus and Jocasta in each of the three plays?

17. Do the writers attempt to make plausible the relationship between Oedipus and Jocasta?

18. Discuss the verbal and circumstantial ironies that occur in the relationship between Oedipus and his mother.

THEME AND CONCEPT OF TRAGEDY

The essential ideas and concepts embodied in the structure and imagery of the plays are explored. One studies the use of symbol, thematic imagery, and symbolic action as stylistic devices to convey the meaning and significance of the myth.

1. The age-old question of how man copes with the power of the gods, or Fate, or the limitations of his existence, if you will, is basic to the Oedipus dramas. What is the function of Fate in the Sophocles and Dryden versions? According to Hölderlin's epi-

graph to his drama, how does Hofmannsthal treat this question?

2. Examine the symbolism in each play. For example, why does Sophocles' Oedipus blind himself? What are the mythical implications of blood, ancestors, the elements, and death in *Oedipus and the Sphinx?*

3. Trace the transformation from golden blood, holy blood, to blessed blood (see Rey criticism) in Hofmannsthal's drama.

4. Do you agree with Lachmann when he interprets the life-ties between father, mother, and child as being created "only through blood"?

5. Compare the criticisms of Lachmann and Rey concerning the role of blood in the ancient and the modern tragedy.

6. Comment on the hermetic (magic) qualities in *Oedipus and the Sphinx.*

7. How does the function and significance of the Sphinx differ in the three plays?

8. Sophocles' second stasimon or choral ode (p. 18) may define his religious position. Is this true?

9. Contrast the religious implication in Sophocles' drama with the biblical allusions in Hofmannsthal's drama.

10. Read the chapters in Nietzsche's *The Birth of Tragedy,* "Apollo and Dionysus" and *The Will to Power,* "Dionysus,"[1] and seek out the Dionysian elements in the dramas.

11. Explain what Rey means when he states in his criticism: "Hofmannsthal's concept is neither identical with the one of Nietzsche nor with the one of the mythological legend. Dionysian elevation for him is more than elemental intoxication of the senses because it is based on the morality of self-sacrifice and on the mysterium of ideal love."

12. The idea of sacrifice plays an important part in Hofmannsthal's *Oedipus and the Sphinx.* What does sacrifice mean to: Oedipus, Jocasta, Creon, and the boy-swordbearer?

13. Discuss the dilemma of Hofmannsthal's Oedipus: the

[1] William Haussmann, trans. *The Birth of Tragedy,* Friederich Nietzsche (New York, Russel and Russel, 1964), Vol. I, pp. 21–28; Anthony M. Ludovicki, trans. *The Will to Power* (New York, Russel and Russel, 1964), Vol. XV, pp. 388–421, esp. pp. 415-417.

significance of a life without a purpose, his attitude toward death, and his struggle to accept the will of the gods.

14. Examine the symbol or motif of the abyss (personal disintegration) in nature and personality.

15. The search for personal identity and integration of personality is an important theme in the versions of Oedipus. According to the three dramatists, is the search to "know thyself" essential to maintain human dignity, is it merely worthwhile, or is the cost too great?

16. Discuss mysticism in *Oedipus and the Sphinx* as a means of overcoming reality.

17. Compare the authors' attitudes toward the gods as expressed in their plays.

18. Do the dramas attain a spiritual plane? Justify your answer.

19. Are the dramas meaningful to us? Are they able to move us aesthetically and purge us ethically, or should this long-forgotten world really concern us?

20. Consider the choice of plot, setting, character, and theme. What is the concept of tragedy of the three authors?

21. It is said that great literature is metaphysical in nature and reflects a universal experience. Do the three Oedipus dramas measure up to these requirements? Justify your answer.

BIBLIOGRAPHY

The following titles suggest possibilities for library research and further criticism. Many of them include bibliographies and references to other works that may be useful.

I. CLASSICAL DRAMA: SOPHOCLES AND ARISTOTLE

Adams, Sinclair M. *Sophocles the Playwright.* Toronto: University of Toronto Press, 1957.

Bowra, Cecil Maurice. *Sophoclean Tragedy*. Oxford: University Press, 1944.

Brooks, Cleanth, and Robert Heilman. *Understanding Drama*. New York: Holt, 1948.

Clark, Barrett H. *European Theories of the Drama*. New York: Appleton, 1925. Rev. ed., 1929.

Cooper, Lane. *Aristotle on the Art of Poetry*. Ithaca: Cornell University Press, 1947.

Else, Gerald F. *Aristotle's Poetics: The Argument*. Cambridge: Harvard University Press, 1957.

Feder, Lillian. " 'The Unwary Egotist': A Study of the *Oedipus Tyrannus*." *The Centennial Review*, V (1961), 260–280.

Haigh, A. E. *The Tragic Drama of the Greeks*. Oxford: Clarendon Press, 1896.

Jebb, Richard C. *Sophocles: The Plays and Fragments. Part I: The Oedipus Tyrannus*. Cambridge: Cambridge University Press, 1893. Third edition.

Jones, Ernest. *Hamlet and Oedipus*. New York: Doubleday, 1949.

Kanzer, Mark. "The 'Passing of the Oedipus Complex' in Greek Drama." *The Yearbook of Psychoanalysis. V, 1949*. New York: International Universities Press, 1950.

Kirkwood, Gordon M. *A Study of Sophoclean Drama*. Ithaca: Cornell University Press, 1958.

Kitto, H. D. F. *Greek Tragedy*. New York: Doubleday, 1954. First ed., 1939.

Knox, Bernard M. W. *Oedipus at Thebes*. New Haven: Yale University Press, 1957.

———. "Sophocles' *Oedipus*." *Tragic Themes in Western Literature*. Ed. Cleanth Brooks. New Haven: Yale University Press, 1955. Pp. 7–29.

Lattimore, Richmond. *The Poetry of Greek Tragedy*. Baltimore: Johns Hopkins Press, 1958.

Lawson, John Howard. *Theory and Technique of Playwriting and Screenwriting*. New York: Putnam's, 1949.

Letters, Francis J. H. *The Life and Work of Sophocles*. New York: Sheed and Ward, 1953.

Lucas, F. L. *Tragedy: Serious Drama in Relation to Aristotle's Poetics*. London: Hogarth Press, 1953.

Mendell, Clarence W. *Our Seneca.* New Haven: Yale University Press, 1941.

Moore, John A. *Sophocles and Arete.* Cambridge: Harvard Uni versity Press, 1938.

Sheppard, John T. *The Oedipus Tyrannus of Sophocles.* Cambridge: Cambridge University Press, 1920.

Thomson, George D. *Aeschylus and Athens.* London: Lawrence and Wishart, 1941.

Velikovsky, Immanuel. *Oedipus and Akhnaton: Myth and History.* New York: Doubleday, 1960.

Waldock, A. J. A. *Sophocles the Dramatist.* Cambridge: Cambridge University Press, 1951.

Webster, T. B. L. *An Introduction to Sophocles.* Oxford: Oxford University Press, 1936.

Whitman, Cedric H. *Sophocles: A Study of Heroic Humanism* Cambridge: Harvard University Press, 1951.

II. JOHN DRYDEN AND NATHANIEL LEE

Adams, Henry H., and Baxter Hathaway. *Dramatic Essays of the Neoclassic Age.* New York: Columbia University Press, 1950.

Addison, Joseph. *The Spectator.* Ed. G. Gregory Smith. London: J. M. Dent (Everyman's Library, 1907) See Addison's essays on tragedy, Nos. 39, 40, 42, 44 (1711).

Dryden, John. *Essays of John Dryden.* Ed. W. P. Ker. Oxford: Clarendon Press, 1926.

Genest, John. *Some Account of the English Stage.* Bath: H. E. Carrington, 1832. See Vol. I for criticism of Dryden's *Oedipus.*

Ham, Roswell G. *Otway and Lee: Biography from a Baroque Age.* New Haven: Yale University Press, 1931. See Chapter XIII.

Jebb, Richard C. "Introduction." *Sophocles: The Plays and Fragments. Part I: The Oedipus Tyrannus.* Cambridge: University Press, 1893. See Pp. xxxviii–xl, xliv–xlvi.

Kallich, Martin. "Oedipus: From Man to Archetype," *Comparative Literature Studies,* III (1966), 33-46.

Nettleton, George H. *English Drama of the Restoration and Eighteenth Century.* New York: Macmillan, 1928.

Nicoll, Allardyce. *A History of English Drama 1660–1900. Vol. I: Restoration Drama 1660–1700.* Cambridge: Cambridge University Press, 1952. Fourth edition.

Russell, Trusten W. *Voltaire, Dryden and Heroic Tragedy.* New York: Columbia University Press, 1946.

Summers, Montague. *The Restoration Theatre.* New York: Mac millan, 1934.

III. HUGO VON HOFMANNSTHAL: BIBLIOGRAPHY OF CRITICISM AND CORRESPONDENCE IN ENGLISH

Baker, George M. "Hugo von Hofmannsthal and Greek Tragedy." *JEGP,* XII (1913), 383–406.

Block, Haskell M. "Hugo von Hofmannsthal and the Symbolist Drama." *Transactions of the Wisconsin Academy of Sciences, Arts and Letters,* XLVIII (1959), 161–178.

Burger, Hilde. "French Influences on Hugo von Hofmannsthal.' *Comparative Literature Proceedings of the Second Congress of the International Comparative Literature Association.* Ed. W. P. Friedrich. Vol. II. Chapel Hill: University of North Carolina Press, 1959.

Butler, E. M. "Alkestis in Modern Dress." *Journal of the Warburg Institute,* I, i (1937), 46–60.

——— "Hugo von Hofmannsthal's 'Elektra': A Graeco-Freudian Myth." *Journal of the Warburg Institute,* II, ii (1938), 164–175.

Gilbert, Mary E. "Recent Trends in the Criticism of Hugo von Hofmannsthal." *German Life and Letters (NS),* V (1951–52), 255–268.

Hammelmann, H., and E. Osers. *The Correspondence Between Richard Strauss and Hugo von Hofmannsthal.* London: Collins, 1961.

——— *Hugo von Hofmannsthal.* New Haven: Yale University Press, 1957.

Heyworth, Peter. "Richard Strauss in Vienna." *The Observer* (12 February, 1961).

Hottinger, M., and T. and J. Stern. "The Letter of Lord Chandos" in *Hugo von Hofmannsthal: Selected Prose.* New York: Pantheon Books, 1952.

Lange, Victor. *Modern German Literature 1870–1940.* Ithaca: Cornell University Press, 1945.

Nagler, A. M. "Hugo von Hofmannsthal and Theatre." *Theatre Research,* II, i (1960), 5–15.

Norman, F. *Hofmannsthal.* London: University of London, 1963.

Steiner, Herbert. "The Harvard Collection of Hugo von Hofmannsthal." *Harvard Library Bulletin,* VIII (1954), 54–64.

Wellesz, Egon. "Hugo von Hofmannsthal and Strauss." *Music and Letters,* XXXIII, iii (1952), 239–242.

——— *Essays on Opera.* Trans. Kean. London: Dobson, 1950.

IV. HUGO VON HOFMANNSTHAL: BIBLIOGRAPHY OF CRITICISM IN GERMAN

Alewyn, Richard. *Über Hugo von Hofmannsthal* 2. Aufl. Göttingen: Ruprecht Vandenhoeck, 1960.

Burckhardt, Carl F. *Erinnerungen an Hofmannsthal und Briefe des Dichters.* München: Rinn, 1948.

Cakmur, Belma. "Hofmannthals Erzählung, 'Die Frau ohne Schatten'." *Studien zu Werk und Innenwelt des Dichters.* Ankara: *Schriften des Institutes für deutsche Sprache und Literatur,* 1952.

Fahrner, R. *Dichterische Visionen, menschlicher Urbilder in Hofmannsthals Werk.* Ankara, 1953.

Jens, Walter. *Hofmannsthal und die Griechen.* Tübingen: Niemeyer, 1955.

Lachmann, E. "Hofmannsthals Drama 'Oedipus und die Sphinx'." *Enzinger Festschrift.* Innsbruck, 1953

Nadler, Joseph. "Hugo von Hofmannsthal." *Deutsche Vierteljahrsschrift für Literaturwissenschaft und Geistesgeschichte,* 23. Halle: a.S., 1931.

Naef, Karl J. *Hugo von Hofmannsthal, Wesen und Werk.* Zürich: Niehaus, 1938.

Naumann, Walter. "Drei Wege de Erlösung in Hugo von Hofmannsthals Werken." *GR,* XIX (1944), 150–155.

Norman, F. *Hofmannsthal.* London: University of London, 1963.
Pestalozzi, Karl. *Sprachskepsis und Sprachmagie im Werk des jungen Hofmannsthal.* Zürich: Atlantis Verlag, 1958.
Rey, W. H. "Geist und Blut in Hugo von Hofmannsthals 'Oedipus und die Sphinx'." *German Quarterly,* XXXI (1958), 84–93.
——— *Weltentzweiung und Weltversöhnung in Hofmannsthals griechischen Dramen.* Philadelphia: University of Pennsylvania Press, 1962.
Schaeder, Grete. "Hugo von Hofmannstal Weg zur Tragödie,' *Deutsche Vierteljahrsschrift für Literaturwissenschaft und Geistesgeschichte,* 23. Halle: a. S., 1931.
——— und H. Hans. *Hugo von Hofmannsthal und die geistige Welt.* Hameln: Fritz Seifert, 1947.
——— und H. Hans. "In Memoriam Hugo von Hofmannsthal." *Die Antike,* V (1929).
Schrögendorfer, K. "Oedipus und die Sphinx bei Peladin und Hofmannsthal." *Festschrift für E. Castle.* Wien: Hrsg. Gesellschaft für Wiener Theater Forschung und Goethe Verein, 1955.
Steiner, H., ed. *Hugo von Hofmannsthal: Gesammelte Werke in Einzelausgaben.* Frankfurt am Main: S. Fischer.
Strauss, Richard. *Briefwechsel mit Hugo von Hofmannsthal.* Zürich: Atlantis Verlag, 1954.
Weber, Horst, ed. *Hugo von Hofmannsthal: Bibliographie der Kritik 1892–1963.* Berlin: de Gruyter.
——— *Hugo von Hofmannsthal: Bibliographie des Schrifttums 1892–1963.* Berlin: de Gruyter, 1966.

V. ORIGINAL LITERATURE AND PLAYS ON THE OEDIPUS MYTH

Homer. *The Iliad,* IV, 378; XXIII, 679f.; *The Odyssey,* XI, 271 ff. (*c.* 850 B.C.).
Hesiod. *The Theogony,* 326 (*c.* 800 B.C.).
Pindar, *Olympian Ode, II.* (*c.* 500 B.C.).
Aeschylus. *Seven Against Thebes.* (*c.* 467 B.C.).
Sophocles. *Antigone.* (*c.* 443 B.C.) *Oedipus Tyrannus* (*c.* 427 B.C.). *Oedipus at Colonus* (*c.* 408 B.C.).

Euripides. *The Phoenician Women.* (*c.* 409 B.C.).

Seneca, Lucius Annaeus. *Oedipus.* (*c.* 50 A.D.) Trans. Clarence W. Mendell, *Our Seneca.* New Haven: Yale University Press, 1941.

Corneille, Pierre. *Oedipus.* (1657).

Dryden, John and Nathaniel Lee. *Oedipus.* (1678).

Voltaire, François Marie Arouet de. *Oedipus.* (1718) Trans. in *The Works of Voltaire,* Vol. XVI. Ed. John Morley. New York: E. R. DuMont, 1901.

Hofmannsthal, Hugo von. *Oedipus.* Berlin: S. Fischer, 1906.

——— *Oedipus and the Sphinx.* (1906) Trans. Gertrude Schoenbohm in *Oedipus: Myth and Drama.* New York: Odyssey Press, 1967.

Gide, André. *Oedipus.* (1931) Trans. John Russell, *Two Legends: Oedipus and Theseus.* New York: Knopf, 1950.

Cocteau, Jean. *The Infernal Machine.* (1934) Trans. Carl Wildman. Oxford: Oxford University Press, 1936.